THE PIANOFORTE

THE PIANOFORTE

W. L. SUMNER
Hon. Fellow of the Institute of Musical Instrument Technology

ST. MARTIN'S PRESS · NEW YORK

AFFILIATED PUBLISHERS: Macmillan & Company, Limited, London –
also at Bombay, Calcutta, Madras and Melbourne – The Macmillan Company
of Canada, Limited, Toronto.

FOR KATHLEEN

CONTENTS

CONTENTS

LIST OF PLATES

The page numbers refer to the text page
preceding the plate

ACKNOWLEDGEMENTS

THE author wishes to express his gratitude to those who have supplied information and illustrations. In particular he wishes to thank Captain Evelyn Broadwood, M.C., M.A., of London; C. and H. Neupert, of Bamberg, Germany; Robert Morley, of London; C. Astell, of Herrburger Brooks, Long Eaton; Dr. W. H. George, formerly of Chelsea Polytechnic; Lady Susi Jeans of Dorking; Karl Bormann, of Munich; and the directors of the eminent firms of: Chappell, Brasted, Challen and Eavestaff, and A. Knight, of London; Bösendorfer, of Vienna; Grotrian-Steinweg and Schimmel, of Brunswick; Bechstein, of Berlin; Blüthner, of Leipzig; Sauter, of Spaichingen; Schmidt-Flohr, of Berne, Switzerland; Steinway, Mason and Hamlin, Knabe, Sohmer, Kimball and Baldwin, of U.S.A.; and Rippen, of Ede, Holland, and Shannon, Ireland. He has to thank Hugh Boyle, Dr. R. E. M. Harding, Mrs. Kathleen Dale, Paul Badura-Skoda and the proprietors of *Musical Opinion* for their permission to quote from their works.

The author owes much to many of the works in the extensive but not exhaustive bibliography given at the end of this book.

W. L. SUMNER

The University
Nottingham, 1970

INTRODUCTION

THIS book is an account of the pianoforte as a link in the chain between the composer and the listener. Inevitably the two ends of the chain have strayed into these pages, although there was no intention in the present work to deal with composers as such, or the detailed study of piano technique.

Although the treatment of the subject is historical in part, because the present can only be understood by reference to the past, no attempt has been made to produce more than an outline of the history of the instrument and its precursors. In fact, a few lines of description of each of the patents pertaining to pianoforte manufacture, amounting to thousands in less than two hundred years, would fill several volumes each larger than this. The quest for the establishment of the priorities of invention is often unrewarding, and is not always to be realised in terms of the dates of patents.

The piano is not an out-classed or effete musical instrument. Throughout the world its popularity is increasing every year, and there are now greater numbers of first-rate performers and competent amateurs than ever before. No other instrument commands such a wealth of great music composed for it; no other can rival it in the quantity of music originally composed for other musical media and then arranged for its keyboard. To this must be added the enormous bulk of music in which the pianoforte appears in combination with other instruments: trios, quartets, quintets, violin, violoncello, flute, sonatas, concerti with orchestra, songs and other forms. Two or more pianos may be played together, and there is a large and useful field of music in piano duet form. Some hundreds of tons of teaching material for the pianoforte alone, much of it of good quality, are printed every year throughout the world.

The possession of even a modest keyboard technique is the key which can open up a storehouse of inexhaustible treasures to the student. To the writer, the gradual discovery, over a period of half a century, of the literature of the piano has been an illuminating and exciting experience, which brought no satiety but only increasing richness over the years and shed light on other music and human activities. The extent of the literature of the piano was impressed on the writer when, at about the time of the end of the first world war, he bought, in a market, copies of the complete piano works of Schubert and a piano arrangement of the four symphonies of Brahms. In the days before broadcasting, visits of orchestras, and good gramophone records, here, for one who had been nurtured on Bach, Mozart and Beethoven, were two rich mines to be opened up and explored. Even with technical equipment of modest quality, the yield was rewarding and durable. It has been well said that the works of Bach for the organ were in themselves sufficient to sustain its claim as the King of Instruments. Similarly, the works of Haydn, Mozart, Beethoven, Chopin, Schubert, Schumann, Liszt, Brahms, Debussy and hundreds of composers of lesser stature are more than sufficient to establish the position of the piano as a musical instrument. The works of only one of the great, such as Beethoven or Chopin, would be enough to demand for the piano a permanent place amongst the important instruments of the Western civilisation.

The piano is the companion of the composer, the class teacher's musical black-board, the easiest method of playing "complete" music and an instrument whose resources are hardly exhausted by the most masterly composers and the most skilful of virtuosi.

The positive qualities of the pianoforte can be stated quite simply. It is not expensive, when it is compared with other instruments which may appear to be simpler in construction. It is durable, and will give decades of service if it is maintained reasonably. It can be obtained in several sizes and shapes, and, apart from its musical functions, can be an acceptable room furnishing of dignified appearance, in keeping with the other appointments of its environment. Though it is not actually portable it is readily transportable, according to its weight and size. It is self-contained and, apart from the performer, no external source of energy is required for its operation. Since the maker and the tuner of the piano have fixed the pitch of each note and the broad limits of its tone quality, it is easy and rewarding to play it even at a rudimentary stage. The usual compass of a piano is 88 notes or more than seven octaves. Its lowest note is a minor third below that of the bottom sixteen-foot pedal note of the organ, and a fifth below the usual extreme low note of the double-bass. The highest sound of the piano is that of the top note of a four-foot stop on an organ of full modern compass, and above the top note of a piccolo.

The piano, at its best, has a great range of dynamics, from a refined pianissimo to the crashing sounds of the large grand, which are not overborne by the orchestral tutti. Further, the piano has a considerable range of tone-colour, which is far greater than is realised by many who regard it as a monochromatic instrument. It is melodic, harmonic and contrapuntal; its keyboard and two or three pedals offer a scope to both composer and player on which it is not easy to set a limit. So great indeed is this scope that the present book, at best, can only be considered as an introduction to the subjects with which it deals.

THE GENEALOGY OF THE MODERN PIANOFORTE*

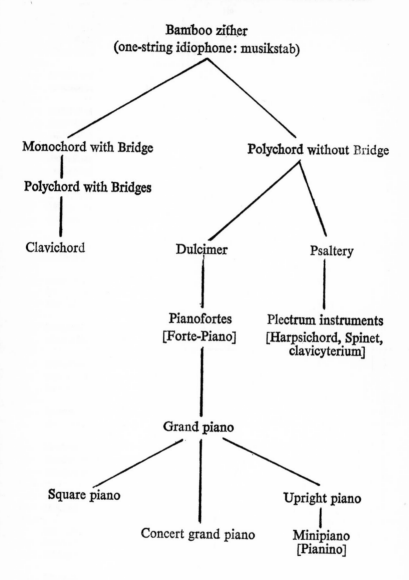

Bamboo zither
(one-string idiophone: musikstab)

Monochord with Bridge

Polychord with Bridges

Clavichord

Polychord without Bridge

Dulcimer

Psaltery

Pianofortes
[Forte-Piano]

Plectrum instruments
[Harpsichord, Spinet,
clavicyterium]

Grand piano

Square piano

Concert grand piano

Upright piano

Minipiano
[Pianino]

*Adapted from H. Neupert, *Vom Musikstab zum modernen Klavier.*

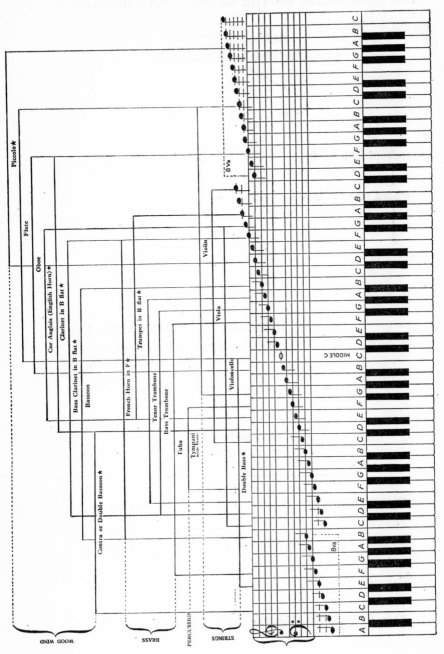

Fig. 1. The compass of the piano and other instruments (Rushworth and Dreaper).

CHAPTER I

EARLY KEYBOARD INSTRUMENTS

"He that fingerithe well the Claricordis maketh a good songe,
For in the meane (middle part) is the melody with a rest longe
If the tewnys be not pleasant to him that hath no skyll,
Yet no lac to the claricorde for he doith his goode will.
He that covytithe in clarisymbalis to make good concordance,
Ought to finger the keys with discrete temperance.

"A slac strynge in a Virginall soundithe not aright,
It doth abide no wrestinge (tuning), it is so loose and light;
The sound-borde crasede, forsith the instrumente,
Throw misgovernance, to make notes which was not his intente."
Leckingfield proverbs. (Yorkshire, c. 1520).

MANY centuries before man recorded his story, some prehistoric music-maker must have stretched a thong or sinew between the horns of the skull of an animal or the fork of a tree branch and, plucking the string, found that it emitted a pleasing sound. No doubt further experiment revealed that the note produced by the vibrating string became higher in pitch as the tension was increased by pulling the string. It is possible—because there is no reason to suppose that, in early man, lack of knowledge meant lack of intelligence and ingenuity—that notes of various pitches were obtained by stopping the string at various points along its length or even by using strings of different length stretched parallel to one another. Also, it might have been noticed that thick strings produced lower and duller tones than light, thin strings. Perhaps, stones, bones or pieces of wood were used as plectra to pluck or strike the strings, and so, not only saved the fingers from fatigue but produced notes of greater clarity and definition.

Hence were born all the stringed instruments, whether of the type of the harp, the lute, the fiddle or those which were played by a keyboard. The harp was firmly established by the year 2000 B.C. in Sumeria, beside the great rivers of Mesopotamia, and in Egypt

19

beside the Nile. Cave drawings, made 40,000 years ago in France, in the Grotte de l'Ariège des Trois-Frères, show horned animals playing stringed instruments.

We travel over many centuries to find records of the first keyboards and these seem to have been used for playing organs. It is probable that crude keyboards, which would be actuated by the whole hand, were known before the time of Christ, but parts of a small organ, which dates from the year A.D. 226 and had lain buried, for many centuries, in the old Roman town of Aquincum, near Budapest in Hungary, included a balanced keyboard, the touch of whose keys was not heavier than that of a modern pianoforte. The organ was used to accompany the singing of those whose duty it was to keep awake the fire-watchers. It is interesting to note that a fire saved the remnants of the organ for posterity because, when the building in which it stood was burnt, it fell into a cellar beneath.

In Greece, several centuries before the birth of Christ, the vibrating string stretched between two pegs, and then appropriately known as the monochord, became the object of scientific or, as it was called, philosophical observation. Pythagoras (c. 550 B.C.), whose earlier ideas insisted upon "putting numbers into everything", and Euclid, who was the editor but not the author of a book on music ascribed to Cleonides, brought music into line with arithmetic. In particular, they seem to have known of the consonances which resulted by stopping the string in the middle (octave), a third of the way along (fifth and twelfth), and a quarter of the way along (fourth and double octave) and so on. Even today the fractions $\frac{1}{2}$, $\frac{1}{3}$, $\frac{1}{4}$, $\frac{1}{5}$, $\frac{1}{6}$, etc., are known as a harmonic series of numbers. These ideas were extended by Boethius (A.D. 500), whose essay was copied throughout the Middle Ages and printed from the end of the fifteenth century until the eighteenth. From the time of the Greeks there have been text-books and treatises on music which emphasised the relationship between music and mathematics, but fortunately even from the time of Aristoxenus (350 B.C.) there were those who insisted that feeling and emotion should be opposed to the "harmony by computation" of the Pythagoreans. Such ideas concerning the nature of music, sometimes in opposition and sometimes complementary, have persisted to the present!

The clavichord, a genuine precursor of the pianoforte, developed from the monochord and, in old documents and in some parts of Europe today, the word monochord is used instead of clavichord. The monochord was a single string of gut or metal stretched between two bridges, placed on a block of wood, or better, a hollow sound-box. The length of the vibrating part of the string could be deter-mined by stopping it by a movable third bridge, placed between the two fixed bridges. The monochord was of great use to musicians for determining the laws of harmonics, fixing the notes of a scale, comparing and determining pitches, tuning other instruments, teaching singing and demonstrating some of the elementary physical laws of sound. In the eleventh century, when the number notation, which the Arabs obtained from the Indians, appeared in the West, Guido D'Arezzo (c. 990–c. 1050) gave his name to the musical notation by placing notes on the staff. Many old manuscripts contain drawings of monochords on which the pitch letters of the Guidonian scale are shown on the side of the monochord. The string could be stopped, to give the notes of a scale, by the fingers or by a thin piece of wood or metal held in the fingers. From this it was an easy step to stop the string by means of a projection at the end of a pivoted piece of wood or a key on a keyboard and so make a clavi-chord (key chord).

The hurdy-gurdy or organistrum was another early keyboard instrument, in which strings were stopped by playing the small key-board with one hand and the barrel, the projections on which plucked the strings, was turned with the other. It would seem that only melodies would be required from these early instruments (although the remarkable Aquincum organ had greater potential-ities), and thus a single string and keyboard could be made to serve.

It is probable that there was less incentive to provide stringed instruments than organs with keyboards, where the larger pipes and their wind supply needed some convenient mechanism for con-trolling them. The strings of the harp and psaltery could be plucked or struck with ease and subtlety with the fingers. Nevertheless, key-board instruments with plectrum action were known in the middle of the fourteenth century at the very latest. Poems by the French poets Eustache Deschamps (1378) and Guillaume de Machaut (c. 1370), the household accounts of Philipp the Brave, Duke of Bur-gundy (1385), and letters of John I, King of Aragon, in the years 1387–1388, all mention such keyboard instruments, but Jean de Muris writing in 1323 in his *Musica speculativa* does not mention them.

In the church in Certosa near Pavia, built in 1472, there is in the basement a pictorial representation of an instrument which is transitional between the psaltery-cymbal and the clavicymbal. This instrument, which is being played by King David, is described thus:

In form it is the well-known istromento da porca (shaped like a pig's head), a trapezoid formed by cutting off the top of an isosceles triangle by a cross-section near the apex. David has the instrument lying on his lap, the base of the triangle towards him, its top facing outwards. The body of the instrument, near the player's right hand, is not closed and within it we see eight keys which relate to a similar number of strings running in the same direction. Under these a sound hole, decorated with a rosette, is to be seen. David operates the keys with his right hand, while the left rests on the strings, apparently as a damper. It is well known that the greatest difficulty in playing the usual form of the psaltery was in having to damp the strings with the same hand that plucked them. The difficulty is solved here quite simply through the use of keys, which leave the left hand free to do the damping while the right can easily perform even double stops. The fortunate accident that an artist here made use of an instrument that he must have seen somewhere fills a substantial gap in the history of keyboard instruments.[1]

Still another psaltery, played upright like a portative organ, is depicted on the altar of the church at Kefermarkt, Austria (1480).

The Clavichord

A monochord, with the compass of about an octave, is mentioned in the manuscript appendix, *Novellus musicae artis tractatus*, to Conrad Von Zabern's printed work *Opusculum de monochord* (Mainz, *c.* 1450), and at that time the instrument must have been known for three centuries at least. By the year 1400 the monochord had developed into a clavichord which had a chromatic scale and up to ten strings.[2] The instrument was popular until the year 1800.

The flat, metal tongues, which strike the strings and at the same time stop off an appropriate speaking length, are fixed to the ends of the keys and are known as tangents (from the Latin *tango*, I

[1] Ambros, *Geschichte der Musik*, III (Breslau, 1864).
[2] Thurston Dart mentions references to the monochord and clavichord in *Le Roman de Flamenca* (1235), *Prise d'Alexandrie*, by Guillaume de Machaut (1333), *Der Minne Regel*, by Eberhard Cersne (1404), and the treatises of Georgius Anselmi (1434), Henri Arnault of Zwolle (*c.* 1455) and Ramis de Pareja (1482).

touch). It is obvious that only one note can be produced at any one time from a single string, and if counterpoint and harmony will be required a number of strings will be needed, though not necessarily to the extent of a string for every note. For instance, in old music it was rarely or never necessary to play simultaneously notes which were a semitone apart, and thus one string could serve for more than one note. Instruments so limited were called fretted or *gebunden* (German: bound or "tied-up") clavichords. Frets were the raised parts of the finger boards which denoted the stopping positions of the stringed instruments which had no keyboards. Where there was a separate string for each note of the scale, the clavichord was called *bundfrei* (free from "tie-ups") or fret-free. The clavichord was a remarkably complete and versatile instrument. Its tone was small but sweet and satisfying. Since the string was struck at the end of its speaking length all the harmonics appeared in its vibration[1] and the tones were gently reinforced by the wooden construction of the instrument. The clavichord was cheap to construct and readily portable. Its tones, though capable of considerable dynamic range, were gentle and intimate. For the exploitation of the qualities of the instrument much subtlety of touch was required. Since the tangent was at the end of the key, a note could be repeated by a slight movement of the finger. This is the Bebung. Also, a lateral movement of the key, after the note had been struck, would give a tremulando effect. This treatment of the instrument, which was only possible because of a small degree of "play" of the key on its pins, would produce wear and the rattling of the keys, and was often considered undesirable. In order to produce fullness of tone, each note was sometimes strung with pairs of strings, and the bass was strengthened by combining each string with one which sounded an octave higher. In both monochord and clavichord it was necessary to have a damper to prevent the speech of the smaller length of string from the tangent. Also, it should be noted that there is a secondary tone, when the finger is taken quickly from the key. The clavichord was a favourite instrument of most of the great composers from 1400 to 1800, including J. S. Bach. It was useful as a teaching instrument, for accompanying the voice and for solo playing. Its sounds would not disturb those who were not sitting near to it, and for this reason it was said to be popular in nunneries. Clavi-

[1] Paradoxically, the striking point of the string is also a node. This is an interesting technical matter, which refutes much which Helmholtz wrote about the vibrations of strings.

chords could be made so that they were played by pedals. Moreover, one clavichord could be placed on the top of another and thus an organist could practise trios and other contrapuntal compositions which needed two manuals and pedals.

The instrument is a real precursor of the piano and, although it does not possess the great dynamic and sometimes destructive power of the latter, it has qualities which the piano does not possess. Even after the clavichord key is depressed there is still control of the tone which has been elicited, but in the pianoforte as soon as the hammer has left the jack in its journey to the string the player has no further control of it until it falls back to the key mechanism again. In the present century, particularly in the last three decades, the clavichord has been played again for its own sake and not merely because of an antiquarian interest in old instruments. Busoni and Howells, amongst other composers, have written significant music for it. Beautiful modern specimens have been made by Dolmetsch, Goff, Morley, Gough, Hodsdon, Goble, in England, Challis, Dowd, Hubbard, in U.S.A., and many craftsmen in Europe, notably Sperrhake, Kemper, Wittmayer, Steingraber, Mändler and Neupert. The instrument is worthy of attention by pianists. Great refinement and versatility of touch have to be acquired. Much music, such as that of J. S. Bach and D. Buxtehude, was composed for the clavichord originally. When such music is played on the pianoforte a problem arises. Ought the music to be regarded as a transcription for the piano, or should the player do the best to imitate the tone and manner of the clavichord as much as possible?

The problem is a difficult one and a general solution is not possible. Many piano transcriptions have played havoc with the ornaments and grace notes which were an essential part of the texture of the old music: others have completely missed the finer points of phrasing in the contrapuntal melodies. Since transcriptions from one musical medium to another were not only condoned but made and played by no less a person than J. S. Bach himself, the subject is important. No other instrument, apart from the piano, can claim a fraction of the music composed for other instruments and then arranged for its keyboard. There has often been a two-way traffic too. Music, which was originally conceived for piano solo or duet, by Brahms, Mussorgsky and Ravel, to mention only three, later appeared in orchestral colours.

The Harpsichord

The harpsichord flourished between 1500 and 1800 and there has been a great resurgence of interest in it in recent years. Since it is an instrument in which the strings are plucked, it stands further from the pianoforte than the clavichord, although the pianoforte seems to have originated by displacing the mechanism of a harpsichord. The harpsichord originated in Italy, then it became popular in the Low Countries and finally spread to other parts of Europe. The name harpsichord applies particularly to the large and more elaborate instrument shaped like an early form of grand piano. The virginal is a smaller rectangular type, and the spinet has a polygonal shape, which has been described as "leg of mutton". The word virginal or "pair of virginals" was usually applied to any instrument of the harpsichord type in seventeenth-century England. Although the larger harpsichords were elaborate instruments with several sets of strings, two or even three keyboards, and various mechanical devices, the action of the smaller virginal was simple. A string for each note was stretched between bridges on a wooden soundboard.

The plucking mechanism consists of a jack, five to eight inches high, placed at the end of each key. A slot is cut at the top of the jack and into this is placed an upright piece of wood about $1\frac{1}{4}$ inches long called a tongue, pivoted by means of a horizontal metal ring. A spring of hog's bristle presses on the tongue so that if it is displaced from the vertical it will return to this position. The plectrum, a quill or small wedge of hard leather, is let into a small slot in the tongue and projects from its front about $\frac{1}{8}$ in. At the side of the top of the jack is a damper made from a small piece of felt. Each set of jacks is placed in registers or holes in a flat piece of wood. These serve two purposes. Firstly, they line up the jacks so that the plectra strike the strings exactly at the right places and, secondly, the register may be moved by stop levers, so that the jacks are rendered inoperable and the strings are not struck. The action of plucking a string is this: when a key is depressed the jack rises and the plectrum is forced past the string and causes it to sound. When the finger is taken from the key the jack descends and the plectrum coming into contact with the string turns the tongue on its pivot, so that the quill passes the string without plucking it. When the jack has descended as far as it can go, the hog's bristle spring restores the upright position to the tongue, the damper descends to the string, silencing it, and then the cycle of operations is complete and can be repeated.

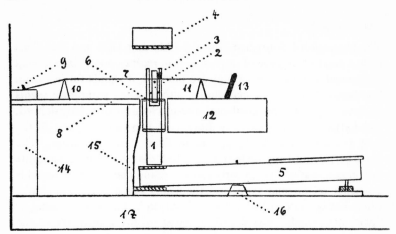

FIG. 2. The Cross-section of a Plectrum Action.
1. Jack, 2. Tongue with plectrum, 3. Damper, 4. Jack rail, 5. Key, 6.
Jack guide, 7. String, 8. Sound board, 9. Hitch pin, 10. Sound board
bridge, 11. Wrest plank bridge, 12. Wrest plank, 13. Wrest pin (or tuning
pin), 14. Hitch pin block, 15. Cross block, 16. Balance rail, 17. Base.
(Neupert).

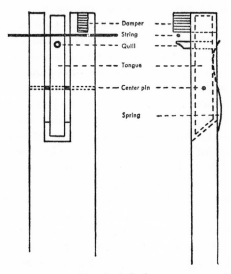

FIG. 3. A jack.

Such is the action of the harpsichord at its simplest and indeed as it remained in the virginal and spinet. In the larger instruments in which the strings were at right-angles to the keyboard, that is parallel to the length of any key, many things were possible. The instrument could have two sets of keys, each of which controlled one or more sets of jacks. (Rarely, three manuals and separate pedal harpsichords were made.) If, following the pitches given to organ stops, the unison pitch is known as 8-ft. pitch, then the octave above it is known as 4-ft. pitch and that below it 16-ft. pitch. Thus, there might be separate sets of 4-ft. strings and, in later times more rarely, 16-ft. strings (always played by the lower keyboard) and 2-ft. strings. Moreover, further sets of jacks with plectra which struck the strings nearer the bridge to produce a lute effect, or plectra of other materials would elicit different tone-qualities from the same set of strings. The lute stop seems to have been peculiar to English instruments made after 1750. Often there was a "harp" stop which caused a small piece of buff leather or felt to mute each string and so cause a dry, pizzicato effect when it was plucked.

In the sixteenth century the compass of most harpsichords was four octaves from C, but this was extended in the eighteenth century to five octaves from F, though a compass of five and a half octaves from C was not unknown. Between these extremes many variations of compass were found. Also, as in organs before the days of tuning in equal temperament, economies were effected by having short octaves in the base. Since long pipes are more expensive than long strings, and organ-builders were generally slower than others to recognise the claims of equal temperament, short octaves in organs persisted into the eighteenth century although they were not often found in harpsichords after the end of the seventeenth century. Such notes as C♯ F♯ G♯ were not often required as bass notes in earlier times and so their raised keys could be used for other notes which were required more often, thus saving keyboard length and mechanism.

Here are examples of short octaves and "broken" octaves:

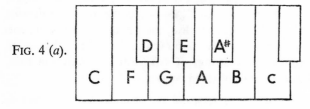

FIG. 4 (a).

The Short Octave

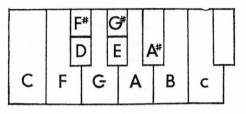

The Broken Octave

FIG. 4. (*b*).

In the earliest pictures of harpsichords we find a diatonic keyboard with two raised keys for B♭, and this is elaborated to a keyboard of thirty-eight notes with five raised keys in each octave. The bass had F as the lowest note in the Middle Ages but, after about 1500, the compass was extended to C. This was achieved by adding a key for the note C and making the D and E raised keys. C♯ and D♯ were omitted since it was impossible to use them as "root" tones with the systems of tuning then employed. This arrangement given above of the "short octave" shows that the keys which seemed to be E, F, F♯, G, G♯, A actually sounded C, F, D, G, E, A. There were other versions of the "short octave".[1] The octave span of these old instruments was about 6⅓ in. (16 cm.), that is, about .17 in. less than the present octave. The keyboard extended upwards to f‴— four octaves and a fourth. Some keyboards were of four octaves compass, and extended to c‴. From the year 1600, the short octave was modified chromatically and this was known as *ravalement*. A short octave was again employed to extend the compass downward to G so that the notes which seemed to be B, C, C♯, D, D♯, E actually sounded G, C, A, D, B, E. Occasionally, the raised keys were divided into two portions, each playing a note. These were known as broken octaves. Thus were the missing notes filled in or enharmonic notes provided. When equal temperament began to be adopted in the eighteenth century there was no need for these enharmonic separate notes. The expansion of the keyboard to five full octaves, usually from F, to f‴, known as the *grand ravalement*, took place about 1700. Nevertheless, the smaller-sized instruments still retained a four-octave keyboard even in the eighteenth century. A large instrument with strings of 4-ft., 8-ft. (unison) and 16-ft. pitch would have a range of seven octaves.

---

[1] Kinsky, "*Kurze Oktaven auf besaiteten Tasteninstrumenten*", *Zeitschrift für Musikwissenschaft*, II, 1919.

The keys were covered with ivory, ebony, bone, boxwood, pear, cedar, tortoise-shell or silver. Usually the raised keys ("sharps") were light in colour and the lower keys ("naturals") were covered with ebony or a dark-coloured wood. It is said that this custom originated in France because it enabled the player's hands to be seen more easily.

Sachs[1] gives the following dates for the development of the registers of the harpsichord:

1514	Two registers with one manual
1538	Eight and four foot registers
1576	Three sets of strings
1582	Four registers

The coupling of the manuals was also possible and was effected in a manner similar to that used in the old organs. The upper key frame could be pushed backwards about half an inch or the lower keyboard could be pulled forward by means of two knobs a similar distance, so that the keyboards engaged with one another. Modern harpsichords use a more complex coupling mechanism.

It is often stated that the tone, as regards quality and intensity, is not susceptible to changes of touch, but this is an exaggeration. A sensitive player, able to feel the movement of the plectrum against the string, will produce a better tone than one who forces down the

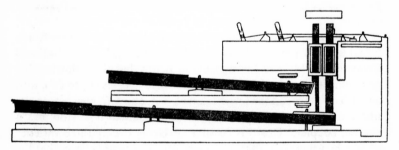

FIG. 5. Action of Two-Manual Harpsichord (Neupert).

keys with violence. Nevertheless, with the harpsichord, like the baroque organ, a carefully calculated use was made of pitch, dynamic and tone-quality differences between its keyboards. In the eighteenth century various mechanical devices such as Venetian swell shutters,

[1] C. Sachs, *History of Musical Instruments*, New York, 1940.

stops of various types and sets of strings in different pitches, tended to obscure the fundamental requirements of harpsichord technique and the beauty of tone which could be obtained from the simpler types, by a sensitive and skilful performer. A similar fate overtook the organ.

Neupert[1] has compiled the following table of harpsichords which he has examined or of which he has obtained reliable information.

Number of Instruments	Sets of Strings	Manuals			Registers
		1	2	3	
4	One	2			1×8'
		2			1×4'
70	Two	59	1		2×8'
		8			1×8', 1×4'
		2			2×4'
65	Three	13	57	4	2×8', 1×4'
		1	7	1	1×8', 1×4', 1×16'
		1	1		3×8'
8	Four		5		2×8', 1×4', 1×16'
			1		2×8', 2×4'
			2		3×8', 1×4'
1	Five		1		2×8', 1×4', 1×16', 1×2'
148		88	75	5	

An interesting type of harpsichord, of which there is a specimen by an unknown maker, known as the Bach-Flügel, in the National Collection of Musical Instruments in Berlin, has the following disposition. It has a keyboard compass of five octaves (F, to f′′′), 8-ft. and 4-ft. registers on the lower manual, 8-ft. and 4-ft. registers on the upper manual, a buff stop for the upper manual 8-ft. stop and a manual coupler. This was capable of giving twenty-three varieties of tune by using the registers and coupler. F. Ernst[2] believes that the Bach harpsichord, left at his death, did not possess a 16-ft. register, but was made in the style of Couchet or Ruckers.

Because of the excellent productions of the Ruckers family, the centre of harpsichord making moved from Italy to the Low Countries. At the beginning of the sixteenth century many makers of keyboard

[1] H. Neupert, *Harpsichord Manual*, Kassel (3rd ed., translated), 1960.
[2] F. Ernst, *Der Flügel J. S. Bachs*, Frankfurt, 1955.

instruments were at work in Antwerp and, in later years, from 1575 until 1667, the Ruckers family (Hans the Elder, Hans the Younger who was usually called Jean, and Andreas) dominated the scene. Their instruments, often decorated on the lid by first-class paintings by Dutch masters, were much prized. Their instruments may be identified by a leaden rosette, depicting an angel playing a harp with the initials HR, IR (Jean) and AR. An AR harpsichord with a painting by Rubens of "Cupid and Psyche" was sold to Charles I of England for £30. In the first half of the sixteenth century the Ruckers harpsichord had manuals of different compasses: the upper manual, with a short octave, was from C to c''', and the lower from C to f''' with the f''' in the treble immediately below the c''' in the treble of the upper manual, but both of these were of the same pitch. Thus, the pitch of the lower manual was a fourth below that of the upper. This device made transposition from *Chorton* (Choir pitch) to *Kammerton* (Chamber pitch) easier.

Ruckers harpsichords were durable and were in use until the end of the eighteenth century. A large instrument, made by Andreas Ruckers in 1651, is mentioned in the will of Handel.

When a harpsichord string is plucked with a hard plectrum a sound with many overtones is produced. Investigations by Meyer and Buchmann revealed that there were thirty-three overtones in the tenor C note of a harpsichord, twenty-three in the note of an early nineteenth-century piano and in a modern piano only fourteen.[1] Couperin says that the attractive qualities of the tone of the harpsichord are *la précision*, an exactness in which every mistake is patent; *la netteté*, a joyful sweetness and the splendour of *le brillant*—the radiant lustre. It is these qualities, like those of the tones of the baroque organs, which are so acceptable to many ears, sated with the opulence of romantic "eight foot" tone, at the present time.

Other Early Instruments

Although, from the point of view of the pianist, who is interested in every period of keyboard music, the clavichord and harpsichord are the most important precursors of the piano, there were several other earlier instruments which, because of their mode of action, were genuine forerunners of the instrument with hammers.

[1] Meyer and Buchmann, *Die Klangspektren der Musikinstrumente*, Berlin 1931; Trendelenberg, Thienhaus and Franz, "*Zur klangwirkung von Klavichord Cembalo und Flügel*", *Akustische Zeitschrift*, 1940.

In 1360, King Edward III of England gave to the French monarch an instrument known as an *echiquier d'Angleterre* or *dulce melos*, the exact nature of which has been a mystery and is still a matter of slight doubt. Henri Arnault, of Zwolle, in the early part of the fifteenth century described an instrument which seems to be of the same type. At the end of each key of a keyboard is a piece of wood weighted with lead. Although the front of the key has a limited distance of travel downwards and its other end upwards, the weighted piece of wood will leave the key, if it is struck with sufficient force, and continue to move upwards when it will meet a string, stretched with others in a harp-like frame. Obviously, the strength of the sound varies with the force with which the key is struck. There is no damping.

A popular instrument in Germany in the seventeenth century was the dulcimer, commonly called the *Hack-brett*, or chopping-board. The cymbalon of Central Europe, beloved by the Hungarian gypsies, is a similar instrument. Strings, stretched on a horizontal frame, were struck by hammers or flexible rods held in the hands of the performer. Rods of wood, plates of metal or even pieces of stone, tuned to give the notes of the scale, were used to make other instruments of the xylophone or glockenspiel type. In the remarkable small organ described by the blind Arnold Schlick in his *Spiegel* (1511) there is a stop called Holzerne Gelachter, which, almost certainly, is a xylophone in which wooden bars are struck by hammers. At the end of the seventeenth century, Pantaleon Hebenstreit constructed a very large hack-brett with two sound boards, the upper side strung with metal strings and the under side with over-strung gut strings. Double-faced hammers, with hard leather on one side and soft on the other, were provided instead of the usual beaters, so that loud and soft tones were possible. The instrument gained the favour of Louis XIV of France who called it the Pantaleon, in honour of its inventor. At the beginning of the eighteenth century there was a desire to experiment to make music more expressive and to improve upon the "block" or "terrace" dynamic of the so-called baroque period. The swell organ was invented in the Iberian peninsula and England, and the seeds of romanticism were sown already. Although it is true that the invention of the pianoforte made no great stir at the time, there can be no doubt that its inventor, Bartolommeo Cristofori, desired to produce an instrument which was more powerful in tone than the clavichord, and was capable of more expression and dynamic range than the harpsichord.

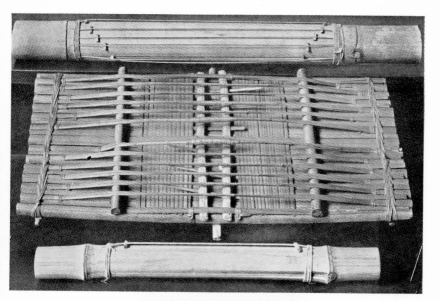

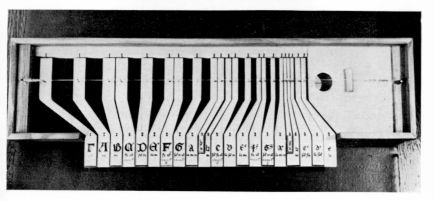

Other influences had been at work, particularly in Italy, towards more expressive, dramatic and lyrical music. In Florence at the end of the sixteenth century, the Cantata had been invented, a secular song in declamatory style accompanied by a single instrument. This resulted from discussions at a meeting of musical amateurs at the Palazzo Barde at Florence.

At the same conference a prominent member, Vincenzo Galilei (1533–91), the father of the great astronomer, had mentioned an instrument in which the harpsichord strings were bowed in an endeavour to make the tone more subtle. Such an instrument, made by Hans Haydn in Nuremberg in the late seventeenth century, is illustrated and described by Praetorius in his *Syntagma*, under the name of Nuremberg Geigenwerk [PLATE 4]. The instrument has the shape of a grand-pianoforte, and a number of revolving drums which hold the lengths of hair[1] for bowing will touch any string when its key is pressed. Reference is made to two instruments called Piano e forte in two letters sent by Paliarino to Alfonso II, the Duke of Modena, in 1598, but no description is given. It is interesting to note that the Italian word *piano* which has come to mean *soft* also means *plane*, *level* or *floor*, as anyone who has stayed in an Italian hotel will know. Thus, the word pianoforte not only means "soft-loud" but also "from a fixed level of tone to loudness".

The violin had been perfected in Italy, and nothing could rival a Stradivarius quartet or string orchestra for its powers of eloquent expression, subtle nuances of tone and beautiful colour; but, even before the master-creations of Stradivarius, the violin was capable of a great range of expression and was an intimate instrument responding sensitively to the artist who played it. The violin and the human-voice were a challenge to other forms of tone production.

A Note on the Names of Keyboard Instruments

Although the *psaltery* and the *dulcimer* have been confused, the former was an instrument in which the strings, stretched between pins on a flat board, were plucked with feather quills or other plectra (*psallein*: the Greek *to pluck*) and the latter was played by hitting the strings or other vibrating bodies with hammers. (*Dulcimer, dulce melos*—a sweet sound.) The psaltery is clearly a precursor of the harpsichord, and the dulcimer of the pianoforte. In spite of the way in which it was played the psaltery was called

[1] Or parchment!

c

cymbal (Greek: *tympanon*), a name which still persists in the Hungarian *cimbalon*, a descendant of the dulcimer. In the fourteenth century, a keyboard (*clavis*) was added to the cymbal, and the early harpsichord was called *clavicymbal* or in Italian *clavicembalo* or *cembalo*. Various opinions have been given concerning the origin of *eschequier*, *exaquier* or *eschaqueil* (in German *Schachbrett*: a chess board), "*semblant d'orgens, qui sona ab cordis*" (resembling the organ but sounding with strings). It is possible that the alternation of black and white notes suggested the chess-board, or it may have been that *Schach* comes from the Low German word *Schacht* (a quill). F. W. Galpin in Grove's Dictionary (Colles' Edition) derives the word from *echec* (to check or stop) and sees in the instrument a rudimentary form of the piano.

The *spinet* or *virginal* was produced when a keyboard was attached to the long side of a rectangular or trapezium-shaped psaltery. Praetorius in his *Instrumentenkunde* says of the harpsichord:

> The clavicymbalum is long and narrow and often called Flügel (a wing) because it is shaped in such a fashion. Some are called Schweinskopf (pig's head) because of the angular shape similar to the head of a wild boar. It has a strong, bright, very sweet sound resonance—more than other instruments of its family, on account of its two-fold, three-fold or even four-fold sets of strings.

Large instruments were called *cembalone* or *gravicymbal* from the Latin *gravis* meaning *large* or by dialectal change from *clavis* to *gravis*. The German term *Kiel Flügel* (*Kiel*=quill) refers both to the shape and to the plectrum action. In France, the larger harpsichord is known as the *claveçin* and the smaller *virginale* or *epinette*. The word *Flügel* is now used in Germany for a grand piano, *Klavier* sometimes for an upright piano.

The name *virginal* for a small harpsichord was used in Virdung's book (1511) and probably earlier. Thus the instrument cannot have been named after the "Virgin Queen" Elizabeth, who was said to be a good keyboard player. In old paintings by Hooch, Molenaer, Steen, Ter Borch, Vermeer, Metsu, Dou, Netscher and others, young women are almost invariably seen playing on virginals, and the viol da gamba and lute are regarded as masculine instruments. Other explanations have been given, although the German term *Jungfernklavier* seems to justify what has been said above. It has been suggested that virginals have a gentle, feminine tone in contrast to more powerful sound-producers. A derivation from *virga*, a wooden plectrum, does not seem to be probable.

A *clavicyterium* is a harpsichord with vertical strings, and in Italy, where it is believed to have originated, it is called *cembalo verticale*.

A Note on Virdung's Keyboard Instruments

Sebastian Virdung, priest of Amburg, wrote *Musica Getutscht* (*German Music*) in 1511. He illustrated, with rather crude woodcuts, four types of stringed keyboard instruments.

1. *Clavicordiu*. This had seven strings of the same length and speaking the same note. This was clearly a development of the monochord which was sometimes the name given to it. There were thirty-eight keys, twenty white and eighteen black:

> There must necessarily be more than one string because on one alone a player cannot sound a consonance simultaneously— but only tones in succession. Consequently, numerous strings are necessarily employed to hear therefrom the sweetness and simultaneous consonances in two, three, four or more parts.... Each string is served by at least three keys but only those two keys cannot be struck together which will sound dissonant.

2. *The Virginal*. This had thirty-eight keys, twenty-three white and fifteen black, which sounded thirty-eight strings, each of different length and separately tuned:

> I have never seen a Psalterium in use but that it was three sided and had ten strings. I therefore believe that the Virginal was derived and copied from the Psalterium. Although it is now played and touched with keys and furnished with quills and, despite the fact that it is now made in the shape of an oblong box like the Clavicordiu, it is, nonetheless, more comparable to the Psalterium than to the Clavicordiu because to each key there is a separate string.

3. *The Clavicimbalu* (*Clavizymbel*). Here the treble strings were at the left and there were forty keys (twenty-four white and sixteen black) and a string for each key.

Clauiciteriū

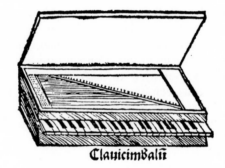

Clauicimbalū

Uirginal

FIG. 6. Three of Virdung's Woodcuts.

4. *The Claviciteriu.* This was an instrument with thirty-eight keys (twenty-three white and fifteen black) with vertical strings with the trebles on the left and the bass on the right:

It is like a Virginale but has strings of sheepgut as well as quills which pluck its strings in harp fashion. It is newly invented and I have seen only one of them.

It has been imagined that the appearance of the last two instruments, with the curve of the strings reversed, was due to an engraver's error. Twenty-five years after the publication of Virdung's book, Luscinius produced in his *Musurgia* an edited version of the account of the keyboard instruments but, while he changed the names or spellings of the names of the instruments, he did not make changes

The strings of two fretted (gebunden) clavichords.[1]

No. of pair of strings	Note(s) given by each A unison pair	No. of pair of strings	Note(s) given by each B unison pair
1	C	1	E
2	C♯	2	F
3	D	3	F♯
4	D♯	4	G
5	E	5	G♯
6	F	6	A
7	F♯	7	B♭, B♮
8	G	8	c, c♯
9	G♯	9	d, d♯
10	A	10	e, f
11	B♭, B♯	11	f♯, g
12	c, c♯	12	g♯, a, b♭
13	d, d♯, e	13	b♮, c¹, c♮¹
14	f, f♯, g	14	d¹, d♯¹, e¹
15	g♯, a, b♭	15	f¹, f♯¹, g¹
16	b♮, c¹, c♯¹	16	g♯¹, a¹, b♭¹
17	d¹, d♯¹, e¹	17	b♮¹, c², c♯²
18	f¹, f♯¹, g¹	18	d², d♯², e²
19	g♯¹, a¹, b♭¹	19	f², f♯², g²
20	b♮¹, c², c♯²	20	g♯², a², b♭²
21	d², d♯², e²	21	b♮², c³
22	f², f♯², g²		
23	g♯², a², b♭²		
24	b♮², c³		
25	c♯³, d³		
	Total 51 keys		Total 42 keys

[1] A. J. Hipkins, *The Pianoforte,* p. 62, Novello, London, 1896.

in the diagrams. It seems clear that there was no mistake in Virdung's diagrams. The first two show the improved forward-looking ideas concerning the scale, whereas the others reveal the conservative and classical principles of those who retained the ancient Greek tone names which read *downward* in the scale: A, G, F, E, D, C, B, A.

CHAPTER II

THE EARLY PIANOFORTE

At the beginning of the eighteenth century, Bartolommeo Cristofori (1655–1731), a harpsichord maker, formerly of Padua and then the Keeper of the Musical Instruments for Prince Ferdinand dei Medici, put hammers in the place of harpsichord jacks and thus made the first pianoforte.

It is known to everyone who delights in music, that one of the principal means by which the skilful in that art derive the secret of especially delighting those who listen, is the piano and forte in the theme and its response, or in the gradual diminution of tone little by little, and then returning suddenly to the full power of the instrument; which artifice is frequently used and with marvellous effect, in the great concerts of Rome. . . .

Now, of this diversity and alteration of tone, in which instruments played with the bow especially excel, the harpsichord is entirely deprived, and it would have been thought a vain endeavour to propose to make it so that it should participate in this power. Nevertheless, so bold an invention has been no less happily conceived than executed in Florence, by Signor Bartolommeo Cristofali, of Padua, harpsichord-player, in the service of the most serene Prince of Tuscany.

He has already made three, of the usual size of other harpsichords, and they have all succeeded to perfection. The production of greater or less sound depends on the degree of power with which the player presses on the keys, by regulating which, not only the piano and forte are heard, but also the gradations and diversity of power, as in a violoncello. . . . This is properly a chamber instrument, and it is not intended for church music, nor for a great orchestra. . . . It is certain, that to accompany a singer, and to play with one other instrument, or even for a moderate concert, it succeeds perfectly; although this is not its principal intention, but rather to be played alone, like the lute, harp, viols of six strings, and other most sweet instruments. But really the great cause of the opposition which this new instrument has encountered, is in general, the want of knowledge how, at first, to play it; because it is not sufficient to know how to play perfectly upon instruments with the ordinary finger board, but being a new instrument, it requires a person who, understanding its capabilities, shall have made a particular study of its effects, so as to regulate the measure of force required on the keys and the effects of decreasing it, also to choose pieces suited to it for delicacy, and especially for the movement of the parts, that the subject may be heard distinctly in each. . . .

This invention has also been effected in another form, the inventor having made another harpsichord with the piano and forte, in a different and somewhat more simple shape.

Thus wrote Scipione Maffei, when he visited Prince Ferdinand in 1709 and saw the new instrument which its inventor called the *Gravicembalo col piano e forte*.[1]

In 1708 a French keyboard-instrument maker, Cuisinié, devised a clavecin in which the strings were kept in motion by being bowed with a revolving resined bow which was rotated by means of a treadle. The tangent which stopped the string and brought it in contact with the bow was called a *maillet* (a little hammer, mallet or club), and it seems probable that these hammers may have suggested to Marius the idea for his own invention of 1716, the *Clavecin à maillets*. The instrument, of which four models were submitted to the Royal Academy of Science in Paris, was welcomed because it could produce *"les sons plus ou moins aigus"*, by different applications of force to the keys.

Beethoven thought that the pianoforte was a German invention and called it the *Hammerklavier*. Thus, it was erroneously believed that the instrument had been invented by Christoph Gottlieb Schröter, a teacher of keyboard playing, who was born in Hohenstein in Saxony in the year 1699. It is said that his pupils complained that they could not obtain on the harpsichord the expression which they had cultivated in the gentle tone of the clavichord. In 1717, Schröter, having experimented with the "hurdy-gurdy" action of the Nuremberg Geigenwerk and heard Hebenstreit perform on the Pantaleon, immediately devised two actions, one up-striking and the other down-striking, for playing the harpsichord with hammers. Schröter did not possess the means to build a full-size model and,

---

[1] Scipione Maffei in *Giornale dei Letterati d'Italia*, 1711.

when support from the King at Dresden seemed improbable, Schröter was forced to leave that city and his project was never realised. Later, in 1738, when the hammer action was well-known, Schröter claimed that it was his invention and it had been stolen by both Cristofori and Gottfried Silbermann ("the ingenious man of Dresden"). Schröter even explained the differences between their actions and his by saying that they were not intelligent enough to understand the nature of his invention.[1]

By the year 1726 Cristofori had so improved his pianoforte action, that it had all the salient features of a modern action: the double lever, an escapement, a check and the una corda ("one string") mechanism; and about the time of Cristofori's death in 1731, Ludovico Giustini di Pistoia seems to have composed the first music, twelve sonatas, expressly for the new instrument. For several decades there was little development of the instrument and in Italy there was a declining interest in keyboard music.

Before real progress could be made a difficult technical problem had to be solved and the way was then open for the remarkable development of the classical grand pianoforte between the years 1770–1830, a period which includes the work of Mozart and Beethoven, as composers for and performers on the instrument.

What was the problem and how was it solved? When a plectrum is applied to a stretched string which is pushed aside until it slips over the plectrum and vibrates, all of the energy which the plectrum has imparted to the string in pushing it aside is then available in the vibrations of the string and thence in the air in the form of sound. In other words, a plectrum is an efficient way of imparting energy to a string. The early pianoforte makers thought of the new instrument as a harpsichord with hammer mechanism instead of plectra. When the light, flexible strings of the harpsichord were struck by hammers little energy was transferred and the hammers bounced back. Nevertheless, the amount of energy which a plectrum will transfer to a string is limited and not susceptible to much variation, whereas the energy which a moving hammer will carry is limited only by the speed with which it can be moved by the finger on the key. The tension of the strings and their thickness had to be increased and the pianoforte frame had to be braced to withstand the new forces. New sound-boards and scalings of the strings had to be devised and ultimately iron frames had to be used, although certain beautiful

---

[1] *Neu-eroffnete Musikalische Bibliothek*, vol. III, pp. 474–6, Leipzig, 1736–54; and Marpurg's *Kritische Briefe*, vol. III, p. 85, Berlin, 1764.

tonal qualities, which resulted from the older wooden constructions, were lost.

Gottfried Silbermann (1683–1753), of Saxony, made clavichords and pianofortes but he did not achieve in this the fame which was his as an organ-builder. He knew of the work of Cristofori and added to the ideas of this inventor by making the external case of the instrument a part of the structure, and extending the keyboard.

Silbermann was the friend of the Dresden court poet, König, who published at Hamburg in 1725 a translation of Maffei's article in the *Giornale* on Cristofori's invention. According to J. F. Agricola (1720–74), a pupil of J. S. Bach, in a treatise on musical instruments which is contained in Adlung's *Musica Mechanica Organoedi*, Silbermann made two pianofortes of an existing model, the origin of which he would not divulge, and submitted them to Bach. To the vexation of Silbermann the great musician disapproved of them, on account of their weak trebles and heavy touch. Pianoforte makers had not yet fully realised that a harpsichord with hammers instead of plectra did not make a pianoforte! Insufficient energy was communicated to the strings until the sound-board and the weight, type and tension of the strings had been radically changed.

Silbermann did not understand his model, nor had he attained the skill to reproduce it. For a time Silbermann did not make, or at least did not show, any pianos, but after some years he made one for the Countess of Rudolstadt and another, submitted to Bach, seems to have given more satisfaction to the master. Forkel (1749–1818) says that Silbermann's pianofortes so pleased the king that he bought fifteen of them. By the end of the nineteenth century there were only three to be found in the palaces associated with Frederick the Great: the Stadtschloss, Sans Souci and the Neues Palais. The last was described by Dr. Burney.[1] At least one of these instruments was preserved at Sans Souci until the last war:

. . . Mr. Gottfried Silbermann had at first built two of these instruments (pianofortes). One of them was seen and played by the late Kapellmeister, Mr. Joh. Sebastian Bach. He had praised, indeed admired, its tone; but he had complained that it was too weak in the high register, and was too hard to play (i.e., the action was too heavy). This had been taken greatly amiss by Mr. Silbermann, who could not bear to have any fault found

---

[1] Charles Burney, *The present state of music in Germany, the Netherlands and United Provinces*, vol. II, p. 144, London, 1773.

in his handiworks. He was therefore angry at Mr. Bach for a long time. And yet his conscience told him that Mr. Bach was not wrong. He therefore decided—greatly to his credit be it said—not to deliver any more of these instruments, but instead to think all the harder about how to eliminate the faults Mr. J. S. Bach had observed. He worked for many years on this. And that this was the real cause of this postponement I have the less doubt since I myself heard it frankly acknowledged by Mr. Silbermann. Finally, when Mr. Silbermann had really achieved many improvements, notably in respect to the action, he sold one again to the Court of the Prince of Rudolstadt. Shortly thereafter His Majesty the King of Prussia had one of these instruments ordered, and, when it met with His Majesty's Most Gracious approval, he had several more ordered from Mr. Silbermann. Mr. Silbermann had also had the laudable ambition to show one of these instruments of his later workmanship to the late Kapellmeister Bach, and have it examined by him, and he had received, in turn, complete approval from him.[1]

We now turn to the development of the action of the pianoforte: the means by which the fingers of the performer cause energy to be transferred to the strings of the instrument. Obviously a good action is of absolute importance to the adequate playing of the instrument; and even at its best a piano action does not offer the intimate contact with the source of sound which is enjoyed by the players of bowed instruments, the clavichord, the harp and the orchestral woodwind. Nevertheless, a pianist playing a piano with a good action should feel that he and his instrument have become an artistic unity and that his instrument is an extension or projection of himself. It is not surprising that pianoforte actions have been the subject of several hundreds of patents in the last century and a half.

The simplest type of keyboard action which is conceivable is that of the clavichord, but it would be impossible to replace the blade of the tangent with a leather-covered hammer. A pivoted hammer must be thrown to the string so that the hammer is free to bounce back even if the key is still depressed, otherwise there will be "blocking", and the hammer will remain against the string and keep it from sounding. The simplest piano action which can be devised [PLATE 15] is the single lever action which was called the "mop-stick" or "old man's head" action, as will be clear when the diagram is examined.

[1] J. F. Agricola, *Treatise on the organ and other instruments*, 1768.

The hammer was knocked up by pads of leather fixed to the ends of pieces of brass wire which were inserted in the keys. Such actions were liable both to block and to miss striking the string, but they were extensively employed in English square[1] pianos until about 1800, and in German instruments until later than 1770. If the mop-stick was too long the hammer would block, and if it was too short it would fail to carry the hammer up to the string. The touch was shallow and the instrument was strung with fine wire.

To overcome these difficulties it was necessary to devise an action which has an escapement, so that near the end of its journey towards the string the hammer leaves the mechanism which has impelled it and is then free to travel to the string, and to fall back after striking it. The attack and clarity of the tone are improved, and most players with a sensitive touch are able to sense the instant when the hammer leaves the mechanism and thereby are able to adjust their control of hammer speed. Such an action does not embody all the factors of Cristofori's invention but, when it was used with a satisfactory damping system, it became the basis of the Viennese action which pleased Mozart [PLATE 16].

The escapement was devised by Andreas Stein (1728–92), a pupil of Silbermann, who, like his master, was also an organ builder. Thus was the eighteenth-century German pianoforte brought to its highest stage of development. Stein's daughter, Nannette, a capable pianist, who had been taught pianoforte-making by her father, married Andreas Streicher of Vienna and assisted her husband in improving the techniques of piano-making.

At a meeting of the Royal Musical Association in 1951, Mr. Hugh Gough, an artistic maker of keyboard instruments, presented a Stein pianoforte—then about 180 years old—in which the sound-board of pine about ⅛ in. thick was in perfect condition. Although such instruments are more suitable for the chamber than the concert hall, they are the pianofortes for which Mozart's, Haydn's and some of Beethoven's sonatas were conceived. It is pleasing to think that the making and playing of such pianos is not a lost art. A sonata or piano-concerto, with small string orchestra, by Mozart has a rare beauty of sound which cannot be imitated on the modern, powerful, iron-framed instruments. The Viennese pianoforte had much of the sensitivity of the clavichord and was perhaps about twice as loud as the largest models of the earlier instrument. It is difficult to know exactly what was the quality of tone which was

[1] These were *rectangular* in shape.

preferred. When the soft leather of the hammers was new, the tone was gentle, singing and flute-like; but when the hammer had hardened from age, dryness or use, the tone was brilliant and metallic. No doubt the *via media* was considered to be ideal.

At the end of the eighteenth century there were three types of pianoforte action. The single action was used in the small square pianofortes which superficially resembled the larger clavichords. It was extensively employed by Johannes Zumpe, who was one of Gottfried Silbermann's workmen, and came with others to work in England about 1756 because of troubles in Germany caused by the Seven Years War. Strangely, he seems to have been content to use the simplest type of action and never adopted the double action which his master used. The Zumpe pianofortes had little more tone than a large clavichord, they had less power of expression and the hammers tended to block and to bounce and hit the strings more than once when the keys were struck with some force. The clavichord had not been a popular instrument in Britain in the eighteenth century and therefore the Zumpe pianoforte must have seemed a useful invention. The dampers were lifted by two stops on the left of the keyboard, one for the treble strings and another for the bass [PLATE 16].

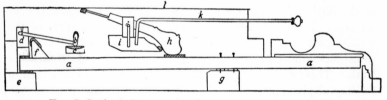

FIG. 7. Socher's Hammerklavier Action, 1742 (Neupert).
a. Key, *b.* Hammer, *c.* Hammer headcheck, *d.* Centre, *e.* Rail, *f.* Jack,
g. Key-rail, *h.* Damper, *i.* Damper rail, *k.* Damper stop, *l.* String.

The Double Action

Cristofori showed extraordinary insight into the problem of designing an efficient action. The double lever multiplied both the speed and distance of the descent of the key by a large factor. Thus, the hammer could be impelled to the string at a large maximum velocity and also had a greater space in which to travel. The escapement allowed good repetition and the check prevented it from bouncing. Thus, the skilful player could have remarkable control of the dynamics of the instrument. Even a gentle pressure on the key would cause the hammer to strike the string softly, and a loud tone was possible without the risk of blocking or of the hammer bouncing on to the string to cause a second sound. Moreover, if the escapement has been carefully adjusted so that the hammer does not leave the mechanism until it is about a tenth of an inch from the string, the touch is refined, there is no feeling of lost motion and wasted energy, and the repetition is good. Pianoforte makers were slow to improve on Cristofori's mechanism, but it became the basis of the actions of the larger concert pianofortes of the nineteenth century, and improvements in design, materials and methods of manufacture have resulted in the robust, reliable yet sensitive actions of the modern pianoforte. The single action became known as the English action and, in general, the English pianos of the early nineteenth century had a deeper and heavier touch than those with the Viennese action [PLATE 15].

The Viennese or German Action

Plate 16 illustrates this ingenious and simple single action in which the hammer was mounted on the key itself. It would have been difficult to fit a check to this action, but good repetition was more easy to achieve than on the English action. The Viennese instrument achieved perfection in itself about the year 1780. It was not capable of the further development which of necessity the English had to undergo. The touch was lighter and shallower than that of the English pianofortes. The hammer-heads were also lighter and were sometimes hollow in construction. They were covered with buckskin leather. There was a better balance between bass and treble than in the English pianofortes in which the bass overwhelmed the treble, unless vastly different touches in each hand could be managed by the performer. The best remembered maker of such pianofortes was Stein, but Walter and others made some good specimens.

Mozart has left a spirited account of Stein's pianofortes:

This time I shall begin at once with Stein's pianofortes. Before I had seen any of his make, Späth's claviers had always been my favourites. But now I much prefer Stein's, for they damp ever so much better than the Regensburg instruments. When I strike hard, I can keep my finger on the note or raise it, but the sound ceases the moment I have produced it. In whatever way I touch the keys, the tone is always even. It never jars, it is never stronger or weaker or entirely absent; in a word, it is always even. It is true that he does not sell a pianoforte of this kind for less than three hundred gulden, but the trouble and the labour that Stein puts into the making of it cannot be paid for. His instruments have this splendid advantage over others, that they are made with escape action. Only one maker in a hundred bothers about this. But without an escapement it is impossible to avoid jangling and vibration after the note is struck. When you touch the keys, the hammers fall back again the moment after they have struck the strings, whether you hold down the keys or release them. He himself told me that when he has finished making one of these claviers, he sits down to it and tries all kinds of passages, runs and jumps, and he polishes and works away at it until it can do anything. For he labours solely in the interest of music and not for his own profit: otherwise he would soon finish his work. He often says: "If I were not myself such a passionate lover of music, and had not myself some slight skill on the clavier, I should certainly long ago have lost patience with my work. But I do like an instrument which never lets the player down and which is durable." And his claviers certainly do last. He guarantees that the sounding-board will neither break nor split. When he has finished making one for a clavier, he places it in the open air, exposing it to rain, snow, the heat of the sun and all the devils in order that it may crack. Then he inserts wedges and glues them in to make the instrument very strong and firm. He is delighted when it cracks, for he can then be sure that nothing more can happen to it. Indeed he often cuts into it himself and then glues it together again and strengthens it in this way.

. . . Here and at Munich I have played all my six sonatas by heart several times. The last one, in D [K. 284] sounds exquisite on Stein's pianoforte. The device, too, which you work with your knee, is better on his than on others instruments. I have only to touch it and it works; and when you shift your knee the slightest bit, you do not feel the least reverberation.[1]

The knee device worked the sustaining mechanism, which was applied by pedal in England, before it became general in the German states. Mozart actually owned a pianoforte made by Anton Walter in c.1784. Its compass seems to have been almost five octaves to e''', a seventeenth above middle C.

The compass of the English grand piano in the early years of the nineteenth century was five and a half octaves, and later six octaves. Because of the demands of composers and performers and the popu-

[1] W. A. Mozart, letter to his father from Augsburg, October 17–18, 1777.

larity of treble octave passages in pianoforte arrangements of operatic and symphonic works, progressive manufacturers adapted their piano designs to include "the additional keys".

What were the reasons for the difference of tone of the two types of piano? The strings of the Viennese piano were thinner than those of the English. The wire of the first was about ·012 in. diameter and that of the second 50 per cent greater. The English grand had three strings to each note and the Viennese piano only two, except for a few notes in the treble where there were three. Also, the sound-boards were differently made and of different kinds of wood. The Viennese sound-board was quite flat but the English sound-board was thicker and was bucked, that is, slightly convex outwards. In the Viennese piano the case was merely decorative, and the instrument was built with a very solid base and system of braces, but in the English instrument the case took most of the pull of the strings and the bottom was only a part of the case. The hammer of the English piano was somewhat heavier than that of the Viennese, which escaped more easily from the key mechanism and had a higher velocity ratio. The dampers of the Viennese instrument were properly weighted wedges and were efficient, whereas the English instruments had relatively poor dampers which rested lightly on the strings. Hugh Gough believes that the English players preferred to have inefficient dampers.

Thus, as Hummel sets forth so clearly, there were shortcomings in both instruments. Improvements were required which would produce a pianoforte which had the sensitivity and repetition of the Viennese action and the fullness of tone of the English instrument. There were external forces which encouraged pianoforte makers to improve their instruments. The influence of Mozart as player and composer and the extension of the scope of the piano in the works of Beethoven generated much interest in the instrument on the part of musicians. A generation of players who derived from Muzio Clementi or his pupil Hummel were anxious to develop pianoforte technique and not infrequently, like a prima donna, were more interested in the technique of performance than in musical content. Also, at the same time there was an increase in popular interest in orchestral music, opera, oratorio, songs and light church music, and there was a demand in Europe as well as in England for piano-forte transcriptions of popular music composed for other media. Most of the manufacturers and vendors of musical instruments, even organ-builders, also printed and sold popular music. Johann

Plate three

a. Fretted (bound) Clavichord (about 1600) with Short Octave (Museum Neupert)

b. "Hammerflugel" such as W. A. Mozart used, by J. A. Stein (1728–92) (Museum Neupert)

c. Virginal, H. Ruckers, Antwerp, 1610

Nepomuk Hummel in the English edition (1827) of his *A Complete Theoretical and Practical Course of Instruction in the Art of Playing the Pianoforte, commencing with the Simplest Elementary Principles and including every information requisite to the Most Finished Style of Performance*, writes:

The German piano may be played upon with ease by the weakest hand. It allows the performer to impart to his execution every possible degree of light and shade, speaks clearly and promptly, has a round fluty tone, which in a large room contrasts well with the accompanying orchestra, and does not impede rapidity of execution by requiring too great an effort. These instruments are likewise durable, and cost about half the price of the English pianoforte.

To the English construction, however, we must not refuse the praises due on the score of its durability and fullness of tone. Nevertheless this instrument does not admit of the same facility of execution as the German; the touch is heavier, the key sinks much deeper, and, consequently, the return of the hammer upon the repetition of a note cannot take place so quickly . . . this mechanism is not capable of such numerous modifications as to degree of tone as ours. . . .

In the first moment [i.e., when first using an English pianoforte] we are sensible of something unpleasant, because, in forte passages in particular, on our German instruments we press the keys quite down, while here, they must be only touched, superficially, as otherwise we could not succeed in executing such runs without excessive effort and double difficulty. As a counterpoise to this, however, through the fullness of tone of the English pianoforte, the melody receives a peculiar charm and harmonious sweetness.

In the meantime, I have observed that, powerfully as these instruments sound in a chamber, they change the nature of their tone in spacious localities; and that they are less distinguishable than ours, when associated with complicated orchestral accompaniments; this, in my opinion, is to be attributed to the thickness and fullness of their tone.

and Friedrich Kalkbrenner, in his *Méthode* (Paris, 1820), says:

The instruments of Vienna and London have produced two schools. The Viennese pianists are particularly distinguished for their precision, the clarity and rapidity of their execution. Thus the instruments manufactured in that city (Vienna) are extremely

D

easy to play. . . . The use of the pedals in Germany is almost unknown. English pianos have a fuller sound and a heavier keyboard action. The players of that country have adopted a larger style and that beautiful way of singing that distinguishes them; and it is indispensable to use the large pedal in order to conceal the inherent dryness of the piano.

Dussek, Field and J. B. Cramer, the chiefs of that school which was founded by Clementi, use the pedal when harmonies do not change. Dussek, above all, was responsible for that, for he used the pedal almost constantly when he played in public.

The Transition from Harpsichord to Pianoforte

Balbastre, a late eighteenth-century French composer, keyboard player and organist of Notre Dame Cathedral in Paris, said to French pianoforte makers: "You toil in vain, this upstart will never replace the majestic harpsichord"; and Voltaire in 1774 described the pianoforte as a "boiler-maker's instrument". Nevertheless the German *Musik Handbuch* for 1782 placed the pianoforte over the harpsichord but below the clavichord: "Though it has more light and shade than the former and can express more varied emotions, it still has no middle tints and lacks the refined details of beauty of the clavichord."

Dr. Charles Burney in his *History of Music* shows how he had grown away from the exotic tones of the harpsichord:

There is no instrument so favourable to such frothy and unmeaning music than the harpsichord. . . . I remember well in the early part of my life being a dupe to this kind of tinsel, this *poussière dans les yeux*, . . . At length, on the arrival of the late Mr. Bach[1] and construction of pianofortes in this country, the performers on keyed instruments were obliged wholly to change their ground; and instead of surprising by the seeming labour and dexterity of execution, had the real and more useful difficulties of taste, expression, and light and shade to encounter.

The transition from harpsichord to pianoforte is reflected in the title pages of printed English keyboard music from 1750 to 1800; a period when England was an important centre for music publishing.[2] In nearly three hundred solo keyboard music editions in this period no publication for piano only appeared during the period

---

[1] i.e., J. C. Bach.
[2] Albert G. Hess, "*The Transition from Harpsichord to Piano*", *Galpin Society Journal*, VI, July 1953.

1750–80, thirty years, though from 1770 more editions mentioned both pianoforte and harpsichord than harpsichord only. After 1785, editions for harpsichord only hardly ever appeared, though both instruments are still mentioned on the title-pages, doubtless to suggest a wider scope for the works for commercial reasons. In 1800, out of thirty-eight works, none appears for harpsichord only, three for both instruments and thirty-five for pianoforte only. The figures are not significantly different for the changes in title wordings in English chamber and vocal music editions during the same period of time, in spite of the fact that it has been asserted that the harpsichord tended to persist as a concerted instrument.

In 1767 Dibden accompanied Miss Brickler's singing at a benefit concert at Covent Garden "on a new instrument called a Piano-Forte" and in the following year John Christian Bach gave a public recital on a Zumpe pianoforte. Two years before this, *Burton's Ten Sonatas*, published by himself, mentioned the pianoforte; and the publishers Bremner, Napier and Welcker soon did likewise. Parrish says that the inclusion of the pianoforte in the titles of English editions became general about the year 1775.[1] There were forty-five firms which manufactured pianos in London alone, before 1800. Broadwood made 6,000 square and 1,000 grand pianos between 1780 and 1800, a large number when the size of the cultured population is taken into consideration.

A leading firm of makers of fine harpsichords, that of Kirkman (Kirckmann) tried to resist the change. They gave away harpsichords to girls who would play them in the London streets. One of the family composed a concerto for pianoforte and harpsichord. In the end they yielded to the pianoforte and became one of the leading firms of manufacturers, holding royal appointments for some years. At the end of the century they were absorbed by Collard and Collard.

Hess has also considered the transition of one instrument to the other in France by reference to the catalogues of instruments confiscated by the Revolutionaries from the houses of the nobles. It is possible that the French showed a certain conservatism although it seems probable that they retained their harpsichords as pieces of furniture or antiques, nearly all of them having been made before 1780. In 1765 Nicolas Sejan, a Paris organist, published *Ariettes*

---

[1] Carl George Parrish, *The Early Piano and its Influence on Keyboard Technique and Composition in the Eighteenth Century*, Harvard University Thesis, 1939.

choisies mises en Sonates pour le clavȩçin ou le piano-forte, and three years later a pianoforte concert was given in Paris.

Here are two letters, by unknown writers, at the time of this transition:

I am favoured with your letter, which was brought immediately to me. I find your daughter is a forte piano player, whence I conclude she has been in the hands of some of the idle, tasteless masters of the day. These wild fellows teach their scholars upon that instrument, because they think if they do but teach them to gabble and chatter, they make fine players of them. But there is as much difference between fiddling and playing, as there is between gabbling and expressive reading. No musical expression can be produced by hammers; it is all tub-work at the best, whether forte or piano. It gives a thumping staccato manner of fingering, that is as ungraceful to the sight, as injurious to expression, and renders the pupils incapable of the touch of a harpsichord; and with an organ, the noblest of all our keyed instruments, they play the very d—l! Set a forte player down to a harpsichord, or a good spinet finely in order, and he will expose himself to a judge of musical expression before he has played five bars; for he has no fine expression of his own, because the instrument he has been used to, is incapable of it, and he avoids fine taste as he would a monster. It affrights the modern fiddler.

You say you are fond of solemn music, and express your predilection for Handel's, for that the general run of your daughter's lessons seems such an empty parade of execution, that the affections of the heart gain no interest in them. You need not have added this, having informed me that she is a forte piano player—I could have told you—solemn harmony! and on a forte piano? It is most murderously insufferable. Mr. Handel's great genius would not allow him to write for that trifling instrument, and of ten of his oratorios which I have by me, I scarcely find anything fit for it. Such pieces as may be played upon it, with any degree of toleration, I have copied and sent to you. But these are all of the talkative kind (except the "Dead March in Saul") and not the music you want. However, they are excellent lessons, not being mere miscellaneous harmony, like the modern compositions; but subject, or air, supported through every piece. It is regular subject, or air only, that can improve musical genius. The modern miscellaneous stuff, however grammatical, will no more make a musician, than novels and romances form the scholar. The former is taught to fiddle, the latter teaches himself to gabble.

As I remember you have a tolerable little spinet, this kept in good order, and evenly, but tenderly pinned, is more fit to practise upon than a forte piano. The spinet or harpsichord equally lead to the proper touch of the organ, to which the manner of touching the forte piano is directly contrary, and I believe never to be got over, if fixed by habit. Handel's finest airs and songs are bearable on a spinet. Let your daughter learn upon the spinet one of Handel's finest songs; for instance, "I know that my Redeemer Liveth", and you will see what vile stuff a forte piano will make of it. This trial will sufficiently prove to you the truth of what I have asserted respecting the great imperfection of that instrument, and will soon convince you, that the way to the organ is through the keys of the spinet or harpsichord, and the road to musical expression of course. . . .

Here is a more favourable view of the pianoforte:

As a source of social gratification, music has no small obligations to the perfection to which mechanical ingenuity has brought the pianoforte. The power of expression it offers to the finger of the feeling performer, and the force and delicacy, the light and shade, the illustration of the composer's designs which it permits, is so prodigious and so delightful an advance beyond the inferior-toned and monotonous harpsichord of our forefathers that, to say nothing of the advantage of the enlarged compass afforded by its additional keys, it may now be said to form the king of stringed instruments. Its various and novel capacities have opened to one species of composition a perfectly new scope; and in consequence, given to it as perfect an originality of character. By skilful adaption, it can even re-model pieces, composed for other instruments, and produce effects transcending their author's first conception.[1]

[1] Susi Jeans, *Musical Opinion*, London, May 1962.

CHAPTER III

NINETEENTH-CENTURY PROGRESS IN PIANOFORTE MAKING

BY the year 1800 composers and performers were seeking to extend the capabilities of the pianoforte. An instrument was required which not only combined the subtlety of the Viennese piano with the fullness and roundness of tone of the English, but also had facilities for speed and repetition in playing, and a tone which would fill a large hall. Sound-boards and frames of greater strength, heavier strings under increased tension and improved actions were required. The type of mechanism which became the basis of nearly all subsequent actions was that devised by Sebastien Érard. Érard was born in Strasburg in 1752, and even as a boy showed extraordinary feats of initiative, as, for instance, in climbing to the top of the spire of the cathedral of his native city. He was one of the greatest of all instrument makers and improvers in Europe, and the harp and organ were developed by him and his assistants.

After his father's death he worked with a harpsichord-maker in Paris from 1768. His desire to explore the fundamental principles of instrument construction led to a dispute with his master and he transferred his services to another instrument-maker, who more properly appreciated the talents and energy of his brilliant assistant. A harpsichord of exceptional beauty of tone and delicate touch established his reputation, and the Duchesse de Villeroi gave him a workshop and comfortable apartments in her château, and here he constructed his first pianoforte in 1777. Soon after this he wished to increase his output of instruments, and so he moved to the Rue de Bourbon in Paris and was joined by his brother Jean Baptiste.

Érard's workshops were raided by the jealous Luthiers of Paris with the excuse that the laws of the Company of Fanmakers, of which the Luthiers were a part, had been infringed; but Louis XVI protected the Érards, so that after a time their pianofortes displaced those of Zumpe. Gradually the Érards improved Zumpe's action.

The Revolution of 1789 disturbed the Érard business and in 1792 Sebastien started a factory in Great Marlborough Street, London, and left his brother to continue in Paris. The first grand pianoforte, which worked with an improved English grand action, was made in 1796. Subsequently, various English patents were taken out by Érard, such as those for an action in which the hammers could be made to strike one, two or three strings of the trichord, and a harmonic device analogous to that of the Cavaillé-Coll organ pipes, but obtained by a different means: that of lightly striking or plucking the strings at their middle points.[1]

At the beginning of the nineteenth century more and more was expected of the piano. The sonatas of Beethoven had explored it but the interest in operatic music, the tremolando of the violin and the prima donna, and the sounds of massed instruments had suggested attempts to imitate these effects on the keyboard of the "household orchestra". The action of the piano had to give improved powers of repetition, so that any note could be reiterated at great speed. The first Érard repetition actions were not easily maintained and the mechanism soon became noisy and needed adjustment. In 1821, the famous "double-escapement" action was completed and was patented in England by Pierre Érard. (The term "double escapement" is perhaps misleading and a better term would be "compound escapement".) At first the action seemed to be too complicated to be sturdy and reliable but it was simplified by Herz and used in a modified form by Steinway, Bechstein, Pleyel, Collard and Broadwood.

Sebastien built piano-organs with two keyboards, pianos with transposing devices and pedal keyboards, patented methods of prolonging the sound of the piano, and used copper wire for the lower octaves. He died on August 5, 1831, and his business was continued by his nephew, Pierre Érard, who lived until 1855. Then his widow and afterwards his nephew, the Count de Franqueville, in partnership with Blondel, directed the distinguished house of Érard.

The Érard pianofortes were favoured by Liszt and later were often played in Europe by Paderewski, Busoni, Sauer, Planté, Bauer, Berthe Marx, Goldschmitt, Risler, Ricardo Vines and many others. Thalberg, Hummel, Moscheles, Steibelt, Herz, Pixis, Mendelssohn and Verdi possessed Érard pianofortes.

Moscheles, a brilliant performer, constantly urged Érard to im-

---

[1] This was also the principle of G. Silbermann's "Cembal d'Amour".

prove his actions, and for many years preferred to play on the instruments of Pape and Petzold. On June 1, 1825, Moscheles wrote:

> Pierre Érard showed and explained to me . . . his Uncle Sebastien's new completed invention . . . It consists in the key, when only sunk half way, again rising and repeating the note. I was the first to play upon one of the newly completed instruments and found it of priceless value for the repetition of notes. In the matter of fullness and mellowness of tone, there is something yet to be desired, and I had a long conversation on the subject with Érard.

Although the Érard pianofortes were so successful in Europe, what almost amounted to a campaign against them in England inhibited the flow of the Érard pianofortes in Britain. A court of enquiry of the Privy Council in 1835 received evidence in their favour, and Érard's patent of 1821 was extended. Monsieur Latour, Director of the Philharmonic Concerts in 1827 and 1828, stated that Érard pianofortes were generally used at their concerts. Signor Scappa, leader of the Opera, remarked that Érard's pianofortes had "a great deal more strength and power than any other instrument and greater effect in accompanying the voice"! Madame Dulcken stated that "they had the same advantages as the German pianofortes with a greater brilliancy of tone, and that when visiting Russia she had observed that they stood the climate, whilst other instruments did not. They also remained in tune better than ordinary pianofortes; her own needed tuning only three or four times a year".

The Piano as Household Orchestra

The organ of the seventeenth and eighteenth centuries, an instrument of rare beauty and individuality, was to give way in the nineteenth century to a romantic-symphonic tendency which almost completely destroyed its identity by the end of the same century. The piano has a shorter history than the organ, and although it was beset with tendencies and devices which were deviations from its real nature, its recovery from contaminating influences was much quicker. The greatest composers for the instrument formed and informed the piano aesthetic and, in the end, determined its optimum structure and appointments. When the organ departed from the ideals of those of Bach it did so at the peril of losing itself completely. In other words, as the decades of the nineteenth century passed, the "trappings" and ancillaries, which had connected themselves with the piano, were seen to be unnecessary. The strung sound-board, with a responsive action, a single keyboard and two or three pedals could offer sufficient scope to the virtuoso of the Liszt, Busoni, Rachmaninoff standards and, at the other extreme, the humble player of songs and hymn-tunes.

The lack of sustaining power of the sounds of the piano (though this was more marked a century and a half ago than it is now) was considered to be a grievous shortcoming in the instrument. It is said that, in the eighteenth century, when keyboard pieces were composed for "organ or harpsichord", young ladies used to go to church in order to hear their music played, "so that the concords may be more fully heard, and the sound will hold on as long as the artist pleases, without the repeating of the stroke".

The Nuremberg Geigenwerk was an early attempt to produce "continuity". Early pianofortes were sometimes combined with chamber organs. Devices were made from time to time, in the eighteenth and nineteenth centuries, for bowing the strings with circular bows worked by treadles. Such an instrument was that produced by John Isaac Hawkins of Philadelphia, U.S.A., in 1802 and called the claviol. When the key was pressed, the string of the instrument was raised to meet the revolving bow. The dynamics of the sound could be varied by pressing lightly or heavily. In England, I. H. R. Mott of Brighton, a music teacher, made a similar instrument in 1817.

Another type of "Sostenente" pianoforte imitated, by a different method, the *Bebung* of the clavichord. In 1800 the father of the Hawkins mentioned above, took out an English patent for a device in which a cylinder with projecting teeth, which was kept revolving while the instrument was being played, caused the hammer to reiterate quickly its motion and thus the sound, as long as its key was kept down. Many pianoforte makers adapted the device in some of their pianos, with modifications. Both Érard and Henri Pape in Paris patented forms of it.

A third method of producing a continuous sound was the employment of currents of air to keep the strings of the piano in vibration. In 1828 Eschenbach devised the Eolodicon, a type of keyboard Eolian harp, on this principle. The idea was obviously that of the organ, with a use of stretched strings instead of the lips and body of organ pipes. In England, Wheatstone, the inventor of the Concertina, a free reed instrument, and Green patented a similar system; and Henri Pape, in Paris, extended the principle to vibrating springs and to strings which were connected to one another with silk threads, so that they would vibrate "sympathetically".[1]

At the end of the eighteenth century, after the treaty of the Russian Empress with the Turks, and with an increasing interest in the customs of former enemies in Austria, Turkish instruments were introduced into Royal Bands. The drums, triangles and cymbals were used, not only in military music, but for the accompaniments of dances. Gluck used the Turkish band in his opera "Iphigénie en Tauride" with terrifying effect. Drums and Cymbelstars, which revolved in the organ-case, were a feature of organ specifications from the sixteenth century. Mozart and Beethoven were attracted by Turkish music, and the March or Rondo in the Turkish style became popular in keyboard music.[2] A similar influence is seen in Mozart's "Die Entführung aus dem Seráil". All sorts of drum devices were fitted to pianos. The crudest was a drum-stick, actuated by a foot-lever, which beat upon the sound-board of the instrument. In another, a drum-skin was stretched over a circular hole in the sound-board and was struck by a foot-actuated drumstick with spherical head. Thus was the now-defunct cinema organ, of the third and fourth decades of the present century, anticipated. Triangles and cymbals were also added to the resources of some pianos.

Even at the beginning of the nineteenth century the artistic pianists and teachers eschewed the use of devices which were imitative of other instruments. Hummel said:

> Though a truly great artist has no occasion for pedals to work upon his audience by expression and power, yet the use of the damper-pedal, combined occasionally with the piano-pedal . . . has an agreeable effect in many passages. All other pedals are useless, and of no value either to the performer or to the instrument.

This is echoed by Czerny in his Pianoforte School. He says that only three pedals are necessary: 1, The damper pedal (forte); 2, Una Corda (Verschiebung); 3, Piano (piano). . . . "All other pedals, such as the Fagotto and Harp pedals, or the Drum and Bells, or Triangle, etc., are childish toys of which a solid player will disdain to avail himself."

Battle and storm music were popular about 1800 and even the organ had to provide it. During Mass in Parisian churches the organ

[1] These systems are described in detail by R. E. M. Harding in *The Pianoforte*, pp. 95 et seq., Cambridge, 1933.
[2] The march in Mozart's popular Sonata in A is well known (K.331).

was made to imitate the roar of the cannon, the trumpets blowing martial strains, together with the noise of arms, the cries of the wounded and the Te Deum of victory, "pour célébrer le Dieu des Armées". Miss R. E. M. Harding[1] tells of a young lady who owned a pianoforte by Astor, with two pedals: ". . . one for sustaining the sound and the other for opening the short side of the lid for the purpose of obtaining a pleasing 'swell'. When playing a battle piece she illustrated the explosion of cannon by suddenly releasing her foot from the swell pedal and allowing the lid to fall with a crash." Somewhat less destructive to the nerves, as also to the pianoforte, was the pastorale fantasia, ennobled by Beethoven in his Sixth Symphony. In the piano pieces, bassoon effects in the bass were supported by flute-like passages in the treble. The delights of country life were interrupted by thunder, lightning and hail, but the storm soon passed and a hymn of thanksgiving made a fitting coda to the work. Both the battlefield and the country village offered immense scope to the composer, particularly if his ability and inspiration were inadequate for the creation of a purer type of musical expression. Nevertheless, even some of the greatest composers did unbend to the extent of providing examples of this programmed, descriptive music when the occasion demanded it.

Here is a brief description of the chief pedal-actuated "effects" which persisted for years after the piano had established itself as an instrument in its own right.

Miss Harding[2] gives a list of the stops which were found on pianos at the end of the eighteenth century. On the grand pianoforte the basic stops were Forte and Una Corda (Verschiebung), which was later called Piano in England. On the square (rectangular) piano there were two stops which raised the dampers in the bass and treble respectively, and often, in more expensive instruments, a lute stop was added.

Forte.—This was a mechanism for raising the dampers first by hand-stops and later, in 1783, by a foot-pedal patented by John Broadwood. Five years later Bury patented a system in which a sliding-board removed the dampers "whereby the tone becomes exactly similar to a Dulcimer".

Piano.—This was called Pianozug by the Germans. Strips of cloth or soft leather were interposed between the hammers and the strings.

[1] *A History of the Pianoforte*, p. 113.
[2] op. cit., page 69.

The device was extended by Isaac Hawkins in 1800, so that the material was graduated in thickness and hardness from one edge to the other, and thus by its gradual introduction and withdrawal between the strings and the hammers, *diminuendi* and *crescendi* could be achieved.

Una Corda (Verschiebung).—By the movement of a pedal, the hammers were made to strike one, two or three strings at the will of the performer. Merlin patented the device in 1774, for his combined harpsichord and pianoforte, to imitate the swell of an organ, but there was also a change of tone quality because of the sympathetic vibration of the unstruck strings. Harpsichord players did not readily adapt their touch to the more responsive mechanism of the piano and would use the Una Corda pedal instead of modern graduated touch-dynamics to secure softer tones. In the finale of Opus 101 (Sonata No. 28 in A), Beethoven asks for *"einer Saite"* (*Seite*) i.e. *una corda* or "one string", and further, *"Noch und noch mehrere Saiten"* (*more and more strings*). In Opus 110 (Sonata No. 31 in A♭), *"poi a poi tutte le corde"* (*little by little all the strings*). The slow movement of the Hammerklavier Sonata (Opus 106) asks for *una corda* ten times and *tutte le corde* an equal number of times, together with two other references to the device.

Harp.—A strip of leather damped the motion of one of each set of unison strings and, at the same time, the hammers were moved to strike the strings which were affected by the leather. The dry, sweet tone of the harp was thus imitated.

Buff Stop.—This was similar to the "harp", "buff" or "Lautenzug" of the harpsichord. It was patented in 1786 by John Geib, who seems to have intended it as a tuning aid for the treble strings. A piece of leather presses and damps one of each set of unisons at the side or, occasionally, from below.

Sordin or Mute.—A piece of wood, hinged to the case and worked by a pedal, lined with "soft leather, hair or silk shagg" damps the motion of the strings. The curve of the wood followed that of the sound-board bridge (Broadwood, 1783). If soft leather is used the effect is that of the Lautenzug (the Lute stop) and if hair or silk the effect is that of the Harfenzug (the Harp stop).

Harpsichord Stop or Cembalo.—Tongues of leather, tipped with a hard substance, such as bone or ivory, are placed between the hammers and the strings, so that the hard substance strikes the strings. It was patented in 1788 by Bury, and there may have been earlier examples in Germany.

Swell.—A pedal raised a portion of the lid or the dust plate. The Venetian blind type of swell, which became popular in organs, was invented in Germany, patented in England by Shudi in 1769, and applied to harpsichords.

Miss Harding[1] points out that *Sordini* and *Sordino* imply different damping methods. In the first movement of Beethoven's Sonata in C♯ minor (Opus 27, No. 2, the "Moonlight"), the instruction "Senza Sordini" means that the dampers are to remain lifted throughout the movement. Sordino is another name for a lute stop. This was often used with the forte pedal, so that the dryness of tone was less in evidence. Schubert uses it in his song "Der Tod und das Mädchen" (Opus 7, No. 3, 1817); and, when the pianoforte lid was closed it was used to imitate "Side drums" played softly.

In the early years of the nineteenth century still more tone-changing mechanisms were added to the piano:

Harmonic Sounds.—A pedal brought into operation a set of hammers or a bar which touched the strings at their central points. This produced an echo effect which was a feature of Pastoral music. This was clearly a new version of G. Silbermann's "Cembal d'amour". It was suggested that other tonal effects could be produced by touching the strings at points one-third of their length.

Dolce Compana (Compana, a corruption of Campana, a bell).—By means of a pedal, weights apply pressure to the sound-board at about eight places. This lowers the pitch of the instrument, so that a rapid operation of the pedal gives the effect of a vibrato, like the tremulant of the organ.

Harmonic Swell.—The piano had two bridges and the raising of dampers allowed the wires between the bridges to vibrate sympathetically with the ordinary speaking lengths of strings. The device was called the swell, because gradations of power could be obtained by: 1, raising the dampers of the harmonic swell; 2, raising the forte dampers; 3, raising both sets of dampers.

Cymbals.—Two or three thin strips of brass were made to strike the bass strings.

Bassoon.—A piece of parchment or stiff paper was placed against

[1] *A History of the Pianoforte,* p. 71.

the strings. Usually this only affected the notes from middle C downwards but, occasionally, it was applied to nearly the whole compass. The effect can be imitated by placing a sheet of stiff paper on the strings of a modern grand piano. The effect is dry, penetrating, reedy and unpleasant to modern ears.

Octave couplers.—These showed the influence of the harpsichord. They tended to become unreliable and spoil the expressive touch of the piano. After their disappearance, for some decades an attempt was made to resuscitate them in the Moor and other keyboards. (q.v.).

Obviously, many combinations of these devices were possible. A giraffe piano which was represented in one of Sir William Orchardson's paintings had eight pedals.[1] A horizontal grand which was also painted by the same artist had six pedals.[2]

Giraffe piano by Van der Hoef of Amsterdam: 1, Bassoon; 2, Una Corda; 3, Bassoon (lighter); 4, Piano; 5, Forte; 6, Piano; 7, Drum and Triangle; 8, Triangle alone. [See plate 9.]

Grand piano by Jeorg Taschta of Vienna: 1, Bassoon; 2, Drum; 3, Piano; 4, Triangle (small bells); 5, Una Corda; 6, Forte.

Other combinations:

Weber's piano by Brodmann of Vienna: 1, Una Corda; 2, Lute; 3, Piano; 4, Forte.

Napoleon's piano by Érard (1801): 1, Una Corda; 2, Bassoon; 3, Forte; 4, Piano; 5, Drum and Triangle.

Pape, for a square piano in France (1826): 1, Forte; 2, Sourdine (a harp sound); 3, Bassoon; 4, Jeu Céleste (piano).

Kisselstein of Nuremberg in a Giraffe piano (1831): 1, Forte; 2, Octave coupler contra F to é; 3, Octave coupler é to f‴; 4, Piano; 5, Pianissimo; 6, Una Corda ("which produces a sound similar to that of the glass harmonica").

The Pianoforte in England

At the beginning of the eighteenth century Fulke Greville bought for a hundred guineas a piano from Samuel Crisp, a friend of Samuel Johnson, who had imported it from Italy where it was said to have been made in Rome by Father Wood, an English monk. The harpsichord maker Plenius tried to copy the action, which was

---

[1] "Music when soft voices die."
[2] "A tender chord."

of the early Cristofori type, but he was not successful and the harpsichord continued to be popular. In 1755 the Reverend William Mason, a poet and musician, brought a little square piano from Germany and he tried to introduce this type of piano with a Zumpe or Silbermann modification of the Italian action. When J. S. Bach's son, Johann Christian, settled in London his free advocacy of the pianoforte encouraged craftsmen to make it and musicians to play it.

Viator, a German, and Americus Backers, a Dutchman, made attempts to improve the action but there was little progress until twelve instrument makers, including several trained by Silbermann, were driven from Germany because of the Seven Years War, and settled in England. The best known of the "twelve apostles" was Zumpe, who brought the Cristofori–Silbermann tradition and entered the service of Burkat Shudi, the harpsichord maker, originally a Swiss.[1] As will be seen in the account of the distinguished firm of John Broadwood, this was an important event in the history of the English pianoforte, for Broadwood married Shudi's daughter and, in 1770, became his partner. Zumpe's square pianofortes became very popular, and those of Johannes Pohlmann were not far behind. Zumpe used a "single" action invented in Germany by him or his master and commonly known as "the English action", whereas his successors used a "double" action derived from that of Cristofori (Zumpe's second action). The treble and bass dampers of Pohlmann's pianos were raised by two stops in the left hand side of the keys and a third stop actuated the lute effect. Sometimes a pedal was provided to give a swell by raising a part of the lid of the piano. A single action was used also by Southwell of Dublin in the closing years of the eighteenth century. Southwell used the "Irish damper", which was hinged directly to the key and was pressed to the string by the weight of the key. John Geib, a keyboard-instrument maker in the workshops of Longman and Broderip, obtained a patent in 1786 for a modification of Cristofori's action of sixty years before. Besides Zumpe and Pohlmann the most distinguished of the twelve were Buntlebart, Beyer, Beck and Ganer. The English square pianos were also greatly prized on the continent. In 1782 a Zumpe piano was offered in exchange for a Stradivarius violin!

The English grand action, which was admired by Beethoven, was invented about 1772 and seems to have been the joint work of John Broadwood, his apprentice Robert Stodart, and Americus Backers. This was an up-striking action, but some piano makers

[1] Also spelt Schudi or Tschudi.

thought that down-striking action, which would not tend to push the strings away from the bridge, would be more conducive to stability of tuning. George Pether devised such a mechanism in which the hammer, in an inverted *prellmechanik*, was lifted from the strings by a lead weight at its end. In other patterns the hammer was returned to its position of rest by means of springs; indeed, some players preferred a spring touch, even with up-striking actions, which was like that of a small organ. With the improvement of the technique of piano-playing, this became unpopular.

The end of the eighteenth century was a time of much experiment to find the ideal striking place on the string length. In 1788 Broadwood adopted a striking place about a ninth of the length of the string, and with some small variation of this in the treble, it was made possible by dividing the belly-bridge. The problems of temperament also occupied the attention of some makers; for instance Clagget, in 1788, with a principle not unlike that of the chromatic harp, used auxiliary bridges to alter the speaking lengths of the strings, and his pianoforte, the Telio-chordon, could divide the octave into thirty-nine pitches. He also devised new forms of keyboards by which he claimed that all keys could be "five-fingered" in a similar manner and trills could be easily and evenly played.

The Pianoforte in America

In 1788 Brissot de Warville, a French lawyer, wrote from Boston:

> Music, which their teachers formerly proscribed as a diabolical art, begins to make part of their education. In some houses you hear the forte-piano. This art, it is true, is still in its infancy; but the young novices who exercise it are so gentle, so complaisant, and so modest that the proud perfection of art gives no pleasure to what they afford. God grant that the Bostonian women may never, like those of France, acquire the malady of perfection in this art! It is never attained but at the expense of the domestic virtues.

The late eighteenth-century pianos were largely imported from England and France, but soon America was able to produce instruments which in tone and efficiency were the equals, at least, of those of Europe. By 1850 imports from England were almost negligible but the Pleyel and Érard pianos were imported from France. The Chickering and later Steinway pianofortes made in America, and

used by both American and visiting virtuosi, became well-established and, in the second half of the century, won first and second prizes at International Exhibitions anywhere in the civilised world. The energetic and well-travelled American pianist, Gottschalk, played exclusively on Chickering's pianofortes, and, as was the custom, the name of the maker was prominently displayed on the instrument. The achievements of the Chickering and Steinway firms have been noticed elsewhere in this book.

Many German keyboard instrument makers settled in America about the year 1840. Sohmer, J. and C. Fischer, Weber, Steck, amongst others, founded good businesses. In 1851 about 9,000 pianos were made in America; in 1860, after the establishment of Steinway and Son, Mason and Hamlin, and William Knabe, the number had risen to 22,000.

At the Great Exhibition in 1876 in Philadelphia many piano-fortes from America and Europe were displayed and this gave scope for comparison. The American pianofortes were said to withstand the climatic changes in America better than those imported from Europe.

It showed plainly the superiority and inferiority contained on both sides in European and native pianos in a detailed and analytical sense of comparison, while it served to illustrate the progress made in this country since 1853 in the art of piano-making. This informal convention of European and native makers was, however, characterised by universal good feeling toward the foreign element, while all the strength of competition seems to have reposed between American manufacturers. While many points of excellence worthy of adoption were noted in the pianos of Brinsmead and Sons and Browne of London; Blüthner of Leipzig; and Debain of Paris, American piano-makers in general had every reason to feel proud of their instruments and the great development reached in the art and craft in this country since 1775, when Behrent announced the first piano in Philadelphia.

While a most courteous and hospitable demeanour was evinced by the judges toward European exhibitors, there was no use trying to conceal the fact that the first-class American pianos exhibited excelled the best instruments of European makers in every respect. At the same time, American makers were bound to admit that in point of finish and detail, in regard to construction

E

and ornamentation, many German, French and English pianos sent across contained points of high excellence.[1]

The Upright Piano

In the eighteenth century, pianos were sometimes arranged vertically on stands, in order to give them an organ-like appearance, to rise in empathy with the music, to save floor space, or to decorate the wall of a room. As early as 1735 upright pianos were made by modifying the action of a horizontal instrument and placing it vertically on a stand, or table. Christian Ernst Friederici, a keyboard-instrument maker of Gera and a brilliant pupil of Silbermann, produced such pianos from 1735, of which a number are still extant in European museums. The curve of the grand piano placed vertically suggested a type of case-work which was called the Giraffe; a little ingenuity of the arrangement of the action and strings could place the tallest part of the case in the middle and this was known as a Pyramid piano. Further modification and oblique stringing could permit the enclosure of the piano in a lyre-shaped case. It was typical of many of the early upright pianos that makers tried to disguise them as, or incorporate them with, book-cases, study-desks or dressing tables.

In 1795 Stodart invented an upright grand pianoforte and, three years later, Southwell of Dublin had placed a small square pianoforte on its side on a stand. At the turn of the century two independent makers produced real upright pianofortes, both of which embodied some new and ingenious principles.

Mathias Müller of Vienna called his piano Ditanaklasis. It was of five octaves from E, the strings were bichord and vertical, the striking point was near their middle, and this was said to be the cause of its mellow tone. The instrument had a check action, and a later model anticipated the tape-check action, which prevented the hammer from giving unwanted repetition and "blocking", by assisting its return from the string.

John Isaac Hawkins, also the inventor of the "ever-pointed pencil", an Englishman living in Philadelphia, U.S.A., patented his "Portable Grand Pianoforte" in America in 1800 and simultaneously, under his father's name, Isaac Hawkins, in England. There was a complete iron frame and the sound-board (belly) was suspended independently of the case. At the back there was a set of metal rods

[1] From the official report of the Exhibition.

to prevent the tension of the strings from distorting the sound-board. There was a hopper mechanism which foreshadowed Wornum's popular action, an upper bridge of metal, strings of equal length throughout and tuning by mechanical screws. The keyboard could be folded up and the instrument was suitable for use in a confined space such as a ship's cabin. Most of the upright pianos were tall and cumbersome and attempts were constantly being made to produce smaller instruments. Thomas Loud of London patented in 1802 an upright piano which was seventy-five inches high and used oblique stringing to accommodate the long bass strings which were considered to be necessary at that time. Southwell produced an improved action for his cabinet piano by which the hammers struck the strings outside the sound-board. The old arrangement, that of the up-striking grand action turned through a right angle, necessitated cutting through the sound-board and this weakened a structure which was under great stress from the total tension of the strings. Ladies liked to accompany themselves as they sang, and it was clearly inconvenient to sing and play facing a tall piano. In 1811 Southwell produced his piano sloping backwards, which was fitted with a pedal known as a Volto Subito for turning over the leaves of the music. At the same time Robert Wornum patented an upright piano in which the strings reached almost to the ground and there was an improved double English action. After this the upright piano became popular. The English pianos inspired the Pleyel–Kalk-brenner firm in Paris to construct "cottage pianos" of their own; and both the English and the French firms, who called them "pianinos", produced pianos which were less than four feet in height. In 1827 Blanchet et Roller of Paris produced an upright only a metre (39·4 inches) high: but at this time the tall, elaborately shaped and decorated upright pianos were still popular in Austria and Germany.

CHAPTER IV

THE PIANOFORTE CONSTRUCTED

*"For the body is not one member but many—and whether
one member suffer all the members suffer with it"*—St. Paul:
Epistle to the Corinthians, I, 12.

The Sound-board

The tone quality inherent in any piano depends on the nature and
tension of the strings, the sound-board, the hammers and their
coverings and even the mechanism attached thereto, the whole
structure of the metal frame and the wooden case of the instrument.
Nevertheless, by far the most important radiator is the sound-
board. Some centuries of painstaking experiment and experience
are behind the skill of the present-day maker of sound-boards. As in
many aspects of musical instrument making, the empiricism of the
traditional craftsman does not owe much to the work of formal
scientific research, though the increasing impact of this is undeniable.

Vibrating pianoforte strings present only a small area in contact with the air, and unless their motions are communicated to a
larger surface their sounds would be quite inadequate. A sound-
board should be sufficiently large to produce air-motions which will
result in adequate volumes of sound; it should not be too large to
respond as evenly as possible to notes throughout the whole range
of the compass, and it must act as the final arbiter of the tone-
quality by modifying and improving it, by adding its own acoustic
characteristics. Although, for the sake of easy description, we discuss
the various parts of the structure of the instrument separately (the
case, the frame, the sound-board, the strings and the action), a
successful instrument must work as a harmonious, integrated whole,
like the finely co-ordinated anatomical structure of a healthy living
organism.

The material of which a sound-board is made should transmit
sound very quickly, because, as far as is possible, there should be no
difference in phase of the sound-waves in various parts of the sound-

board; otherwise the sounds from various parts of the sound-board will tend to neutralise each other. Also the material should have the property of transmitting the sounds with the minimum of absorption of their energy. All sound, in the end, is lost by being turned into heat, and it is necessary, therefore, to find a material with a low acoustic resistance. At all stages, between the finger, which imparts energy to the mechanism, and the sound-board which projects it, the efficiency of the processes of transmission should be maintained to the greatest degree. In other words, the piano should maintain a maximum energy-conversion rate.

Rumanian pine (*Picea abies*) and Canadian sitka, Norway spruce (*Picea excelsa*), often known as Swiss pine, silver fir (*Abies pectinata*) and *Picea alba*, used in America, are used in making sound-boards. Sound is transmitted along the grain at a speed of about 15,000 feet per second, which is nearly fourteen times the speed of sound in air. The plastic substances such as Perspex, Nylon and Alkathene transmit sounds at much lower speeds, and are unsuitable for sound-board making. Light metals, such as magnesium and aluminium alloys, have high velocity sound transmission properties but their densities are greater than that of pine (aluminium 2·7, pine ·43). With the decline of the Rumanian timber, "resonance" wood was obtained both from Bavaria and Russia. The wood must be most carefully selected, seasoned and prepared. Since resins in the wood absorb and resist the sound-waves, the wood is chosen and cut so that it contains a minimum of these substances or else it is treated by steam, salt or solvents so that all resinous substances are removed. In an early chapter we have noted Mozart's description of Stein's care in the preparation of sound-boards. Sound-board wood is chosen from straight-growing trees which have had little sunlight in the middle of a forest. The wood is carefully cut so that there is a matching of the annular rings and the grain of the pieces. The Grotrian-Steinweg firm was early in the field of matching the pieces by carefully measuring their acoustic properties. Old trees are felled in the winter, and the lower part of the trunk is split and then sawn into planks several feet long, five to fifteen inches in breadth and a third of an inch thick. The sound-board is built from thirteen to twenty-five carefully-matched, narrow planks. The older pianos had sound-boards which were somewhat thicker in the treble than in the bass, but in general today the board is of uniform thickness, and varies according to the maker, from between 7 mm. and 10 mm. (·28 and ·4 in.). The grain of the sound-board or bellywood is arranged to run parallel with the line of the long bridge. Since the speed of sound across the grain of the wood is only about 4,000 feet per second, bars of wood, about ten in number and 2 cm. to 3 cm. (·8 to 1·2 inches) square are fixed at right angles to the grain of the sound-board. The bars distribute the sound energy quickly to all parts of the sound-board, and also support it. There is an optimum size for a sound-board, and if it were too large, various parts of it would vibrate in different phases and mar its effect. Triangular pieces may be cut away in the bottom treble and top bass corners, or dumb bars may be applied to stop all motion of these parts of the sound-board. The shape of a grand piano sets a limit on the treble of the sound-board. The vibrations of the strings are transmitted to the sound-board by the bridge, which is made of Swiss pine or maple. The strings meet the sound-board at a "down-bearing" angle of about 1·5 degrees below the line of their main length, and the sound-board is curved slightly towards the strings in order to compensate for the down-bearing pressure. The down-bearing force may be calculated by multiplying the tangent of the down-bearing angle by the string tension. The total pressure to the sound-boards is probably about half a ton. There must be an even distribution of pressure of the strings on the bridge. The optimum down-bearing and curvature of the sound-board have been worked out by various makers in decades of experiment. Too great a down-bearing produces a "tight, short tone", too little a thin, false, irregular, unmusical tone. The bearing angle is graduated because of the greater flexibility in the middle of the sound-board. The strung sound-board is a highly sensitive apparatus: "a mass of nerves responsive to the most minute shocks."[1]

In the Blüthner aliquot-scaled pianos (q.v.) a small extra bridge for the unstruck string is "floated" or suspended to carry the contact nearer to the main bridge and away from the dead end of the sound-board. The notches on the sound-board have to be cut with great accuracy to the middle of the bridge-pin hole at least, so that there is a good clearance between the string and the wood.

Time and use tend to cause the loss of the curvature of sound-board and the consequent deterioration of the tone of the instrument.

An ideal sound-board should not dissipate the energy of the strings too quickly or the piano tone will lack sustaining power. Moreover, it should be so coupled to the strings that its motion ceases almost

[1] L. Nalder, *The Modern Piano*, London, 1927.

immediately when that of the strings is quenched. Some piano-makers glue a bridge to the sound-board on the reverse side of the sound-board to the main bridge. This limits the vibrations of the sound-board and its rate of dissipation of energy, and thus prolongs the tone but diminishes its power.

The Metal Frame

In a desire to produce larger volumes of tone from their instruments, piano-makers tended to increase the thickness and therefore the tension of the strings, as the nineteenth century progressed. Moreover, the increased number of tensioned strings, because of the extended compass of the keyboards, and the rise in pitch which followed that of the wind instruments, ever seeking more brilliance, added to the tensions. The total tension of the strings increased considerably and a wooden structure tended to buckle and become distorted. The up-striking actions of the grand pianos necessitated that the sound-board should be curtailed or cut through so that the hammers could reach the strings from below. The progressively increasing forces were soon to become too much for an all-wooden structure such as generally prevailed in pianos until 1820. Many makers felt that the introduction of metal for strengthening the structure would be deleterious to the tone quality and so they resisted the use of iron or brass. Pianos were even made with strings on both sides of the sound-boards; and two sets of hammers, with elaborate actions, were devised to try to obviate the necessity of metal bracings. Already we have noticed the iron frame which John Isaac Hawkins used in his upright piano. Iron bracings and struts were patented in London, in 1799, by Joseph Smith, but probably because they occupied less space than the equivalent pieces of wood. In 1808, and again ten years later, James Shudi-Broadwood tried, but not very successfully, to fix iron bars to resist the great strain caused by the treble strings. On January 15, 1820, James Thom, a foreman, and William Allen, a tuner in Stodart's piano factory, took out a patent for a combination of parallel metal tubes, with metal plates: iron over the iron strings, and brass over the brass and spun strings in the bass part of the instrument. The metal plates were grooved to slide upon balls fixed to the bent side, and to hold the hitch pins to which the farther ends of the strings were attached. This system was inspired by the use of different metals to correct the lengths of the pendula of accurate clocks which were subject to varying thermal conditions. It was intended to keep the piano in tune when the temperature changed.

The principle of compensation in this invention was that the different thermal expansions of brass and iron wire would be correlated by similar differences in the brass and iron bracings respectively. The invention was widely acclaimed, but more because of its value in resisting the string tensions than for its differential thermal properties. William Stodart, who took over the patent from his employees, was generous enough to allow his competitors to develop iron-framing if they wished to do so. The tuning of the piano was much more stable when the structure was strengthened by the application of metal bars. Rollings used a metal frame in 1795 to strengthen his portable piano, and Joseph Smith used a metal structure shaped like the frame of a harpsichord.

The Great Exhibition of 1851, in Hyde Park, contained a considerable collection of pianofortes, and was the occasion for a controversy in *The Times* concerning priority claims in the introduction of metal bracings and frames. Érard of Paris was early in the field and, in 1825, obtained an English patent for fixing iron bars to the wooden braces of the piano, by using bolts passing through holes cut in the sound-board, and sheet-iron between two sides of the case for uniting the "wrest-pin block with the key-bottom". Broadwood obtained a patent in 1827 for four metal bracing bars, but insisted that his firm had used tension bars to the trebles in 1808, and three to five bars in grand pianos in 1821, in which year a metal hitch-pin plate had been used by Samuel Hervé in their factory in a square piano. Only at a later date had they sought a patent.

In the third and fourth decades of the century, patents were taken out for metal frames in Europe and America. An iron-frame with diagonal tension-bar and transverse suspension bar was invented in 1847, by Broadwood for their concert grands, and was used by them for the next half century.

In 1837 Thomas Loud of Philadelphia patented metal tubes or bars to strengthen the frame and these became general in New York piano factories within a few months.

The next step was to cast a complete metal frame with hitch-pin block in a single operation. This, an outstanding achievement in the history of the instrument, was undertaken by Alpheus Babcock of Boston, U.S.A., on December 17, 1825.

In the account of the Fourth Annual Exhibition of the Franklin Institute of Philadelphia (1827) "especial mention is made of a horizontal piano by A. Babcock, of Boston, of an improved construction, the frame which supports the strings being of solid cast-iron and strong enough to resist their enormous tension".

Babcock patented an iron framing for square pianos with cross-stringing in 1830. Another claim to have invented the metal frame in a single casting was made by Conrad Meyer of Philadelphia in 1833. In 1831 Allen invented a cast-iron grooved frame with a wrest-pin block between the grooves, and a single cast-iron brace to give further strength. Little use was made of this invention. Miss Harding[1] says that the cast-iron frame, an American invention, found favour with the French and Danish makers but apparently not with the English, Germans or Austrians, who preferred the composite frame, and this was evinced in the construction of the pianofortes from various countries which were shown at the Great Exhibition of 1851. Four years later Steinway and Sons of New York produced a pianoforte, with over-strung scaling, and a solid iron frame, and the volume and quality of tone of the instrument were much admired. Thereafter, the iron frame construction became standard.

In 1828 Henri Pape, formerly of the firm of Érard, and one of the most fertile inventors in the development of the piano, made a number of pianos with "cross-stringing", or "over-stringing", so that the long bass strings crossed over those for the treble. This artifice was a milestone in the history of the instrument; not only could pianofortes become more compact, but the longest bass-strings were almost as long as the diagonal of the case; and a new tone quality, rich in overtones, pleasing but less chaste than that of the parallel strung pianos, resulted. Soon the principle was applied to upright and horizontal pianofortes in England, Europe and America. Bridgeland and Jardine used it in America from 1833. Greiner, of Munich, Kaspar Lorenz and Samuel Meiszner and C. L. Jahn of Vienna, Fischer and Gerock, in England, J. F. Vogelsands, of Brussels, employed cross-stringing and many secured patents for what appeared to be modifications of Pape's method. In order to compensate for the weak tones of some of the bass strings of the small pianos, Fischer, Greiner and others used tuned springs and thin vibrating pieces of wood, as had been suggested by Hawkins, to reinforce the tone.

Devices have been patented so that, by tightening rods by means

[1] R. E. M. Harding, *A History of the Pianoforte*, p. 208. This book contains a full account with diagrams of many of the patents.

of screws, the original arched form of the sound-board could be restored when age and wear had caused a sinkage. The Mason and Hamlin grand pianos are fitted with metal rods for maintaining the bearing between the strings and the belly. There have been other inventions which attempted to sustain the resistance of the sound-board to the downward pressure of the strings. For a time the Ibach firm supported sound-boards with steel springs. An important part of the design and creation of a good pianoforte is the provision of well-graduated downbearing, which is neither excessive nor inadequate.

Attempts to improve the tone of the piano by providing double sound-boards, connected by posts, do not seem to have been successful. Moreover, the use of varnish, considered to be so important in violin manufacture, does not appear to add to the acoustical qualities of the piano sound-board. However, it acts as a preservative, increases its resistance to changes of humidity, and thus is well worth while.

Strings and Stringing

Although the strings of a piano radiate comparatively little energy, they are an important medium between the action and the sound-board and, to some extent, to the frame and the case of the instrument also. They convert the direct kinetic energy of the hammer into vibrational energy, and this is distributed to the sound-board via the bridge. The length, weight and tensions of the strings must be worked out carefully. Many thousands of experiments, over many decades, have contributed to the improvement of the efficiency of the whole system between the key and the vibrating wooden surface of the sound-board or belly, which transmits the sound to the air.

Until 1834 wire was made from iron or brass, and had poor tensile strength and could yield only comparatively quiet, piquant tones. No great energy output was possible with such wire, and the tensile strength was so little that heavy playing would cause it to break. The best wire was made first in Nuremberg and then in Berlin. Steel wire was introduced by Webster, of Birmingham, but by the middle of the nineteenth century the wire of Müller of Vienna was said to be the best. In 1854 the wire of Webster and Horsfall, of Birmingham, made from tempered cast steel, again took the lead; but towards the end of the nineteenth century the wire of Pohlmann, of Nuremberg, became the most popular amongst the pianoforte makers. Steel wires, whose tensile strength almost reaches the theoretical limits, are made today in Britain, U.S.A. and several European countries, but there is no standard agreement concerning the way their diameters or gauges are described. When the gauge of wire is printed on the frame of a piano it is necessary to know exactly what type of gauge is intended. Such wire has made possible the modern concert piano with its great tonal output.

The rate of vibration is given theoretically for an "ideal" string without stiffness by Mersenne's formula

$$F = \frac{1}{2l}\sqrt{\frac{T}{m}}$$

where F is the frequency in cycles per second, l is the length of the string in centimetres, T is the tension of the wire in dynes and m the mass of unit length of the wire in grammes per centimetre.

It will be seen that the frequency is inversely proportional to the length, inversely proportional to the square root of the mass and proportional to the square root of the tension. If wire of the same type is used, the frequency will be halved every time the length is doubled. Thus a length of two feet at middle C would mean one of four feet at tenor C, eight feet at C below the bass clef and sixteen feet at the lowest C on the piano. This is not practical and therefore the bass strings are made thicker and are weighted with close-fitting coils of copper wire in order to keep them to more convenient lengths. Sometimes this causes the strings to sound with a dead or "tubby" tone because non-harmonic overtones are produced. If the mass of a unit length is quadrupled by doubling the diameter of the string, its frequency is halved and it will sound an octave lower. The opposite effect takes place with tension: if this were to be increased four-fold, the frequency of the wire would be doubled and it would sound one octave higher. However, this is purely theoretical since an even tensioning of the strings at about 170 lb. weight each is desirable for the stability of the structure of the instrument, and the simple formula ignores the stiffness of the wires. Up to a certain limit a well-tensioned string requires more energy to set it oscillating than a slacker string, and thus the tensioned string will continue vibrating for a longer time, and will have more energy to hand on to the sound-board.

A string under tension will produce overtones because not only does it vibrate as a whole, but there are vibrations which are an aliquot fraction, $\frac{1}{2}, \frac{1}{3}, \frac{1}{4}, \frac{1}{5}, \frac{1}{6}, \frac{1}{7}, \frac{1}{8}, \frac{1}{9}$, etc., of its length, and these produce a series of harmonics whose frequencies are respectively 2, 3,

4, 5, 6, 7, 8, 9, etc., times the frequency of its fundamental vibration. Actually, because of the stiffness and the great tension of the strings, the overtones tend to become sharper than those which are calculated theoretically. Moreover it must be remembered that even the theoretical overtones, apart from the octaves, are out of tune with the notes of the tempered scale.

In the first half of the nineteenth century there was as much experimenting with strings and stringing as with other parts and operations in pianoforte building. Strings were covered with silver, gold and platinum in order to protect them from rust and corrosion; indeed, it was often imagined that the tone was improved thereby. The number of strings to each note was increased in an endeavour to produce louder tones. Mechanisms were made so that two hammers for each note should strike two or three strings each. Beethoven had a piano, with four strings to each note, made by Graf of Vienna. The use of several strings for each note made the difficulties of tuning and keeping in tune greater. A committee of musicians and physicists, appointed by the Académie Royale des Sciences in France, decided in favour of bichord stringing because of the increased tension and dangers of distortion with trichord stringing. Moreover, an uneven hammer would tend to strike one string more than the others and put it out of tune; or it would not strike the strings simultaneously and this would result in an unsatisfactory tone. Müller of Vienna used a tuning fork to which the strings of a bichord were attached and tuned to them, to obviate the use of a third string. Originally, each string had an eye twisted in it at its end, which was fixed to the hitch-pin, and the other end of the string was wrapped round the wrest-pin for tuning. This was not a very satisfactory arrangement, for the twisted wire and eye were not stable under the increasing tensions which were becoming necessary when more power was demanded from the instrument. In 1827 James Stewart, the first partner of Jonas Chickering, the American piano maker, discovered a method of stringing which has been fundamental to all subsequent methods. In this the eye and twisted end were eliminated, and a wire, double the length of a unison, was made to serve for two unison strings: it passed over the hitch-pin and the friction there was quite sufficient to prevent slipping if there were differences of tension in the two portions of the string. In the trichord portion of the compass, the third string was returned at the hitch-pin and the remaining portion served as the first string of the next trichord. This method of stringing did not prevent many others appearing. Ingenious devices, like spring balances, were connected to the strings so that their tensions could be maintained, and elaborate and expensive wrest (tuning) pins and other tuning methods were devised, but none has survived. With a metal frame, good steel strings and overstringing, the structure of the piano was so stable that it might stand in tune for months, and thus many of the ingenious but elaborate devices which became associated with it were seen to be redundant. Nevertheless, there were three important inventions for fixing the strings and increasing their efficiency as vibrators of definite pitches. In 1808 Sebastian Érard invented the Agraffe, a metal stud, in the head of which were bored three holes for the trichord or two for the bichord. This not only defined the speaking length of the string but also the angle of its bearing. Open-headed Agraffes have been introduced by Sauter recently. The harmonic bar was used to define the length of the string at the wrest-plank. The Capo Tasto ("head fret"), invented by A. Bord in 1843, was another method of defining the speaking length of the string. The Capo d'Astro bar serves a similar purpose (Capo d'Astro is a corruption of Capo Tasto).

The Wrest-plank

This is a block of very hard, bonded wood, made of beech or other hardwood in thicknesses, glued together with the grain of alternate layers running at right angles, as in ply-wood. Into this, holes are bored to receive the wrest- or tuning-pins, which are equal in number to the strings. The wrest-plank, guarded by metal, has to be absolutely firm, for the strain on it is many tons. The wrest-pins, which have very shallow threads, should fit the holes tightly and should allow an even motion of the tuning hammer without slipping or sticking. No greasy lubricant should be applied to wrest-pins or this may ruin the wrest-plank permanently.

Of the eighty-eight notes of the piano a suitable division might be sixty trichords, fifteen covered bichords, and thirteen single copper-covered strings.[1] We can now trace the course of a string on its way to the hitch-pin and back again. It starts firmly twisted round and anchored to the wrest-pin, it is defined in length and position near the wrest-plank by the pressure of the Capo d'Astro bar or by the Agraffe. Soon after this we reach the point where it is struck by the hammer, and nearer the hitch-pin it passes over the bridge, to which it imparts its energy, which is transmitted to the

[1] There are many other ways of making this division.

sound-board or belly. Thence it reaches the hitch-pin, round which it turns through two right angles and, as before, reaches another wrest-pin, adjacent to the former. It is convenient to string the lowest notes separately.

The Action

> "*How oft, when thou, my music, music play'st,*
> *Upon that blessed wood whose motion sounds*
> *With thy sweet fingers, when thou gently sway'st*
> *The wiry concord that mine ear confounds,*
> *Do I envy those jacks that nimble leap*
> *To kiss the tender inward of thy hand.*
> *Whilst my poor lips, which should that harvest reap,*
> *At the wood's boldness by thee blushing stand!*
> *To be so tickl'd, they would change their state*
> *And situation with those dancing chips,*
> *O'er whom thy fingers walk with gentle gait,*
> *Making dead wood more bless'd than living lips,*
> > *Since saucy jacks so happy are in this,*
> > *Give them thy fingers, me thy lips to kiss.*"[1]

—Shakespeare: Sonnet CXXVIII.

The essentials of a good action are:

(*a*) There must be absolute control over the blow, enabling its intensity and so the volume of tone to be varied with facility and certainty.

(*b*) There must be immediate withdrawal of the hammer from the string, otherwise the hammer becomes a damper.

(*c*) This withdrawal must be irrespective of whether the player continues the depression of the key or otherwise.

(*d*) Once the blow is struck, there must be no bouncing backwards or forwards of the hammer. The hammer must not only leave the string, but must be checked. Yet:

(*e*) There must be the facility for immediate and continuing repetition of the note, should the player so desire.

(*f*) This repetition must be fully possible whether the key has returned to its normal level or not.

(*g*) The right-hand pedal must raise and lower each and every damper instantaneously and without noise.[2]

---

[1] Jack=key, and not another part of the action.
[2] L. Nalder, *The Modern Piano. Musical Opinion*, London, 1927.

Truly a formidable list. Yet the grand action fulfils these duties very nearly to perfection. How are these mechanical desiderata reflected in the mind and touch of the player? To a sensitive player a good action should contribute to a feeling of extension of the arms and hands and of intimacy with the string: it should be a medium whereby the slightest nuances of expression initiated by the mind and translated into changes of muscular energy are communicated without sensible loss to the string. It should be capable of transmitting effectively energy at a considerable range of dynamics, graduated imperceptibly from the level of a toneless whisper to that of a forceful and noble fortissimo. Again, the player should feel that the energy of his fingers is being converted into sound efficiently. Although other factors contribute to this, a feeling that there is a good conversion of muscular to acoustical energy is most encouraging and even inspiring to the player. If a piano key is pressed down gently a momentary change of touch will be perceived at the instant of "set-off", that is, when the hammer has left the jack. This can be demonstrated more effectively by pressing down a number of white keys at the same time, by means of a wooden ruler laid on them. In a well-regulated action the change of weight of touch at "set-off" is readily apparent. Players differ in their attitude to this property of the piano action. It cannot be ignored by any sensitive pianist. Some great pianists, such as Schnabel, preferred to play on instruments where this change of weight was reduced to a minimum; others like to sense it deliberately, because it seems to give them final control of the hammer at the moment it frees itself from the mechanism. Of course, any sensation of friction, loss of energy or speed at this moment would be undesirable and would denote an action which was imperfect in design, manufacture or maintenance.

Of the many types of action which were made from the end of the eighteenth century only three and modifications thereof survived. (The ingenious Viennese action in which the hammer is pivoted in a kapsel at the end of the key, used by Stein, was improved by Bösendorfer and persisted in his cheaper pianos during the nineteenth century, and it still appears in Renner's catalogue.)

The types of action were: 1, the English improvements of the old "Stoss-mechanik" or "old man's head" action: this developed into the English direct-lever action of Broadwood; 2, the improvements and modifications of Érard's double escapement repetition action, such as the Herz-Érard action—modifications and even simplifications of Érard's action were necessary because originally it soon

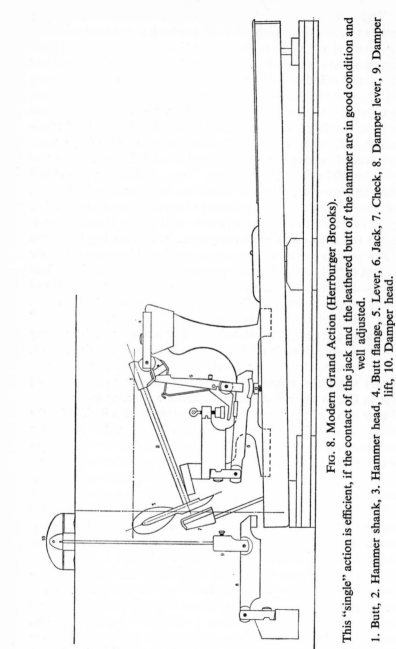

FIG. 8. Modern Grand Action (Herrburger Brooks).

This "single" action is efficient, if the contact of the jack and the leathered butt of the hammer are in good condition and well adjusted.

1. Butt, 2. Hammer shank, 3. Hammer head, 4. Butt flange, 5. Lever, 6. Jack, 7. Check, 8. Damper lever, 9. Damper lift, 10. Damper head.

Plate eight

a. Broadwood Square Pianoforte
b. Pianoforte by William Southwell, Dublin, 1784, for Countess of Grafton

required adjustment; 3, the upright action patented by Wornum in 1826 and introduced in his pianos three years later. This was known as a tape-check action because a tape, tightened by the movement of the hammer, pulls back the hammer, makes the hammer blow "clean", and helps repetition.

All actions have in common a "set-off" device, so that the hammer leaves the action and is free to move to the string, a check to stabilise and catch the hammer when it has left the string, and a repetition device so that it is not necessary for the key to return to its position of rest in order that the note can be sounded again. The movements of each part of the mechanism can be followed from the diagrams by imagining the key depressed and its other end raised. Much research has been undertaken in order to perfect piano actions as regards sensitivity, mechanical efficiency and durability. The modern action is a marvel of design and precision engineering.

All the movements and their interplay have been worked out carefully by geometrical and mechanical principles. It is a pity that more regular attention is not given to piano mechanism, since all good actions are capable of refined adjustment. Some firms of makers, such as Steinway, issue booklets which give precise instructions concerning the adjustment of their piano actions. Modern developments in making actions include the use of light alloys and plastics; but, in particular, new types of centres, which replace the old metal pins which worked in cloth bushings, have been developed. The Kastner-Wehlau Floating Centre, used by Barratt and Robinson, and the centres made by Herrburger Brooks, which are resistant to humidity, are examples of developments which constantly take place in the actions of all makers.

A good action and keyboard are very inviting to the fingers.

Keyboards and Keys

The organ shown in a painting by Hugo van der Goes (1476) [Plate 2] has a keyboard which is remarkably similar to those in use at present, nearly five hundred years later. Until the beginning of the nineteenth century the length of the natural keys, from their fronts to those of the sharps, was shorter than at present. When, until the time of J. S. Bach, the use of the thumbs on the keys was eschewed, the keys were much shorter in length; but, apart from this, our present keyboard, with its alternating blocks of two and three raised keys, is similar in shape to one depicted by Praetorius in the Halberstadt

F

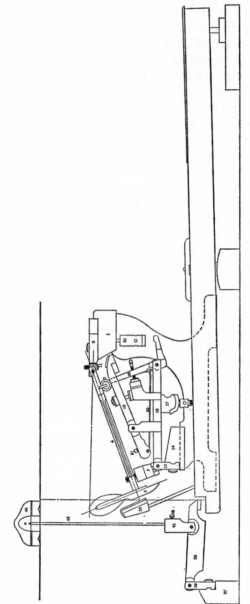

Fig. 9. Modern Double Lever Grand Action (Herrburger Brooks).

1. Hammer shank rail, 2. Hammer shank flange, 3. Knuckle, 4. Hammer shank, 5. Hammer head, 7. Hammer rail, 11. Drop or repetition screw, 12. Wippen, 13. Wippen flange, 14. Wippen flange rail, 17. Capstan block, 18. Repetition lever, 20. Repetition spring, 21. Repetition spring regulating screw, 25. Repetition lever regulating screw, 26. Jack, 30. Set-off dowel, 33. Backcheck head, 37. Damper lever rail, 38. Damper lever flange, 39. Damper lever, 41. Damper lever wire flange, 42. Damper lever wire flange screw, 43. Damper head, 45. Damper wire.

Cathedral organ of 1361. For more than six hundred years musicians have produced music by communicating their ideas via such an arrangement. Keys have been covered with ivory, bone, porcelain, mother-of-pearl and other substances; rare, coloured and polished woods have been used and the fronts of the keys have been carved beautifully and inlaid with precious metals. Until the end of the eighteenth century the use of black keys for the naturals became general and, in modern clavichords, harpsichords and sometimes organs, the naturals are usually black.

The wood, of which the keys are made, must not twist or cast because of climatic change. Linden (lime) was popular, but Swiss pine and American bass, amongst other types of wood, are satisfactory.

Standard modern measurements for piano keys are: the complete length of a long key is 16 inches of which 14·12 inches is operative. The front balance is 8·5 inches and the surface covering of the natural key is 6 inches and this is ·25 inch beyond the end of the sharp keys. The length of the key-head is 2 inches (5 cms.). The length of seven and a quarter octaves is almost 4 feet (122·94 cms.). The width of a natural key is ·9 inch. The sharps are ·4 inch broad at the level of the naturals and ·04 inch ($\frac{1}{25}$ inch) less at their tops. The sharp keys are usually cast in moulds from plastic, but ebony keys are buffed and the edges rounded. The depth of touch is $\frac{3}{8}$ inch (·375 inch); this is multiplied by a factor of about five by the action, and this is the distance travelled by the hammer from its position of rest to the string. The weight of touch is generally about two and a half or three ounces graduated to two ounces in the trebles.

In order to secure a properly balanced action the keys are weighted at their ends under the action. There is a certain amount of inertia in the keys and the action, and there is an upward jump of the key when it returns to its position of rest. Too light an action may offer facilities for rapid playing, but most performers require some sense of resistance to the touch in order to define it carefully and produce sensitive graduations. Some manufacturers balance the keys by means of springs, thus obviating the use of weights.

The beautiful keys made by Herrburger Brooks and Hermann Kluge, for instance, are a delight both to the fingers and the eyes. Ivory is still the material *par excellence* for covering the natural keys: it takes a high polish, is durable and possesses an exquisite velvety quality to the touch of sensitive fingers. Strangely, makers and players of pianos prefer to have the ivory bleached white,

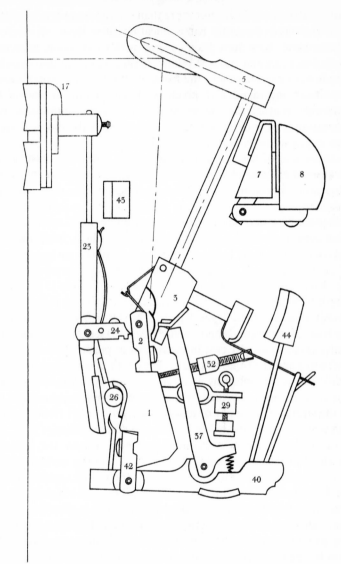

FIG. 10. Under-damper Upright Action (Herrburger Brooks).

1. Hammer rail beam, 2. Butt flange, 3. Hammer butt, 4. Hammer shank, 5. Hammer head, 7. Half blow rest rail, 8. Hammer rest rail, 17. Damper head, 23. Damper stem, 24. Damper stem flange, 26. Damper rod, 29. Set off rail, 32. Jack check rail, 37. Jack, 40. Lever or wippen, 42. Lever flange, 43. Damper check rail, 44. Check head.

although the unbleached substance lasts longer, has a rich appearance and shows beautiful figurations similar to those of expensive woods which have been planed smooth. Various imitation ivories made from modern plastics are extensively used for key covering. The covering can then be made in one piece and, when special circumstances demand it, both the vertical front and the main key covering can be moulded together. In modern pianos the sharp keys are moulded from a black plastic. Good ebony has become scarce and expensive. Ivory tends to discolour in the dark, but soon bleaches again when it is exposed to bright light. The keys should be cleaned by wiping with a moist chamois leather, and polished with a very soft cloth. Cleaning substances, which contain spirit and powerful detergents, are usually harmful to the surfaces of ivory and some forms of plastic. Ivory coverings cost a little more than plastic but the extra expenditure is amply justified. The heads and tails of ivory keys are made separately.

The Hammers

In the later Cristofori pianofortes, the hammer heads began to approach the modern tapered form in shape. Various substances such as leathers of many kinds, cork, sponge, tinder, woven materials and compressed rabbit's wool were tried as covering materials for the wooden head of the hammer, but leather was not entirely displaced by felt until after the middle of the nineteenth century. In 1839 Henri Pape, a Paris musical-instrument maker, exhibited pianofortes with hammers which were covered with hair felt, but even after this, for some years the Viennese pianoforte makers preferred to use soft leather. The hammer covering must be durable so that it will withstand the cutting resulting from many thousands of blows on the wire. The hammer must also possess good elasticity so that it will recoil quickly to leave the strings free to vibrate. The surface must be resistant so that it will not be destroyed by fortissimo playing, and it must be smooth and elastic so that it may caress the strings in very soft playing. The best wool for making hammer felt comes from the North American merino sheep. The wools of various countries are mixed so that the desirable qualities already mentioned are obtained as far as possible. American wools which had been bleached were thought to have lost their elasticity. Merino wool was esteemed for making dampers. The making of pianoforte hammer felts, by compressing wools and using only their natural binding qualities, became separate industries. Whitehead first specialised in this, and later Naish, of Wilton, after 1859, became even more famous. The hammers were generally covered by hand until 1880, but thereafter this was done with machines, of which an effective type was patented by Alfred Dolge in 1887.

The best quality hammers were doubly-covered, starting with a hard core so that there was a gradual decrease of firmness from the wood outwards. This allowed for a well-graduated musical tone between the merest whisper of tone and fortissimo. The hammer could not be considered in isolation, but only in relation to the strings on their sound-board and the action of the instrument. The whole was a complex system which had been perfected by decades of

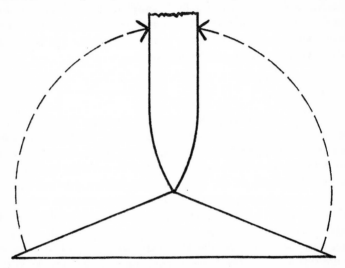

Fig. 11. The section of the felt is triangular, graded in thickness in a single length, to cover the 88 hammers.

experiment. Many experiments were made with covering materials. Sometimes leather or gutta-percha was used for the immediate covering of the wooden head, and over this there were layers of felt. In 1846 Woolley, of Nottingham, patented detachable hammerheads, so that a new quality of tone might be obtained by refitting a set with a different type of striking surface. Circular hammer heads fixed into a clamp were suggested, so that they could be turned to present an unworn surface to the wires.

A set of hammers is covered from a roof-shaped length of felt and then bent over the wood and glued [Fig. 11]. This prevents the noses of the hammers from flattening. The hammers are separated by vertical cuts in the felt. The width of the striking face of each hammer is one centimetre (·4 in.), and if the surface is slightly convex the tone is better than if the surface is flat or concave. This may be secured by sandpapering the surface of each hammer after it has been separated. The felt must be so made that it is hard and thick in the bass and harder and thinner in the trebles. The "weight" of the wool, from 9 to 16 lb., is the weight of about a square yard. Sometimes the felt is touched with collodion at the striking point because it is thought that this produces a brighter tone. The shafts of the hammers are made of hickory, white beech or maple: woods which are elastic and acoustic but do not bend easily. A slewing of

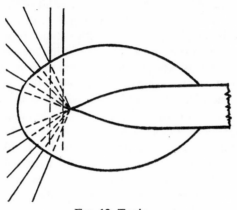

FIG. 12. Toning.

The needles may be inserted radially for deep toning without touching the striking surface. Another method uses needles parallel with the nose of the hammer and at right angles to it. Thereafter, fine needles may be used to produce a surface for soft playing.

the hammer along the string would produce an unmusical tone. Light metal hammer shafts have been used. The easy but definite movement of the hammer, so that there is neither resistance nor looseness at the little "axle", known as the centre, on which it moves, is absolutely essential.

The felt of the hammer head is toned by inserting needles, but this is a task for an expert. Over-toning can be corrected to some extent by pressing the surface of the felt with a hot iron, but enthusiastic amateurs have sometimes ruined sets of hammers. No toning, however skilfully done, will disguise other tonal faults in the piano. To some degree, tone-quality is a matter of taste, but a piano in which there has been indiscriminate needling of the hammer heads will produce an indefinite "woolly" quality of tone, will neutralise the value of a discriminating touch and will give the performer the feeling that his physical efforts are producing a disappointing result. A bright, or even an incisive tone, gives scope for finely regulated playing.[1]

The Pedal

> *"Without the pedal the piano is only a dulcimer."*—Liszt.

The function and uses of the sustaining or "loud" pedal can best be understood by considering the behaviour of the strings of the piano when all the dampers have been raised. The lid of the grand piano should be lifted or the front of the upright removed. The strung sound-board is obviously a very sensitive sound producer. It will resound to a note sung near it and it will even imitate a sung or spoken vowel sound. Strings, whose frequencies are those of the harmonics of a note, will vibrate sympathetically when that note is struck. Further, the non-harmonic and noise components of a note are analysed by and cause sympathetic vibrations in other strings. The matter is even more complex where there is over-stringing, because of the proximity of one set of strings to another at different angles.

If some of the notes which represent the harmonics of a lower tone are put down silently, and that note is struck and then released, the upper notes can be heard sounding. For instance, if middle C and the G above it are pressed down silently and tenor C is then played and released, the notes middle C and G will be heard distinctly. The considerable difference in both power and tone-colour between a note played without pedal and with pedal is well known. In the latter case, all the strings which represent harmonic or non-harmonic components add their radiance to the tone.

The modifications to the tone and dynamics of a single note and chords, of various types in different parts of the compass, should be heard by the critical musical ear when (i) The pedal is put down before the note or chord is struck; (ii) the pedal is put down simultaneously with the playing of the note or chord; (iii) the pedal is put down after the note or chord is struck. In (i) all the components of the tone activate other strings on the sound-board which are in a sensitive, responsive condition waiting to receive impulses. In (ii)

[1] J. W. Little, *Toning*, Institute of Musical Instrument Technology, London, 1963.

Plate ten

a. *Italian Spinettino, c. 1700 (Museum Neupert)*

b. *Two Manual Cembalo, Hans Ruckers, 1602 (Museum Neupert)*

c. *Action of Modern Clavichord, by Morley of London. The tangents and string dampers can be seen*

Plate eleven
Modern Instruments by Morley of London
a. Clavichord
b. Two Manual Harpsichord

the sound is still full but less lively and only some of the sound components are apparent in forced vibrations or resonance. In (iii) the noise components have had time to die away but the harmonic components of the note are available to activate other strings by resonance. Then the resulting sound is purer and more bell-like than the others.

The dampers of a piano, raised as a whole when the sustaining pedal is down, or severally, when the notes which correspond to the dampers are played, are usually more efficient in grand pianos because the dampers fall on the strings under gravity, or are pushed up by leverage from the key in under-damping, and the movement is sometimes assisted by a spring. In upright pianos the dampers, which work under the hammer, are more efficient than the more easily contrived "over dampers", because the former system gives to the damper the power of quenching the string nearer a point where its amplitude of vibration is greatest. The dampers of an upright piano have to be pressed against the strings by a spring; they may require adjustment, and to most pianists produce an effect which is less definite and controllable than those of the grand. There is no reason why they should not be efficient, if the action is carefully adjusted.

The Soft Pedal

The left pedal no longer produces a *una corda* effect. In most grand pianos it shifts the whole mechanism, including the keyboard, to the right, so that the hammers strike only two of the three strings in the trichord range and one of the two in the bichord. The unstruck strings resound to those which are energised by the hammers and sometimes, when the hammers are worn, softer parts of their heads touch the strings and the tone quality is mollified. The abuse of the soft pedal on the grand can lead to uneven wear on the hammer heads and disturb fine adjustments to the action. In the upright piano the soft pedal causes a horizontal bar to push all the hammers nearer to the strings. Since they then do not have so far to travel, it is easier for the player to cause them to strike the strings with less velocity and so produce a quieter note. Nevertheless, since a sensitive, skilful performer can control the speed, throughout a wide range, at which the hammer strikes the string, the "half-blow" action does not give any further tone colouring possibilities to the instrument. In some piano actions, which have not been designed, or adjusted skilfully, the half-blow action can produce "lost motion", which gives the performer the uncomfortable feeling that part of his finger movement and that of the action is wasted and counts for nothing.

Sostenuto Pedal

Some pianos, notably those made in America, are fitted with a third pedal. This is the tone-sustaining or sostenuto pedal. This device catches and holds any dampers which are raised at the moment it is put down. Thereafter, while it is still down, it will not interfere with any other dampers which are raised, either by playing their notes or using the general sustaining or right-hand pedal. A thin and accurately regulated metal rod is moved by the third pedal to catch the dampers which are off the strings. Thereafter, these strings will be left vibrating and everything else can continue as usual. Such a device has many uses: it can sustain a chord, leaving melody notes unblurred; it can catch the lower note of an extended skip, or a foundation note of an arpeggio chord can be maintained through rapid changes of the ordinary sustaining pedal. If a chord is sustained by both of the sustaining pedals and then the righthand pedal is suddenly released, there is a distinct change in the tonal colouring. Half-damping, which is sometimes called half-pedalling, becomes easy when the piano has a third pedal. In half-damping the aim is to prolong a bass note against clear moving harmonies above it. When there is no sostenuto pedal this is only possible when the harmonies or melody are sufficiently high in the keyboard and the sustained note is low in pitch. The dampers, particularly of an upright piano, are less efficient in quenching the vibrations of the heavier bass strings, with their high energy content, than those of the thin treble strings. In fact, in the extreme upper part of the scale it is usual to dispense with dampers altogether because the sustaining power of such strings is so small.

The Case

The case of a piano is important not only for its appearance but because it acts as a sounding board. A poor case, badly joined and of inferior wood, can ruin the tone. All should be worthy and well made. It is true that the frame and mechanism of the instrument can be made in a rigid unit and then clothed by the case, but it is still necessary that this should retain sound acoustical properties. In grand pianos, curved sides are made by bending a number of thin pieces of wood and bonding them with glue or plastic adhesives under pressure and temperature. Such a curved part is very strong but still retains some elasticity. It is braced below by trusses. The Bechstein and Steinway curved sides were made by uniting more than twenty thicknesses. The plastic-bonded woods tend to be very resistant to climatic change.

The cases of pianos have reflected their contemporary styles in general furnishing. In the nineteenth century there were the over-decorated cases with dust-holding filigrees and frets, with painted or inlaid figures, and restless designs. These have given way to plainer and more functional cases, in which comparatively large surfaces of wood are polished so that the beautiful natural figurings are retained. For those with highly-polished surfaces, resistant cellulose polishes are employed.

The black ebonised style is still popular for concert grands, but the fret-work of the music desk and the elaborately turned heavy legs have given way to something simpler and more elegant. There is an appropriate case for every décor and environment of the instrument; and beautiful cases are made in Chippendale, Louis XIV, Bieder-meier, American Colonial and other styles. The shapes which are popular are the small grand, the upright, the console and the spinet; but some of the very small grands do not have the string lengths which a moderately-sized upright can accommodate, and thus they lack adequate tone, particularly in the bass.

A note concerning Figs. 8, 9 *and* 10

The weight of key touch can be adjusted by putting pieces of lead in the keys; but touch weight must not be confused with the inertia which results from the weight of the mechanism and only manifests itself when the key is moved and increases with the speed of motion. Thus, the moving parts of the action should be as light as is conformable with strength, stability and durability.

A well-designed and constructed action is susceptible to refined adjustment. For instance, there is no need for the sensitive player to feel that there is a separate change of touch when the key begins to move its damper. Unhappily, the skilled and patient attention, which is necessary for such adjustment of the whole action, is not forthcoming as often as it should be.

CHAPTER V

SOME LINKS IN THE CHAIN OF MUSIC

The Chain of Communication

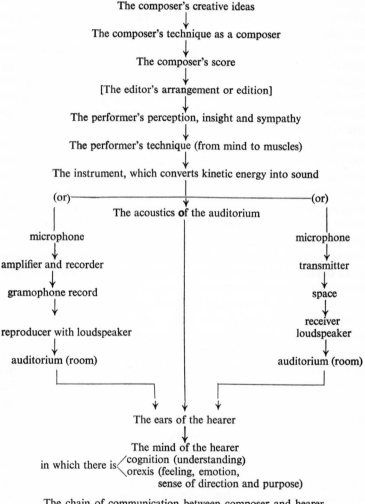

The composer's creative ideas

↓

The composer's technique as a composer

↓

The composer's score

↓

[The editor's arrangement or edition]

↓

The performer's perception, insight and sympathy

↓

The performer's technique (from mind to muscles)

↓

The instrument, which converts kinetic energy into sound

(or) ——————— ↓ ——————— (or)

The acoustics of the auditorium

microphone   microphone

↓   ↓

amplifier and recorder   transmitter

↓   ↓

gramophone record   space

↓   ↓

                                         receiver
reproducer with loudspeaker   loudspeaker

↓   ↓

auditorium (room)   auditorium (room)

↓ ↓ ↓

The ears of the hearer

↓

The mind of the hearer

in which there is ⟨ cognition (understanding)
                    orexis (feeling, emotion,
                    sense of direction and purpose)

The chain of communication between composer and hearer.
Good communication will not be possible if there is a weak
link in the chain.

FROM the physical point of view the piano is merely a machine for converting mechanical energy, supplied by the performer, into acoustical energy in about ninety separate frequencies, used selectively. Pianoforte makers have endeavoured to improve from time to time the efficiency of the instrument as an energy transformer. Physical apparatus only becomes a musical instrument when the sounds which it makes are perceived as music in the minds of the listener. This may seem to be trite, but a failure to appreciate the difference as well as relationship between what is objective (physical) and what is subjective (psychological) has resulted in a tendency to seek explanations of the basis of music in physical phenomena, rather than in the perceptual experience of them.

The science of acoustics, which should be that of hearing, has tended to be limited to the physical aspects of sound. Helmholtz's classical work, *Tonempfindungen* (the sensations of tone), was an attempt to seek a physiological and psychological basis of music; in spite of the fact that subsequent research has failed to corroborate almost anything which he wrote about the piano. Frequency (vibration number), amplitude (extent and energy of vibration), wave form (harmonic composition) are three, though not the only, physical properties of a sound. Formerly, each of these was supposed to be uniquely related to pitch (the sense of highness or lowness of a note), loudness and tone-quality (tone colour) respectively, which are perceptual qualities. It is now known that pitch, loudness and tone-quality are all related to frequency, amplitude and wave-form. For instance, the perception of pitch of a note changes when its loudness is increased, and this change is related in its extent to the tone-quality of the note. A tone which is rich in harmonics is less subject to such a pitch change than a "pure", dull sound, such as that of a tuning fork or a fundamental note produced by loudspeaker and electronic valves.

The most important fact about any musical instrument is that it is a link in the chain between the mind of the composer and that of the hearer. A link cannot be considered in isolation, but only in relation to the other links in the chain. The worthiness of every link must be appraised. Music which begins in the mind of the composer is translated by means of an elaborate symbolism into marks on paper, copies of which are then multiplied by the printing press. The relations between ideas and symbols are known as semantics. In general, semantics is a part of the theory of communication, and a systematic study of the creation and transmission of music as an aspect of communication is important, and some very useful work has been done already.[1]

A sympathetic appreciation of the intentions of a composer is necessary before his work is published, and often, in the history of music, arrogant and ignorant editors have stood between the composer and the player.

The next link in the chain is the performer, whose task is to try to understand the composer's ideas by studying the printed pages, and by means of a technique, in which muscular movements are governed by cultured mental processes, to transmit movements to the vibrating parts of an instrument, which basically is a machine for changing energy from one form to another. Instruments, where there is an intimate connection between the performer and the vibrating medium, such as the violin and wood-wind instruments, are susceptible to the finest nuances of performance but demand much subtlety in manipulation; whereas in those organs, where there is an elaborate mechanism and a considerable distance between instrument and player, a sensitive performance is difficult or impossible to obtain.

Thus, it is important to consider the nature of the sounds which the piano, as a link in the chain of music, can produce.

Tone Colour

In general, tone colour is a function of the number and strength of the harmonics and non-harmonic components which combine with the ground or fundamental tone. To these must be added the initiation and collapse phenomena at the beginning and ending of each note. The attack of the bow on a string, the chiff of the flute, the "bubble" of the horn are all part of the tone qualities of the respective instruments. In the piano, as in other stringed instruments, there are further complications. These are associated noises, especially during loud playing, and they cannot be ignored when we are considering the complete tone-colour picture. Moreover, when once struck, the sound of the piano dies away, but the ingredients of the tone do not necessarily diminish at the same rate. When the sound of a note of a piano is analysed by physical apparatus, it is seen to be of great complexity. For many years, following the publication of Helmholtz's book,[2] the quality of a sound was

[1] e.g., Deryck Cooke, *The Language of Music*, Oxford, 1959; V. Zuckerkandl, *Sound and Symbol*, London, 1956.

[2] *Tonempfindungen* (*The Sensations of Tone*).

thought to be determined completely by its harmonic contents. An interesting and simple experiment will suffice to show how inadequate such an idea is in connection with piano tone. If a few bars of a simple tune are played backwards, by starting with the last chord, and the sound is recorded with a tape recorder, it is easy to change the direction of the tape and replay it so that it travels in the opposite direction and the tune is then heard from its beginning. Although, as would be expected, the tune is recognised, the nature of the sound seems to bear no relation to that of a piano. The sound is that of a broken-winded harmonium, in addition to which, each note ends with a click.

What are the factors inherent in the nature of the pianoforte which influence its tone colour?

1. *The nature of the sound-board and the general construction of the instrument.* The area of a string in contact with the air is not sufficient to radiate a tone of adequate volume. The vibration of the large area of the sound-board, in direct communication with the strings, increases the volume of the sound and purifies and enriches the tone quality of the string. The wooden construction of the old Viennese pianos contributed to their peculiar tone quality.

2. *The nature of the string.* The type of sound emission differs between steel, brass and gut strings. Steel strings with copper windings for the lowest notes are general in pianos today, but experiments have been made with other substances. Thin strings give a brighter and more penetrating tone than thick strings. The reason is that the harmonics of the thin string are able to develop themselves, but because of the stiffness of a thicker string the upper partials are not only less in evidence but are not true harmonics of the fundamental. (This produces difficulties in the tuning of such strings.) Bass strings, whose excessive shortness has been compensated by a heavy loading of copper winding so that they vibrate slowly enough to secure the requisite pitch, yield a tone which is often devoid of interest. It is comparatively free from real harmonics but contains noise and non-harmonic elements, and is generally known as "tubby" tone. The bass notes of a large grand piano, on the other hand, may have an impressive organ-like sonority.

3. *The action, including the hammers:*

(*a*) The point at which the hammer strikes the string is of importance, but it has been determined by years of empiricism. The theoretical explanation given by Helmholtz is not sufficient. (If

Helmholtz had been correct in this matter, the clavichord, in which the string is struck at the point where its speaking-length is determined, a node, would not play at all.) A distance of a seventh to a ninth of the length of the string is a suitable striking place.

(*b*) The hammer mechanism should work easily, but should be free from other movement apart from that which permits the hammer-head to move in the arc of a circle. The nature of the covering of the hammer-head is a fundamental factor in tone production. A small, hard hammer will produce a bright, incisive and wiry tone. A soft large head will produce a dull tone because the striking area is too large to produce acute vibrations, and the hammer is in contact with the string for too long a time and the higher harmonics are damped out. All subtleties of touch are destroyed by the use of hammers which are too soft.

In many instruments, including the piano and the organ, distinctive tone colours tend to disappear at the extreme ends of the scale.

The perception and appreciation of tone colour is a subjective matter, and the feelings of musicians will differ. Some pianists prefer an instrument with a harp-like tone, others require a more incisive tone which retains its piquant quality even when played softly, and others the full, round sound of the Bösendorfer, Bechstein, Blüthner, Steinway or of the Broadwood.

4. *The pedals* give opportunities for tone colouring.

5. *Overstringing.*

6. *Aliquot Scaling.* These matters have been considered separately in other parts of this book.

Tone Colour and the Player

Some experiments, by which different weights were dropped on piano keys (or the same weight from different heights) and the resulting sound analysed by means of an oscillograph, seemed to show that there was only a single tone colour at any particular dynamic level. While it is impossible to deny the findings of these experiments, it is false to believe that they prove that the piano is a monochromatic instrument. The ear is not very sensitive to changes of dynamics but it can be very critical of comparative pitch and tone colour. The differences of tone colour are more readily heard than the changes of dynamics which accompany them. In addition to this there are other important factors.

Plate fourteen
a. Table Piano (Sheraton) by John Broadwood
b. Forte Piano by Wm. Stodart

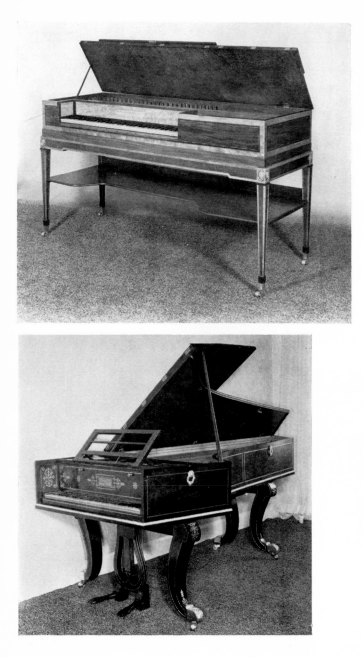

In many pianos there is a certain flexibility of the action by which a sharp, unsympathetic blow on a piano key will prevent the hammer from being impelled to the strings, by gaining velocity steadily until it leaves the jack, as it should do. A sharp blow may cause a bending wave to travel up the hammer shank so that the hammer head travels along the string a short distance at the time of striking. This produces a noisy, unpleasant tone and, to say the least, is bad for a well-adjusted mechanism.

Tuning and temperament also affect tone-colour. In the ears of uncritical listeners an untuned piano may seem to have a rich, interesting tone, and the clash of overtones and differential tones produces an effect which is lively and exciting. When the piano has been tuned they feel that "all the colour has gone out of it". In a pianoforte tuned to equal temperament, the thirds and the minor sixths, which are respectively wide and narrow, have a distinctive colour which they lend to any chord or interval in which they appear: such chords have a reedy growl. A good test of the worthiness of equal temperament tuning, when the instrument is fresh from the hands of the tuner, is to play sixths up and down the scale, listening carefully to the reedy sound of the tempered sixths, which should be graduated evenly from note to note.

Every chord has a characteristic colour. On the pianoforte this may be modified by playing the constituent notes at different powers. Even the apparent pitches of the notes may be modified slightly by playing them at different dynamic levels.

Chords and notes in various parts of the compass of the piano may suggest the colouring of other musical instruments. The tone quality of a chord may be modified by playing its constituent notes with different attack and timings.

It has been said by some modern composers that the piano can never produce a melody. The sense of melody is always subjective: the combining of notes in a linear manner to make a melody, as the Gestalt psychologists have shown, is a function of the mind, which tends towards pattern and completion. Some long melodies built on new patterns are not immediately recognised as tunes, even when their notes are joined and phrased, because the mind of the listener has not been trained to accept them as patterns, or else there is defective memory, so that the beginning of the tune is forgotten in an attempt to perceive the end of it. Actually, the melodic possibilities of the piano, with its notes which die away, are greater than those of some sustaining instruments, the organ for instance.

In the piano the most refined phrasing is possible, because the agogics of carefully contrived note lengths and timing can be combined with touch dynamics. If the melodic sound of a Stradivarius violin played by a master may be compared with a beautiful silken cord, that of a good piano may appear as a string of iridescent pearls.

Piano tone has a well-spread frequency spectrum and this, added to the effect of its transient tones, ensures that it will not quickly exhaust the ear of the listener. The considerable range of tone quality which may be found in different instruments offers a wide choice to the sensitive musician. Questions of historically appropriate tone quality arise in the performance of the works of various composers, but in addition to this there is the matter of personal preference. Generally, modern cultured taste, concerning the tones of keyboard instruments, demands more and more clarity and brightness. The increasing popularity of the harpsichord and neo-baroque organ is symptomatic.

Dynamics and the Sensation of Loudness

It is obvious that the sensation of loudness depends on the energy of a source of sound and its distance from the hearer, but there are other important and subtle factors which determine the subjective response to dynamic level. Musical sounds have many qualities: fullness, richness and brilliance combined together are generally more satisfactory than loudness. Beauty of tone is best appreciated at a mezzoforte level that is neither a toneless pianissimo nor a noisy fortissimo, though doubtless both of these are valuable for occasional use. The most natural increase in loudness is due to the progressive addition of harmonics to a fundamental or ground tone which itself is little altered in power. An increase in fundamental tone without the addition of harmonics gives a sensation of flattening. We not only live in a noisy age, but at a time when concourses of people and the sizes of the auditoria in which they listen to music, have become vaster. The loudspeaker blares everywhere. Most human ears have lost, or never had, the sensitive analytical powers to listen so that they appreciate and love the beauty of quiet sounds. Two examples will illustrate this. In the side of the cliff above Salzburg in Austria is a mechanical organ, known as the Stierorgel or Bull organ, because when it has finished playing its tunes, many pipes sound together to give a bull-like roar. It still plays three times a day, as it did in Mozart's childhood. Then, it was clearly heard in every part of the City of Salzburg; but now, although it is probably more powerful than it was in the eighteenth century, it has been heard by comparatively few visitors and many have not even realised the existence of this remarkable instrument at the end of a week's visit. Again, in the early part of the same century, Gottfried Silbermann, the organ-builder, completed his organs, voicing and tuning them in the churches, throughout the night. He insisted that all traffic, which at its worst must have been very moderate and quiet in comparison with that of today, should be diverted from roads in the vicinity of the buildings in which he was working.

Sound is only soft or loud by comparison. The sensation of loudness does not increase directly with the energy which radiates from a sound-producer. If the energy radiated by a pianoforte string has been doubled, the increase in loudness is only comfortably discernible: in fact, it is about three decibels. If the energy of a piano-hammer is effectively transferred to the strings, this energy varies as the square of the speed of the key at the instant at which the hammer leaves the mechanism. A law of perception, known as the Weber-Fechner law, states that in order to give an equivalent increase of loudness at any dynamic level, the extra energy required to do this will always be the same fraction of the unincreased sound. This means that a small increase in the energy given to the key and therefore to the hammer at a low dynamic level will produce a much greater increase in loudness than a similar increase of energy at a higher level. The thrilling and sometimes almost terrifying passages which occasionally appear in pianoforte music have to be anticipated by periods of quiet though varied tone or even silence.

These principles have many applications in pianoforte playing. If a note on the pianoforte is sounded forcibly some noises at first accompany the sound which quickly loses its powerful qualities, but as long as the key is depressed or the dampers are lifted from the strings, the note continues to sound, firstly for a longer period as an *mf* tone and then for an even longer time as a diminishing soft tone. The matter can be depicted in the oscillogram on following page. The beautiful cantabile of pianoforte tone is obtained in regions B and C. Region A will sound both loud and noisy and often unmusical in comparison with region B, and, in its turn, region B will sound louder and richer in tone than region C.

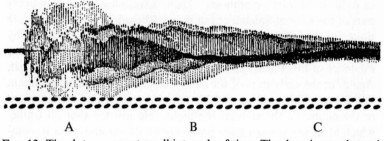

A   B   C

FIG. 13. The dots represent small intervals of time. The duration as shown is about one second.

Temperament and Tuning

"Music came first; then the scales after ages of experiment; then came the theorists to explain them. And as they knew more of mathematics than of musical history they laid down laws which, in actual fact, no human being had ever obeyed."[1]

"A scale is merely a method of classifying and labelling the musical material used by composers and skilled artists. It can never be produced by a keyboard instrument unless the aural perception of the trained musical ear enables it to hear the tuning as something different from its physical original. The available evidence suggests that many of us hear the intonation of the piano in this way."[2]

The problems of tuning each note of the scales of various instruments have exercised musicians, instrument makers and acousticians for more than two thousand years. A number of treatises devoted solely to these problems have been written, particularly in the seventeenth and eighteenth centuries.[3] It is substantially true to say that in the pianoforte, as in other keyboard instruments, the frequency of vibration of each note is controlled by the maker and tuner, and not, as in the case of the violin, by the performer. A tempered system of tuning is necessary on a keyboard when it is desired to play music in any key, to modulate freely, to make use of the properties of the keyboard in which one note and frequency may serve for several nominal notes or symbols, for example D♯ and E♭ or F♯, E♯♯, G♭, and, finally, to take advantage of the composite tone-colour of chords with tempered intervals. Pure intervals, which

[1] Sir Percy Buck (1871–1947), *Acoustics for Musicians*, Oxford, 1946.
[2] Ll. S. Lloyd and Hugh Boyle, *Intervals, Scales and Temperaments*, London, 1963.
[3] e.g., Robert Smith, *Harmonics*, 2nd ed., London, 1758.

are represented by simple mathematical ratios, give no beats (heterodyning) when their notes are sounded together. Here, before we go any further, two points should be made clear. Although in the case of the three strings of a note on the piano, which should be in unison, beating will take place between their fundamental notes if they are out of tune, in other intervals, such as a fifth, the beats take place between the harmonics (or upper partials) of the two notes. In this case, the "third" harmonic (reckoning the ground tone as the first) beats with the second harmonic (the octave) of the higher note. The second point is that tuners sometimes speak of flattening or sharpening an interval and this may lead to confusion. More properly, we should speak of *narrowing* or *widening* an interval. In the first case the lower note is sharpened or the top note flattened; in the second, the lower note is flattened (lowered) or the top is sharpened (raised).

We can make a simple diatonic scale by taking C, E, G, with pure third and fifth and adding the dominant triad G, B, D, and the sub-dominant F, A, C; but other intervals would be out of tune. Moreover, the intervals of a second C to D, F to G and A to B, are larger than the seconds D to E and G to A. With instruments, where the performer has some control over the pitch of the notes which he is playing, he modifies his intervals slightly to suit the nature of the melody which he is playing, and for purposes of modulation. (The possibility of seeming to do this on keyboard instruments is mentioned elsewhere in this book.) At first sight it might appear that, if instead of the twelve notes of the present key-board octave (omitting the octave of the lowest note), it were possible to provide sufficient keys to give pure intervals in every key, all difficulties of temperament would be solved (provided, of course, that the keyboard could be played and the great increase in size, mechanism and cost of the instrument could be met). This is by no means the case, for successive modulation changes without the use of enharmonic change (i.e., a change of note without the change of pitch) might commit the music to a constant change of pitch as it progressed; and it is necessary, in most music, that a general pitch norm should persist throughout its performance. Because of this, and in order to provide a keyboard which is convenient to play and an octave which does not embrace too many pitches, the scale has to be tempered.[1]

---

[1] "Enharmonic" organs, with more than twelve notes to the octave, are in the University of Edinburgh (McClure organ), the Teyler Museum, Haarlem, Holland, and in the South Kensington Science Museum, London.

The Mean-Tone Temperament

This system of tuning, or something approaching it, was found in various keyboard instruments from mediaeval times until the middle of the nineteenth century, though it is only fair to say that the systems of tuning in the seventeenth and eighteenth centuries were legion. The change from mean-tone temperament came gradually by a progressive widening of the thirds. The Broadwood pianos were tuned to equal temperament from 1846. Johann Snetzler's first English organs (1746) were so tuned, but in the last decade of the nineteenth century the older temperament was still found in a few English parish church organs. The large Willis organ in St. George's Hall, Liverpool, was tuned to mean-tone temperament for a number of years after its erection in 1855 and it was not tolerable to play Mendelssohn's first organ Sonata in F minor on it.

In mean-tone temperament the major thirds are in tune, the fifths are slightly narrow and the differences between the major and minor seconds are smoothed out, which is the reason for the expression "mean tone". The relative consonance of intervals in a few keys (B♭, F, C, G, D, and A major and G minor, D minor and A minor) has been secured at the cost of dreadful dissonances elsewhere. For instance, the differences between C, B♯ and D♭♭ have become great and the difference between A♭ and G♯ is considerable. The G♯ is nearly one-third of a semitone from the just fifth with E♭. This fifth, which hurts the ears even of the uninitiated, was known as the "wolf".

Equal Temperament[1]

This is now almost universally employed in the pianoforte and organ, but owing to "rule of thumb" techniques of tuning, mathematical accuracy is not attained, and many instruments still produce the perception of key-colour, which theoretically should not arise. With this temperament only the octaves are in tune, and every other interval has a constant pitch ratio, according to its kind, throughout the compass. With equal temperament the fifths are slightly narrow and the thirds are considerably wide; intervals in all keys are equally mistuned and the "wolf", by being distributed, is rendered more

---

[1] Robert Smith, Master of Trinity College, Cambridge, a leading acoustician of his time called equal temperament in 1749 "that inharmonious system of 12 hemitones which produces a harmony extremely coarse and disagreeable!"

or less innocuous. A moment's thought will show that when equal temperament has been achieved throughout the keyboard the beats which can be counted between, say, Middle C and G above it will have just half the frequency of those when the fifth is played an octave higher, and so on.

Although the arithmetic which is required to deal with the problems of equal temperament is not difficult, some very simple ideas will serve to show its main characteristics. If, starting with the bottom C of the pianoforte keyboard we ascend in fifths: C – G – D – A – E – B – F$\sharp$ – C$\sharp$ – G$\sharp$ – D$\sharp$ – A$\sharp$ – F – C – we shall have reached the top C of the keyboard and ascended by seven octaves which, on the keyboard, are the same as twelve fifths. The ratio of the vibration frequency (rate per second) of any note and its octave is 2 and therefore of seven octaves is 2^7. The vibration frequency ratio of a pure fifth is $\frac{3}{2}$ and therefore of twelve fifths is $(\frac{3}{2})^{12}$, which is larger than 2^7.

It will be seen that, if the fifths are pure, twelve of them will exceed seven octaves by a small amount (known as a Pythagorean comma). On the keyboard where the top note of the seven octaves and that of the twelve fifths is the *same note*, it is necessary to narrow each fifth slightly to fit into the scheme of preserving all octaves as pure intervals and retaining the twelve separate pitches (or thirteen if we include the octave notes of our present keyboard) of each octave. If each fifth is slightly flattened by distributing the Pythagorean comma between them, other results appear in the scale. If the fifths are slightly narrow the fourths must be slightly wide, but the thirds become quite wide, so that the beats between a note and its major third in the middle of the keyboard are too frequent to be recognised as separate pulses, and the minor sixths accordingly become equivalently narrow. Only the octaves are strictly in tune. If the tuner has achieved real equal temperament the two notes of every similarly named interval throughout the keyboard, e.g., all the sixths, or semitones, or minor thirds, have respectively the same frequency ratios. Thus, if we know the frequency of any note we can calculate that of the semitone above it, and so on throughout the keyboard, by multiplying that frequency by the number 1·05946, that is $2^{1/12}$.

How to Calculate Beat Rates on the Tempered Scale

The beats are given between the frequencies of harmonics of nearly the same pitch of the two notes. The fundamental pitches of the two notes are multiplied by simple numbers according to the interval employed.

e.g.: fifths: by $3 \times$ (lower note), by $2 \times$ (upper note).

fourths: by $4 \times$ (lower note), by $3 \times$ (upper note).

thirds: by $5 \times$ (lower note), by $4 \times$ (upper note).

If N is the frequency of the lower note of the interval the number of beats per second in a tuned fifth interval is given by $N(3 - 2 \times 2^{7/12})$, that is, the frequency of the third harmonic of the lower note, from which is subtracted twice the frequency of the tempered fifth, seven semitones above. A simple working by logarithms gives about one beat per second for the interval middle C to G.

In the case of thirds, the higher note of the interval is sharp to the true third. The number of beats is given by $N(4 \times 2^{1/3} - 5)$ where N is the frequency of the lower note. Five times the frequency of the lower note is subtracted from four times the frequency of the tempered third.

With the interval middle C to E the beats are rather more than 10 a second.

The general pitch of a pianoforte is given by that of its middle C, or more usually by the A above it. International standard pitch was fixed in 1939 at A $= 440$ complete vibrations (cycles) per second at 60 degrees Fahrenheit. Although the temperature coefficient for wind instruments, including the organ, is considerable, it is negligible in the pianoforte, within reasonable temperature changes. In fact the A pitch of the pianoforte is *lowered* by less than one vibration for 10 degrees Fahrenheit rise in temperature. This standard pitch of 440 cycles per second is radiated in the tuning note of the B.B.C. Third Programme, and by the German and some of the American broadcasting stations.

Old pianos would tend to have a lower pitch, firstly because they may have been made to give such a pitch and secondly, unless tuners have kept them up to pitch, and not merely corrected the intervals, they would show a progressive decrease of pitch because of the shrinkage of the frames or the relaxation of string tensions with age. It is almost certainly unwise to pull up to pitch such a piano at one tuning session, if, indeed, it can be done at all. The strain on the strings, wrest-plank, and frame of the piano may collectively become too great, if the tension of all of the strings is considerably increased.

Pianoforte Tuning

Pianoforte tuning is an art which requires training, experience and acuity of hearing. Piano-tuners should be regarded as skilled technicians; and those who play and value the piano should do everything in their power to encourage tuners to acquire not only the greatest competence but also the dignity of a profession. It is not to be expected that the patient adjustment of the pitches of two hundred strings, and the careful examination of an instrument can be dismissed in half an hour. Incompetent piano-tuners have not only failed to leave instruments standing well in tune, but have damaged, sometimes permanently, the mechanism or structure of the instrument. Piano-tuning is not the business of an amateur. At its best, the pianoforte is a beautiful, valuable and sensitive instrument and should be maintained in the best possible manner.

The tuner may begin with note A above middle C. By means of tuners' wedges or dampers the centre and right hand strings of the trichord are silenced and the left hand string is brought up to the pitch of the tuning fork, A—440, so that no beats are heard. The tuning lever is usually known as the tuning hammer, and its star-shaped aperture fits neatly over the wrest-pin. If the fullest leverage allowed by the tuning hammer is used a better control of the motion of the wrest-pin and less fatigue of the hand will result. The tuning hammer should fit easily on the pin and care should be taken to see that only a turn and not a lateral motion, which would tend to bend the pin, is given to it. Good tuners quickly sense the feel of the pin and tend to bring the string slightly above pitch and then "spring the pin", that is to say, allow the torsional strain on it to twist out. During tuning the keys should be struck with reasonable force so that subsequent heavy playing does not quickly cause the note to go flat. Then the central string is tuned to its neighbour while the third is muted and finally the third string is brought into true pitch with the other two. Forcible, but never brutal, testing of the note should show that the three strings are in tune with one another and that there is no sign of beating. The A, an octave below, is now tuned by damping with wedges two of its strings and tuning the left hand string to be the true sub-octave of the first A to be tuned. Some very experienced tuners narrow this octave by an extraordinarily small amount and hardly enough to make its presence felt as beats before the notes die away. In any case, any slight widening of this octave is fatal to subsequent tuning. The next note to be tuned is the

E above this lower A. This interval, like all other fifths, must be slightly narrow, and beats should be listened for, between harmonics of the two notes. Musicians, who have a good sense of relative pitch, often need practice for weeks before they can detect and estimate the frequency of the beats. This E may be tested by its beating with the first A to be tuned. As will be seen in the table, the beats of fourths are somewhat quicker than those of fifths in the same parts of the scale. The octave below E is then tuned; and some advanced tuners will tune this octave very slightly narrow, but it should be noted that the tables of beats which are here given assume that the octaves are absolutely true. The fifth B above this, then F♯ a fifth above B are tuned, and so on, as is shown in the diagram of the great circle of fifths. F♯ may be tested against A for it will produce the characteristic sound of the tempered sixth, which should become familiar to the ear by repeatedly listening to sixths played on a well-tuned instru-

FIG. 14. Tuning (top) in fifths and octaves. Tuning (lower) in fourths and fifths.

ment. When C♯ has been tuned the A major chord may be tried and should yield a full, satisfying sound. As the process of fixing the pitches, known as "laying the bearings" proceeds, tests with various sixths may be made. Tempered tenths are more easy to listen to than thirds, and their particular type of sound should become familiar to the ear. When the tuning proceeds downwards and G♯ becomes available the E major chord may be played and savoured. As thirds and sixths become available they should be tested. The last octave is the downward G and the final note is the D above this, which should be tested as a slightly narrow fifth against the first A to be tuned. This method of laying the bearings is known as tuning the great circle of fifths. Another method using fourths and fifths is given in the diagram, and this does not exhaust the possibilities. The upper and lower notes of the scale are then tuned as octaves.[1]

[1] Step by step details of the method of tuning by the cycle of fifths are given by Otto Funke in *The Piano and How to Care For It*, Frankfurt/M., 1961.

Some tuners widen the octaves slightly (less than one beat per second) towards the trebles, and this for two reasons. Firstly, it seems to give a brightness and vitality to the treble register because it tends to bring this into tune with the sharp harmonics of lower strings, and, secondly, the treble notes tend to flatten with playing and time more quickly than those in the bass.

The tuning of the extreme treble is a matter of some difficulty because the notes have little volume or sustaining power. Striking three octave notes for each pitch may assist perception of these high sounds. Some tuners slightly narrow the bass octaves. Again, particularly in those pianos where the extreme bass strings are comparatively short, there is difficulty in hearing the real pitch of the note. Frequently, inexperienced tuners have broken bass strings in tensioning them in a vain endeavour to find the appropriate pitch of the string. It is easily evident that the general impression of the tone colour of a piano depends on the state of its tuning. Uncritical people think that good tuning has "taken all the colour out of the instrument".

For more than a hundred years various devices have been used to assist tuners, but apart from tuning forks few have survived. In particular, in one system strong springs were interposed between the strings and the wrest-pins. The strain on the spring, measured on a dial plate, could be adjusted to bring the string to its original tension. A modern aid to tuning, which is used in America more than elsewhere, is an electronic generator which will produce audible pitches with great accuracy. A refinement of this apparatus uses a microphone which picks up the sound of the vibrating string and shows on a dial when the note is in tune with one of the pre-determined pitches of the pianoforte scale.

A mathematically perfect system of equal temperament would prevent the possibility of "key-colour". The very slight narrowing of the octave within the cycle of fifths distributes the comma more generally than in equal temperament. Tuners usually work empirically, and not with the aid of electronic apparatus. Thus a certain amount of key colour may remain because they allow slightly more consonance to some of the white note intervals. Thus, it may happen that the keys of G and D major are open and bright and those of D♭ and G♭ are veiled and introspective. Suggestions that differences in fingering between the keys may account for the phenomenon of key-colour do not seem to be plausible, since, in spite of their shorter length, the black keys have similar leverage to that of the white keys.

Hipkins,[1] as a young man of eighteen working for the Broadwood firm in London, found that the tuners made unsatisfactory attempts "to relinquish what passed for the old Meantone system of tuning". He found an explanation of "equal temperament" in an appendix to Crotch's *Harmony* and two years later, in 1846, at the request of Mr. Walter Broadwood, the English tuners were instructed by Hipkins in the method of tuning to equal temperament. S. S. Wesley, the organist, was opposed to the system and although the Walker organ at the Exeter Hall, Strand, was tuned in equal temperament in 1848 at the request of Michael Costa, many organ-builders and players in England objected to the system for years, preferring to eschew certain keys altogether, in order to secure a juster tuning in others.

The date 1846 can be taken as that which marks the systematic introduction of equal temperament in English pianos, but there must have been attempts at a progressive sharpening of the thirds before this date. In Germany, pianos were tuned to equal temperament—or an approach to it—at an earlier date.

The late Sir Henry Wood, an orchestral conductor who had great experience in piano concerto "accompaniment", maintained that the pianoforte should be tuned so that its A frequency was about 4 cycles per second above that of the orchestra *as it was at the start of a concert.* "The piano concerto generally comes in the middle of the programme, when the orchestra has risen in pitch four or five vibrations in the heated concert room." If changes of temperature do not greatly disturb the pitch of a piano, changes of humidity affect it considerably.

The British Broadcasting Corporation and other European and American radio stations transmit a pure tone of 440 cycles per second as a tuning note. Although the frequency of this note is maintained at all dynamic levels, an apparent rise or fall of pitch may be secured by adjusting the volume of the receiver. This simple observation shows that the sensation of pitch depends not only on physical frequency but on dynamic level also. Actually, the matter is more complex than this, for the apparent change of pitch is also a function of the harmonic content, that is, the tone quality of the note. The pitch change which takes place with an alteration of dynamic level is less apparent with a bright sound, rich in overtones, than with a relatively dull sound.

[1] Alfred James Hipkins: Some autobiographical notes given to the editor of *The Musical Times* and published in September 1898.

To secure a good crescendo, free from any sense of loss of pitch or dullness of sound, harmonics should be added and increased in strength as the note becomes louder, with relatively little increase in the power of the fundamental tone. The addition of mutation and mixture stops to the diapason stops of the organ gives a much better sense of crescendo than the use of the swell-pedal, which sometimes produces a subjective sense of flattening. The crescendo of the orchestral horn gives little increase in the ground tone of the instrument. In the pianoforte, hammer-coverings which have been overtoned by too much needling produce a most uninspiring sound when attempts are made by the performer to secure a louder tone. As has been noticed, the subjective change of pitch, produced by altering the loudness of the sound, has considerable significance in the playing of keyboard instruments with a fixed temperament.

Enharmonic change does not imply a fixed pitch in spite of the fact that physically the frequency of the sound of the two notes on a keyboard instrument is the same, since they are provided by playing one key. It is the mental perception of the pitches of the sounds implied by the changing harmonic background which differ. If the progressions C, Db, C and C, C♯, D accompanied by suitable respective harmonies, are played, the same black note on the pianoforte may appear to have different intonations in the different musical circumstances.[1] More than a century ago Hauptmann wrote, "In the two passages C, Db, C and C, C♯, D it is certain that the Db will be sung flatter than the C♯. This is the psychological view of intonation that the keyboard can know nothing of."[2] Hauptmann objected to the piano, not because of equal temperament but because of its fixed intonation.

Thus, enharmonic modulation must not be considered as belonging specially to tempered scales. The singer or string player is able to make small changes in the frequency of the changed note: on the keyboard the change of intonation is perceptive and subjective.

The last word has not been said about temperament. It is often supposed in error that Bach's "Well-Tempered Clavier" implied equal temperament. No doubt with the progressive sharpening of the thirds in the scale, which was a feature of keyboard tuning, particularly of stringed instruments in the second half of the seventeenth century, equal temperament was approached; but there can be little doubt that there was still distinctive key-colour in Bach's

[1] *Proc. Mus. Ass.*, vol. LXXVII, p. 50.
[2] Moritz Hauptmann (1792–1868), *Letters of a Leipsic Cantor.*

clavichords. In other words, "well-tempered" meant that each prelude and fugue sounded well, in its own appropriate key-colour, with the empirical system which Bach, as a tuner, employed. We have already mentioned a method of tuning which departs somewhat from equal temperament. The colour of a chord on the pianoforte may be changed by altering the dynamics of each component note by skilful fingering; but it is also changed by altering the tuning of one or more of its notes. The chord C, E, G, with almost mathematically perfect intervals in the frequency ratios of 1, $\frac{5}{4}$, $\frac{3}{2}$, has a chaste, clean effect. When the third (E) is sharpened as in equal temperament a reedy growl, which destroys the former transparency, appears.

In 1957 yet another principle of tuning, and one easy to achieve, was suggested. In equal temperament each of the fifths is narrowed by $\frac{1}{12}$ of a Pythagorean comma. Thus, the fifths, starting with A–E (straddling middle C) and going up to A♭–E♭, have a beat-rate graduated between ·76 to 1·41 beats per second. In the new method the fifths in this sequence have the same beat-rate which is calculated for the formula: Beat Rate $= \dfrac{7,153 \times F}{1,568,693}$, where F is the lowest note (A) of the sequence. An octave sequence is convenient. This is a useful method of tuning and it gives distinctive key colours. Leigh Silver believes that it is closer to Bach's method of tuning than equal temperament.[1] We must remember that tempered scales evolved from the making of music, and the motivation was that of the advancing needs of music. Music is not a form of communication thrust into a fixed system of vibrations. In the framework of music, the cultured ear of the sensitive musician must stand in advance of the use of logarithm tables!

The nature of temperament has been summed up by Ll. S. Lloyd, in the following passage:

Theorists, obsessed with the arithmetical niceties of temperaments and the manifestations of the twelfth root of 2, often failed to realise that the keyboard, as we know it, imposed on all choice of temperaments an over riding limitation from which there was no escape. Ever since Zarlino's day there have been those who have attempted to improve the musical resources of keyboard instruments by adding to the number of keys in the octave. These

[1] A. L. Leigh Silver, "*Equal Beating Chromatic Scale*", *Journal of the Acoustical Society of America*, vol. XXIX, no. 4, April 1957.

attempts have always failed to win permanent acceptance. As Robert Smith observed in his *Harmonics* (1758):

> The old expedient for introducing some of these sounds (D♯, A♯ . . . A♭ D♭ G♭ etc.), by inserting more keys in every octave is quite laid aside by reason of the difficulty in playing upon them.

It is often said that equal temperament has made a marked contribution to the art of music. That statement calls for some qualification of its literal meaning. The mistuned intervals of this temperament make no contribution to the art of music. Good violin players are conscious of them on the pianoforte, and some pianists of sensitive hearing are well aware of differences between the intonation of a good string quartet and that of a pianoforte. A good orchestra does not play in equal temperament, nor must the faulty intonation of a poor one be identified with equal temperament. The real contribution that equal temperament has made to the art of music is indirect: it lies in the fact that, in spite of its mistuned intervals, equal temperament made possible the continued use of a keyboard with twelve notes to the octave, such as had been used for mean-tone tuning. To that continued use of a twelve-note keyboard is due the nineteenth-century development of pianoforte technique and pianoforte music.[1]

Relative frequencies of intervals

		No. of Semitones	Interval
$2^{1/12}$	$=1{\cdot}05946$	1	semitone
$2^{2/12}$ $(=2^{1/6})=1{\cdot}12246$		2	tone
$2^{3/12}$ $(=2^{1/4})=1{\cdot}18921$		3	minor third
$2^{4/12}$ $(=2^{1/3})=1{\cdot}25993$		4	major third
$2^{5/12}$	$=1{\cdot}33484$	5	fourth
$2^{6/12}$ $(=2^{1/2})=1{\cdot}41421$		6	tritone (augmented fourth)
$2^{7/12}$	$=1{\cdot}49831$	7	fifth
$2^{8/12}$ $(=2^{2/3})=1{\cdot}58740$		8	minor sixth
$2^{9/12}$ $(=2^{3/4})=1{\cdot}68179$		9	sixth
$2^{10/12}$ $(=2^{5/6})=1{\cdot}78180$		10	diminished seventh
$2^{11/12}$	$=1{\cdot}88775$	11	seventh
$2^{12/12}$ $(=2\ \ )=2{\cdot}0000$		12	octave

[1] Ll. S. Lloyd and Hugh Boyle, *Intervals, Scales and Temperaments*, pp. 60 et seq., London, 1962.

Beat rates

Beat rates for similar intervals are proportional to the frequency of the higher (or lower) notes of the intervals.

Fifths (in equal temperament the fifths are slightly narrow): The beat rates for fifths which include or enclose middle C are

C to G	9 beats in 10 seconds
A to E	7·6 beats in 10 seconds
G♯ to D♯	7·15 beats in 10 seconds
G to D	6·75 beats in 10 seconds
F♯ to C♯	6·37 beats in 10 seconds
F to C	6·00 beats in 10 seconds

[about 2 beats in 3 seconds for the "middle" intervals].

Fourths (in equal temperament the fourths are slightly wide):

B to E	11·25 in 10 seconds
A♯ to D♯	10·61 in 10 seconds
A to D	10·00 in 10 seconds
G♯ to C♯	9·45 in 10 seconds
G to C	8·9 in 10 seconds
F♯ to B	8·4 in 10 seconds
F to A♯	7·9 in 10 seconds

[about 1 beat per second for the "middle" intervals].

Major Thirds (in equal temperament the thirds are considerably wide):

C to E	10·5 in 1 second
B to D♯	9·9 in 1 second
A♯ to D	9·35 in 1 second
A to C♯	8·85 in 1 second
G♯ to C	8·35 in 1 second
G to B	7·87 in 1 second
F♯ to A♯	7·44 in 1 second
F to A	7·02 in 1 second

These are too frequent to count. In the octave above middle C these numbers are doubled.

"Pitch" of various instruments[1]

Vibrations per second (*A*)		*Date*
	LOW PITCH CHURCH	
391	Andreas Silbermann's pitch, Strassburg Minster	1714
392	Euler's clavichords, St. Petersburg	1739

[1] From A. Ellis, *History of Musical Pitch*, London, 1881 [with modifications].

Plate fifteen

Three Early Pianoforte Actions

a. Cristofori action, 1709

b. Cristofori, 1726. Note the double leverage, escapement and check

c. "Stossmechanik" (Stoss=Blow, push or thrust). A crude action in which the hammer was thrown to the string by the "mopstick" or "old man's head", c. 1780 (Museum Neupert)

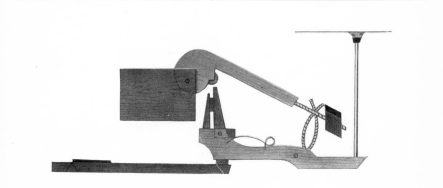

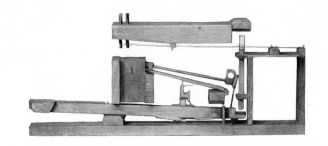

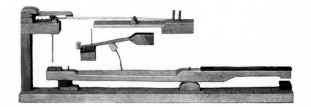

Plate sixteen

Early Pianoforte Actions
a. Prellmechanik (German or Vienna action). The hammer is attached to the key and is pivoted within a little case (Kapsel) fixed to the end of the key. The end of the hammer engages with the Prelleiste
b. Schröter action 1721
c. English action 1795 (Museum Neupert)

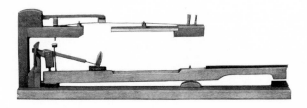

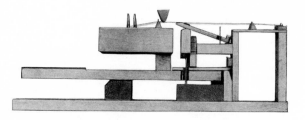

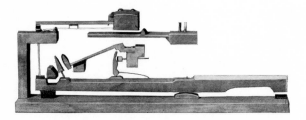

Vibrations
per second   *Date*

395	Trinity College Organ, Cambridge	1759
396	Organ in Versailles Chapel	1789

LOW CHAMBER PITCH

407	Pitch of Spinet measured by Sauveur in Paris	1713
408	Pitch for tuning Stringed instruments (Mattheson) Hamburg	1762
409	Court Claveçins, Paris	1783
414·4	Clavichord, Breslau	1776

"MEAN" PITCH

415	G. Silbermann's organ in chief R.C. Church in Dresden	1722
422	Mozart's pianos (Stein's tuning fork)	1780
422·5	Handel's tuning fork	1751
to 423	Dresden Opera under Weber	1815–1821
	Opéra Comique, Paris	1820
	Westminster Abbey organ	1820
427	Paris Opéra	1811

"COMPROMISE" PITCH

433	Sir George Smart's tuning fork	1828
435	French Diapason Normal	1859
	[Diapason is the French word for a Tuning Fork]	
439	New Philharmonic	1896

MODERN ORCHESTRAL AND "ANCIENT MEDIUM" PITCH

440	International Standard pitch	1939
440	Paris Conservatoire	1812
440	Paris Opéra Comique	1829
440	Dresden Opera	1862
440	Scheibler's Stuttgart pitch for music industries	1834
441	Covent Garden Opera	1878
444·6	St. Paul's Cathedral Organ	1877
446	Broadwood's Medium Pitch	1849–1880
447	Vienna Opera	1878
	Paris Opéra	1858
449	Leipzig Gewandhaus Concert	1859
451	British and Belgian Instruments Standard	1879

H

Vibrations per second		*Date*
452	International Exhibition of Inventions and Music, London	1885
453	Kneller Hall Military School	1878
	London Philharmonic Concerts	1846–1854
455·3	Pitch of Érard, Broadwood, Steinway and Brinsmead pianofortes	1880
	Highest Philharmonic Pitch	1880
457	American Steinway Pianofortes	1890

Acoustics of auditoria

It is beyond the scope of this book to deal in detail with the acoustics of buildings and the reader is referred to the standard works which are listed in the bibliography. Nevertheless, it is important to mention the chief factors which may influence piano tone. Each auditorium and piano presents its own acoustical problems. Moreover, the absorption of sound in an empty hall, unless it has been specially treated, as in many cinema theatres, is less than when the hall is full. In some cases this is a most serious matter; for instance, in the McEwan Hall of the University of Edinburgh a $6\frac{1}{4}$ seconds reverberation period in the hall, when it is empty, almost vanishes when it is filled. The absorption of sound by auditoria and their contents is hardly ever uniform throughout the pitch range. Thus, some halls will seem to amplify the sounds from one part of the keyboard and absorb others. Some "dead" buildings fail to carry the tone of the instrument and the performer has the unpleasant feeling that his expenditure of energy is not producing an equivalent sound and that there is a lack of projection. On the other hand, a lively hall, particularly if there is an echo in addition to a long period of reverberation, will cause a jumbling of sounds which will render rapid part-playing indistinct. Both of these troubles tax the skill of the performer to the utmost and add to the strain of playing memorised works.

Pianos not only differ in touch, but in their tone production in relation to their acoustical environment. Touch, dynamics, pedalling and even the choice of compositions which are to be played may have to be modified to suit acoustical conditions. Pianos should stand directly on a good wooden floor, which in itself should be substantial enough to act as a sound-board. Curtains, carpets and woven

	A	A#	B	C	C#	D	D#	E	F	F#	G	G#
No.	1	2	3	4	5	6	7	8	9	10	11	12
Freq.	27·5	29·1	30·8	32·7	34·6	36·7	38·9	41·2	43·6	46·2	49·0	51·9
No.	13	14	15	16	17	18	19	20	21	22	23	24
Freq.	55·0	58·3	61·7	65·4	69·3	73·4	77·8	82·4	87·3	92·5	98·0	103·8
No.	25	26	27	28	29	30	31	32	33	34	35	36
Freq.	110·0	116·5	123·4	130·8	138·6	146·8	155·6	164·8	174·6	185·0	196·0	207·6
No.	37	38	39	40	41	42	43	44	45	46	47	48
Freq.	220·0	233·1	246·9	261·6	277·1	293·6	311·1	329·6	349·2	369·9	391·9	415·3
No.	49	50	51	52	53	54	55	56	57	58	59	60
Freq.	440·0	466·2	493·8	523·2	554·2	587·2	622·2	659·2	698·4	739·8	783·8	830·6
No.	61	62	63	64	65	66	67	68	69	70	71	72
Freq.	880·0	932·3	987·7	1046·4	1108	1174	1244·4	1318	1397	1480	1568	1661
No.	73	74	75	76	77	78	79	80	81	82	83	84
Freq.	1760	1865	1975	2093	2217	2348	2489	2636	2794	2960	3136	3322
No.	85	86	87	88								
Freq.	3520	3730	3950	4186								

The numbers, names and frequencies of the notes of an 88 note pianoforte.

material absorb sound; and although their deliberate use may be necessary to correct over-reverberation, their effect on musical tone is usually undesirable.

The sound of a musical instrument is transmitted to the hearer by waves in the air. When the instrument is enclosed with the hearer in a room or auditorium, complications arise because of the reflection and absorption of the sound by the walls, floor and ceiling and the contents of the auditorium which includes, of course, the clothes of the audience. Physicists who work in conjunction with musicians know much concerning the acoustics of buildings and also the optimum conditions for listening to speech and music of various kinds. With piano tone, the metallic ("tinny") thin quality of a piano played in the open air can be contrasted with the heavy, lifeless tone of a piano in a heavily draped and carpeted room. The importance of the acoustical link in the chain between composer and hearer is often overlooked: and good performers and instruments are placed at a disadvantage.

Absorbent plaster, plaster boards in which are punched numerous small holes, and surfaces broken into small parts will tend to absorb high notes and harmonics. Large panels tend to absorb low notes, particularly when backed with sawdust or sand. Generally speaking, low notes travel with less sense of attenuation, and with a greater capacity to bend round corners than high notes: in a church porch, often only the low pedal notes of the organ can be heard.

Sometimes a note of a piano will cause sympathetic vibration in a nearby object such as a vase, a lamp shade, an electric fitting, a music-stand or a loose panel. To the uninitiated this may cause some mystification because the vibration of the object may not be apparent, and the effect is that of an unpleasant change in the tone-quality of a particular note of the piano. Even the orientation of a piano with regard to the position of an audience may be an important factor. Experiments should be done with the reflecting lid of a grand piano, which may not always be in the optimum position when the reflection projects the sound along the centre line of the hall. The wave length of the lowest note of a piano is more than forty feet. Such notes cannot be expected to develop themselves in small rooms, and sometimes unpleasant effects caused by a confusion of nodes and antinodes may result. Alternatively, the lower notes may seem to be amplified in large halls, whereas the high-pitched sounds are absorbed by the wall surfaces and a lack of pitch-balance in various parts of the hall may result.

Much trial and error in (*a*) the placing of absorbent and reflecting material, (*b*) the position of the piano, and (*c*) touch, tone balance and the use of the pedal may be necessary in order that the optimum conditions may be obtained in the given circumstances.

The subjective estimate of loudness is not simply an expression of the energy of the source of sound and the distance of the listener from it. The psychological phenomenon of loudness is a complex matter governed by a number of factors, all of which are important to the performing musician and the listener. If a melody is played first legato and then staccato on an organ whose pipes stand on an open sound-board, the melody played legato seems to be much louder than when it is played in short, detached notes. It is well known that accents, known as agogic accents, can be obtained on organs and other instruments by giving careful attention to note lengths. If tones are allowed to overlap they seem louder than if they are played staccato. The perception of the loudness of a note, the duration of which is a second or less, is given by the product of its dynamic level and its duration. It is easy to see why the sustaining pedal has popularly been known as the loud pedal. The sustained sounds, which might result in a blurred mass of tone, give a sensation of loudness greater than tones which are precisely defined in length.

Noise
An important part of the ingredients of pianoforte tone is "noise" caused by the impact of the hammer on the strings, the mechanism and even the fingers on the keys. When the noise elements are filtered away by electronic means, pianoforte tone seems to become uninteresting and emasculated. The word noise is used in its older sense. The only definition of noise which can be accepted today is that it is unwanted sound.

CHAPTER VI

GREAT PIANOFORTE MAKERS

Carl Bechstein

Carl Bechstein was born in 1826 and settled in Berlin as a piano-forte maker in 1853. In 1856 Hans von Bülow inaugurated the first Bechstein grand piano by playing Liszt's sonata. This very successful concert was Bechstein's stepping-stone to fame. In 1860 Bechstein sent to Liszt at Weimar a grand piano and earned a glowing testimonial from the master. In 1861 Von Bülow asked Klindworth to see that the Bechstein piano was properly demonstrated at the International Exhibition in London, and this was the cause of much appreciation in Britain. In 1901 the Bechstein Hall, now the Wigmore Hall, was opened in London and became a small concert hall of the utmost importance to the music of the metropolis and, in particular, to many young artists seeking fame. Carl Bechstein died in 1901, and the business continued to prosper in the hands of his sons. At the time of his death Bechstein claimed special appointments to many of the royal households, including that of Queen Victoria. In spite of the upheavals caused by two wars and subsequent troubles the firm still continues to produce first-rate instruments in the city of its birth. The Bechstein pianos were treasured because of their beautiful, interesting trebles, their singing tenor registers and their rich, resonant basses.

Hans von Bülow wrote to Alexander Ritter in 1857:

Bechstein is, in my opinion, the foremost maker of grand pianos in Germany, although he has built only three so far.

The firm was awarded the English Grand Prix at the London Industrial Exhibition in 1862:

Bechstein's instruments are distinguished by outstanding freshness and breadth of tone, quality of play and uniformity of the different registers, and would seem to be able to withstand even the most vigorous treatment.

In 1864 Richard Wagner wrote to Carl Bechstein:

When I returned to Germany from exile for the first time, with my friend Liszt in Weimar, I came one day by chance upon an instrument which by its delightful, crystal-clear tone so charmed and enthralled me that my dear friend, Hans von Bülow, wishing to console me on my unhappy departure, had the inspired idea of providing an identical instrument to gladden me in my new abode.

In 1883 the firm employed 500 workers and made approximately 1,200 instruments, but in the years before 1914, with 1,100 men, the annual production grew to 5,000 and one factory in Berlin had produced a total of over 152,000 grands and uprights before the second world war.

Schiedmayer

This distinguished family of makers was descended from Johann David Schiedmayer, of Erlangen, who died in 1806 at Nuremburg. His son, John Lorenz Schiedmayer, went to Vienna in the year of his father's death to gain experience. On his return to Stuttgart he started a piano-making firm in 1809, with C. F. Dieudonné (who died in 1825) as a partner. Until that time there was little piano-making in Germany, which relied on Viennese, French and English instruments, and thus the Schiedmayer firm did excellent business in their own country. There were four sons of J. F. Schiedmayer but Julius and Paul left the firm and started independently in Stuttgart in 1854. Unhappily, there was acrimony as a result of this, but it led to the type of rivalry which stimulates improvement and healthy competition. For some years they practically had the German trade to themselves. The Schiedmayer piano won the Grand Prix at the Paris Exhibition of 1900 and was the favourite instrument of Hans Richter, the distinguished conductor. The British agency was held by Archibald Ramsden of London and many northern towns.

Johannes Adolf Ibach

Ibach was born in Barmen, and began piano-building in 1794. He was not only a skilled craftsman, but also an excellent amateur performer on both the piano and organ. In the early years of the nineteenth century, when there was much political strife and poverty, Ibach managed to continue his work, and even in the starvation conditions in 1811, fourteen pianos were made. In 1834 the firm developed under two sons of the founder, Carl Rudolf and his younger brother Richard. Later, Carl had a factory in Cologne and became Purveyor to the Russian Court. A branch was opened in London in 1880 and the Ibach piano was much esteemed in England. Today the firm still flourishes as one which has a long history in Schwelm in Westphalia. Some of the most beautiful instruments presented at the annual Frankfurt Exhibition are the work of this firm. The Ibach piano, whether a grand or upright, is a durable work of art.

Blüthner

Julius Ferdinand Blüthner was born in 1824 in Falkenhain near Merseburg. In November 1853, almost at the same time as Bechstein in Berlin, he opened a piano-factory in Leipzig. The finest workmanship and musical judgment were used to make the pianofortes, and soon they were used exclusively in the Leipzig Conservatorium, which had known the enthusiasm of Mendelssohn and was to have a line of distinguished teachers of the piano and other instruments. Here, for instance, Teichmüller made his piano classes world-famous. Leipzig, the city of Johann Sebastian Bach, was a centre of music-making, music-publishing and music-teaching. Here Wagner had been born and, in 1916, Reger had died. Both the place and era were favourable for the production of Blüthner's first-class instruments. These pianos were well-known throughout Europe, and there was a branch of the firm in London, opened in 1896.

A distinctive feature of the Blüthner piano was the use, from 1873, in the more expensive instruments, of *aliquot scaling*. The principle was not new, since G. Silbermann had used strings played harmonically by being struck in the middle in his keyboard instrument called Cembal d'Amour. The Steinway family had sought to incorporate the sympathetic vibrations of the unstruck part of the strings into the main tone. Blüthner advertised this system as follows:

It is a matter of common knowledge that the ordinary grand piano is provided with three strings for each of the treble notes. This fact notwithstanding, the treble section of many pianos is apt to be overpowered by the bass, and pianoforte manufacturers have for many years turned their attention to means of improving the tone of the treble section. In the Blüthner grand the problem has been solved by the introduction of the aliquot scaling, which consists of a fourth string added to the three strings generally employed. This extra string is not struck by the hammer head, but operates in accordance with the law of sympathetic vibration, sounding the overtone when the note itself is struck. This blending of overtone and parent note produces an increased richness and sympathy of tone; it enhances the beauty of the treble section and has, in fact, greatly contributed to the fame of the Blüthner pianoforte.

Chickering and Sons

"Today I played upon Liszt's glorious Chickering."—Edvard Grieg.

This firm has the longest history of any piano-making establishment in America. Jonas Chickering was born in Mason Village, New Hampshire, in 1796. In 1817 he repaired the piano made for Princess Amelia and, becoming interested in the instrument, he went to Boston the following year and was apprenticed to a piano-maker there. Four years later he joined James Stewart to establish the firm of Stewart and Chickering. The first Chickering piano made by them is still preserved in the Edison Institute at Dearborn, Michigan. From 1828 Jonas continued as sole owner of the business, and two years later made the first Chickering upright piano. In 1833 Captain John Mackay became a partner and the firm began the export of their instruments to other countries. Four years after this, the full iron plate for grand pianos was invented and used. A disaster at sea removed the captain from the business and Jonas continued again as its sole owner. In 1845 overstringing was applied to both grand and upright pianos. The sons were soon taken into partnership and, from 1848, the firm was known as Chickering and Sons, which style remains to this day. In 1852 the Boston factory in Washington Street was destroyed by fire. A new factory, which, apart from the Capitol in Washington, was the largest building in America at the time, was erected in Tremont Street the following year. Jonas died suddenly in 1853 and the business was continued by the sons with increasing distinction.

The Chickering pianofortes were awarded the first Gold Medal at the International Exhibition in Paris in 1867, and the Emperor Napoleon III bestowed upon Francis Chickering the Imperial Cross of the Legion of Honour. Thomas E. Chickering, the eldest son, died in 1871, a second son, Charles F., twenty years later and George H., the third, in 1899, but during all this time there had been great development with many inventions and a great extension of the business. In 1904 the firm produced a "quarter" grand piano, which was then the smallest of its type. The firm became affiliated to the United States Pianoforte Company. During the period 1913 to 1919 remarkable strides were made in improving the tone and volume of both upright and grand pianos. So famous had the firm become by the time of its centenary celebrations, that these were regarded as a national occasion. In 1928 the factory was moved to Rochester, New York.

Steinway and Sons

The Steinway story starts in Wolfshagen in the Harz mountains in 1797, when Heinrich Steinweg was born to a humble forester who already was the father of fifteen children. The Napoleonic Wars took away the father and the elder brothers, leaving the mother and younger children to fend for themselves in the mountains. It is hardly surprising that when the father returned, only Heinrich and two other children had survived to greet him, for the rest had perished from hunger and exposure. Shortly after this the remnants of the family, save only Heinrich, were killed by lightning while working by the road-side. By a miracle, Heinrich survived the Battle of Waterloo, with hundreds falling around him; and he even won a medal for bugling in the face of the enemy. In the post-war days he filled his time in the boredom of the garrison by wood-work, in making a mandolin, a dulcimer and a zither. He had an inborn skill with wood and its ways, and this was further enhanced by his work as a cabinet-maker in an organ factory. On his marriage to Juliane Theimer, he presented her with a piano of his own make with two strings to each note. Another piano, with three strings to each note, took thirteen years of devoted evenings in its manufacture; but it was not until Heinrich had won a first prize at a State Fair that he decided to devote the rest of his life to piano-making. The Revolution of 1848 threatened to ruin the Steinwegs again, and now there were ten children. Tired of the political unrest of Europe, the son Charles, knowing something of the democratic ideals of Franklin and Jefferson, left for New York and soon persuaded his father to bring the family and settle permanently in the New World. Thus, Heinrich Steinweg of Wolfshagen became Henry Steinway of New York.

Henry was a perfectionist; he made disciples of his sons and in them he sowed the seeds of his own principles, purposes and ideals. A central point in all Steinway manufacture has been the understanding of the nature of the various types of wood. Great care has been taken in selecting their timber or, as it is called in America, lumber. In addition to mahogany and walnut, there is used the west coast spruce from Vermont for the sound-board, tulip wood from the south Appalachians for core stock, maple from Indiana, Wisconsin and Canada for rims, wrest-planks and bridges, sugar pine from California for the keys and rosewood from Brazil for an action-part.

The Steinway sons proved to have a good mixture of talents: they combined aptitude as musicians with skill as engineers and craftsmen and ability in research. In 1859 Henry Junior made piano history by combining the single-cast metal plate with the overstrung scale. Theodore's research notes would occupy many volumes, and he had about three dozen patents to his credit. Constant research into every aspect of pianoforte manufacture continues today. The firm has maintained its high artistic ideals during the most difficult times, and on one occasion shut its factory for two years rather than produce instruments which fell short of the best. In the darkest days of the depression Steinway refused two million dollars for the right to use its name on domestic equipment. The Steinway piano stands today amongst the world's finest musical instruments. It is not confined to the American continent but is found in concert-rooms, private houses and teaching institutions throughout the world. The Steinway firm sponsored concerts and tours which featured the best pianists of Europe and America. Thus, the fine qualities of the instrument became well-known. The firm's records show that up to the year 1968 it had produced nearly half a million pianos.

Mason and Hamlin

Professor Lowell Mason, a descendant of one of the *Mayflower* families, was a Boston music teacher who was largely responsible for the introduction of music in the curriculum of the American schools in 1837. He had two sons, one of whom, William, became a pupil of Liszt and another, Henry (1831–90), after instruction in a German University, returned to America in 1854 with a strong wish to provide the best musical instruments for his native country. With

Emmons Hamlin (1821–85), the firm was founded and became famed for the production of free-reed instruments known as the Organ Harmonium. Henry in his turn had two sons, one of whom, Daniel Gregory Mason, became one of the most distinguished composers and teachers in America. Henry L. Mason followed his father as a musical instrument-maker, and the firm started to build pianofortes of the finest quality, the reputation of which was quickly established and has continued to the present. The firm, a division of the Aeolian American Corporation, is now at East Rochester, New York. Mason and Hamlin used a Duplex scale, by tuning the string length beyond the bridge and by the placing of thirty-seven small bars, called *aliquots*, which add to the sonority and clarity of the treble. For a number of years the firm has used a tension regulation to preserve the curvature, or "crowning", of the sound-board. This nullifies the effects of changes of temperature and humidity and resists the effects of time and wear on the curve of the sound-board. Steel rods fastened to the frame are pre-set for the exact tension when the piano is made.

Grotrian-Steinweg

Friedrich Grotrian was born in Brunswick, where the firm still flourishes, in 1803, and as a young man he went to Moscow where he was associated with the leading piano-making industry. In 1835 he and Heinrich Steinweg, of Seesen, a member of the family famous under the name of Steinway, completed the building of Grotrian's first square piano. That instrument, created with the artistry of the true craftsman, was the first of the superb pianos which have won for the house of Grotrian-Steinweg the great reputation they enjoy.

When Heinrich Steinweg emigrated to America in 1850, his son Theodore remained behind to continue piano-making, transferring it from Seesen to Wolfenbüttel, and thence to Brunswick. Eight years later Friedrich Grotrian finally returned from Moscow and joined forces with him. Friedrich Grotrian died in 1860.

Many German pianists preferred the instruments of the firm to all others; and Clara Schumann used them exclusively for her recitals after 1870. In 1872 there was a complete separation of the Steinweg interests in Brunswick and the Steinways in New York. In 1866 William Grotrian became the sole proprietor; and in 1895 his sons Willi and Kurt became partners.

William died in 1917, but after the first world war a third factory and saw-mills were opened in Holzminden. The Grotrian-Steinweg pianofortes are known for their "homogeneous sound-boards". The firm gives the following explanation of this:

Every piece of wood that goes into a Grotrian-Steinweg sound-board must match exactly its neighbour. By matching is understood matching the pieces of wood from the point of view of the acoustic properties of internal rhythm. Formerly, this sameness for each and every element of the sound-board was sought after by using pieces of wood from the same tree. This kind of matching gave homogeneity as far as sameness of wood was concerned. Some manufacturers, in striving for the perfect sound-board, used for their sound-boards only pieces of wood of the same age— pieces of wood taken, perhaps, from the same year-ring or rings of the same or different trees. Here homogeneity was secured from the viewpoint of age of wood. Because sound can be measured scientifically, Grotrian-Steinweg fixed as the standard of homogeneity for their sound-boards, not similarity of wood, or similarity of age, but similarity of reaction to sound waves.

Other patents held by the firm concern a "violin technique" in frame and sound-board surface—the violin shape of the frame and the sound-board surface ensures a perfectly harmonious oscillation of the sound-board over the whole area. The firm also claims a chromatically regulated scale, in which the striking point of each string is at an exact fraction of its length; and a freely balanced static metal frame, which is screwed only on the outside of the sound-board. Further, the use of crossed, centralised bracings gives maximum stability to the foundation, and presents an even resistance to tension throughout the entire scaling, and thus contributes to the stability of the tuning of the instrument. The firm has paid particular attention to details of mechanism, whereby the slightest whisper of tone may be obtained; and has even remodelled the upper surfaces of the black-keys to aid the certainty of the player's touch.

At the time of writing this book the firm continues to produce beautiful instruments in many patterns. The writer possesses one of their grand pianofortes. It is a superb instrument.

Bösendorfer

Ignaz Bösendorfer, the founder of the firm, was the son of Jacob Bösendorfer (called also "Besendorfer" and "Pesendorfer"), a cabinet-maker of Number 4 Wieden (fourth district) in Vienna, and his wife, Marthe. He was born on July 27, 1794, and became a pupil of Joseph Brodmann. The latter had been registered in the Court and State Record Department in the year 1805 as Organ and Piano-Maker; and in the *Lexicon of Musicians 1812*, by Ernst Ludwig Gerber, we find: "Joseph Brodmann, instruments-maker, excelled in the year 1800 in constructing horizontal fortepianos of solid finish." In the *Bureau de Musique*, by A. Kühnel, Leipzig, one could always find instruments of his workmanship. In the *Essay on the History of Piano-Making*, by Joseph Fischhof (1853), one may read: "Brodmann in 1825 improved the sounding-board by giving it the necessary stiffness, so to avoid its tearing and bursting." He owned the house, No. 43 am Glacis, Joseph City (8th district), later 226 Johannes Street, and today 10 Lenau Street, in which he also had his workshop. Ignaz Bösendorfer studied in the workshop of Joseph Brodmann, from his nineteenth year, where he also finished his apprenticeship. A good master found an ingenious pupil, who already in the year 1815 won the first prize for ornamental drawing by the Academy of Plastic Arts; and in 1828 the Body of Magistrates in Vienna had granted Bösendorfer, by decree of July 25, 1828, "the right to trade as piano-maker together with the title of a Burgher and Master".

The young Liszt, who at that time was well-known because of his then incomparable technique and his enormous demands as regards the piano, used, in one of his recitals in Vienna, grand pianos of another but well-known make, which, however, could not withstand his strength, and after the performance of a few pieces were rendered unplayable. Annoyed at the poor resistance of these instruments, and upon the advice of friends, Liszt decided to play on a Bösendorfer grand. The piano withstood his touch, remaining undamaged after the close of his recital. This event created so much sensation that it established the reputation of the young Bösendorfer house in the concert hall, and it was also the beginning of friendship between Liszt and the Bösendorfer firm.

On the occasion of the Industries Exhibitions in Vienna in the years 1839 and 1845 Bösendorfer obtained the Golden Medal as a first prize, and the Emperor of Austria bestowed upon him, in 1839, the title of "Piano-Maker appointed to the Royal and Imperial Court", an exceptional distinction conferred upon no other Austrian piano-maker before him.

He enriched his knowledge by travelling in Germany, France and

England, and the continual increasing demand for his pianos induced him to build a new factory on a site near the "Schottentor" (Scotch gate), called "No. 377 New Vienna" (now 9 Türken Street), which, for those days, was considered to be of great dimensions. It was inaugurated in the year 1859. He was not destined, however, to see this building completed, for he died on April 14th of the same year.

Ignaz Bösendorfer appointed his son Ludwig, born in 1835, as his successor, and he was predestined to develop the firm and to introduce his instruments to all the world. In the year 1860 Ludwig Bösendorfer appears as sole proprietor of the workshop, and secured for himself in the same year a "patent on the invention of a peculiar piano action". At the same time he transferred his workshop into the new, already completed, factory at No. 377 New Vienna, to which there was also attached a concert hall for two hundred persons. The following ten years were devoted to most intensive work, and the factory soon proved to be too small.

Hans von Bülow inaugurated a new Bösendorfer Hall, converted from the riding school of Prince Liechtenstein, with a piano recital on November 19, 1872. The wonderful acoustics of the Bösendorfer Hall, as foreseen by Ludwig Bösendorfer, created general admiration, so that it became the most favoured concert hall in Vienna for more than forty years. For the proper acoustic effect, however, two-thirds of its capacity had to be occupied; with less attendance there issued a disturbing echo because of its extraordinary acoustics.

On the occasion of the jubilee of the Bösendorfer House, Wilhelm Backhaus paid tribute to the Bösendorfer piano:

I have been immensely taken with the Bösendorfer pianos from the very day my fingers touched one of them. Again and again I have been confirmed in the feeling that they practically possess a playing efficiency all their own, never offering the slightest resistance to the intentions of the pianist in sound and touch. The medium section has a subtle, delicious sound, regaling as the early dew, supported by a mighty bass register and a brilliant glittering treble thus permitting a perfect rendering of every mood from the pathetic to playful grace. I see, however, in the Bösendorfer more than merely a magnificent piano; for me, it represents straight away the ideal embodiment of Viennese Music Culture. It is not by chance that this piano has found its origin in this city, which has always exerted an irresistible magnetic force upon the music heroes. Since the year of its inception still found Schubert on this earth I may be so presuming as to consider him the godfather of your House.

This wonderful hall, in a city which was the centre of the musical culture of central Europe and world-famous for its piano-teaching, was the scene of the first recitals and other performances of the greatest solo artists of the world. The Bösendorfer records have accounts of about 4,500 concerts given in this hall.

Unhappily, in 1912, the site of the building was needed for the reconstruction work which was then going on in Vienna and, on May 12 of the following year, it closed its doors. This was a sad blow, but the Society of Music Friends in Vienna, formerly the Royal Imperial Society, made other buildings available. The Bösendorfers were more than piano-makers. They encouraged every form of musical activity, gave away many pianos to teaching institutions, established prizes and gave other help to young musicians. Unfortunately, after the first world war the inflation of the Austrian crown evaporated a large bequest made to advance the teaching of music in the city.

Ludwig received not only the highest international awards for his superb instruments, but he was honoured as a man, and in the great days of the Austrian Empire his pianos were used in the imperial and noble residences. He was given the rare Austrian title of Councillor of Commerce and amongst many other honours he was a member of the Order of the Knights of Saint Joseph and the Golden Cross of Merits with the Crown. Truly, he was one of Austria's most honoured citizens.

The war of 1914–18, which brought the end of both emperor and empire, affected the musical life and prosperity of the city and consumed Ludwig's vitality. He died on May 6, 1919.

Periods of economic and political difficulty, another world war, the division not only of Austria but also of the city itself did not destroy the ideals, artistic vision and competence of the firm, which today stands honoured by the musicians of the world, as a monument to the best in art. If this account of Bösendorfer's may seem to be disproportionately long, it is because its wonderful achievements, which have encouraged musicians in central Europe and elsewhere for so long, have not been well-known in the English-speaking world.

Plate seventeen

a. Erard Repetition action
b. Early English Upright action
c. Frederici's Pyramid Piano action, 1750 (Museum Neupert)

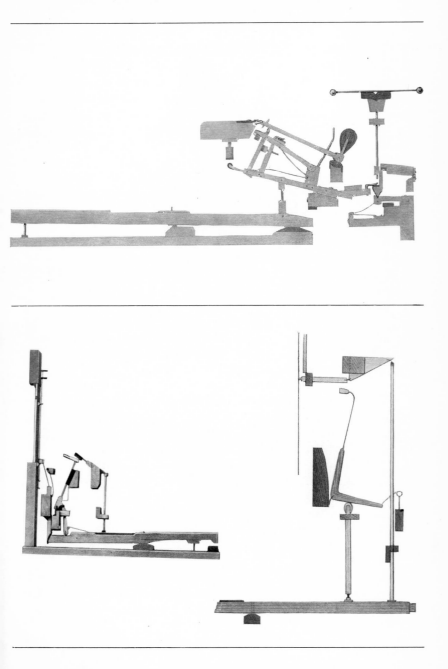

Plate eighteen

Two of Beethoven's Pianofortes
a. The Restored Graf Piano at Bonn (Neupert)
b. The Restored Broadwood at Budapest

Some French makers

In Chapter III we have mentioned the outstanding work of Érard. Another Paris firm of pianoforte makers of great eminence was that of Pleyel. Ignace Pleyel, the twenty-fourth child of a father of thirty-eight children, was born in Ruppersthal on June 1, 1757, and died in Paris on November 14, 1831. Ignace, sub-organist at Strasbourg Cathedral at an early age, was precocious both as composer and pianist, and was one of Haydn's favourite pupils. Mozart spoke highly of his quartets. He loved to travel, and visited England, where in 1807 he established a factory and shop. In his early days as a pianoforte maker he was helped by Henry Pape. In 1821, he was joined by his son Camille, himself a brilliant musician, and the pianist Kalkbrenner. They learnt much from the English pianoforte manufacturers, and produced an instrument which became one of Chopin's favourite pianofortes. The Pleyel piano was used by Mme. Camille Pleyel, Berlioz's beautiful Ariel, an excellent performer, Kalkbrenner, Hummel, Hiller, Moscheles, Rubinstein, Mathias, Fissot, Ritter and Schulhof. At the Salle Pleyel, in Paris, the young Saint-Saëns made his debut at the age of ten.

The Salle Pleyel was a concert room which had excellent acoustics and was famous for the playing of Kalkbrenner and Chopin. When Camille Pleyel died on May 4, 1855, Auguste Wolff, pianoforte professor at the Conservatoire, became director of the house, and he was followed by Gustave Lyon, a former student of l'École Polytechnique. He developed metal frames and made double keyboard pianofortes of the type devised by Emmanuel Moor. Another type of double keyboard piano, with a keyboard at each end of a rectangular body, was used by teachers and duettists. Raoul Pugno, the distinguished pianist and teacher, had such an instrument. The firm had an agency in London from 1876, and was known as Pleyel, Wolff and Co.

It is convenient to mention here other distinguished French pianoforte makers of the nineteenth century.

The firm of Gaveau was founded in 1847 by Joseph Gabriel Gaveau, who was born in 1824. He improved piano actions and experimented with piano constructions designed to amplify the sounds. He was followed by his sons Gabriel and Stephen, who died in 1943. The firm has premises in the Rue de La Boétie and at the Salle Gaveau in Paris, and is noted for the successful production of small pianos.

I

Another ingenious piano maker was Jean Georges Kriegelstein, who was born at Riquewihr in 1801 and after working with Pape established his own business in 1831. He experimented with simple and compound escapement actions, with methods of stringing the piano, and extended the compass of his instruments to seven and a quarter octaves.

John Broadwood and Sons

The House of Broadwood has the longest history of any firm of pianoforte manufacturers in Britain and probably in the world. The story of the Broadwood instruments reflects that of the music of the piano in all the great periods of composing for and playing it. Beethoven, Chopin, Liszt and other masters appear in the annals of this distinguished firm.

John Broadwood was born in 1732 at Cockburnspath, in the seaside village of Haddington in Scotland. As a young man he quickly became skilful as a joiner and cabinet-maker, and in 1761 left Scotland to join Burkat Shudi, the harpsichord maker, in London. At once his skill, inventive genius, and remarkable workmanship became apparent. An excellent relationship existed between master and apprentice, and eight years after his arrival in London Broadwood married Shudi's daughter Barbara, became his partner in 1770 and eventually the proprietor of the business. He and his sons and thereafter the family were notable for their creative skill in producing piano actions and frames. The word Broadwood in Britain and the Colonies was synonymous with pianoforte. Since the reign of King George II (1727–60) to the present day, the firm has been honoured with the royal appointment. During the whole of this period the family nature of the Broadwood business has continued without interruption, and the present chairman is Captain Evelyn Broadwood, M.C. This is a record unique and unequalled in the pianoforte industry. The Broadwood firm has been known, in its long history, for its generosity to musicians. A Broadwood piano was given and sent to Beethoven in Vienna, another was made expressly for Chopin in 1848, and used in his last recitals in London. The firm has commanded the services of some of the most skilful craftsmen, designers and acousticians. It maintains its high standards of production and development. "Tropicalised" pianos, sent to places with extreme climates, stand up to the most severe conditions. Broadwood produces, amongst other models, special school pianofortes, which are built for extreme durability, safety and easy transport.

The firm had premises in 33 Great Pulteney Street for a century and a half, and now has offices and showrooms in Hanover Street, Mayfair, London.

Charles H. Challen

Charles H. Challen made and sold his first piano in 1804. One hundred and sixty years later pianos bearing his name are probably heard by more millions throughout the world than any other piano. Today, as for the past three decades, about two hundred Challens, from large concert grands to small studio upright pianos, are in daily use by the British Broadcasting Corporation in sound and television studios. In the face of international competition, Challen pianos are sold to new radio and television studios in many parts of the world, universities and other education establishments.

John Brinsmead

John Brinsmead was born at Wear Gifford, near Torrington, in 1814. His firm was notable for its upright pianos and the excellence of the action work. The firm had premises in several parts of London. The Brinsmead piano was awarded many honours at British and European exhibitions. The firm is one of the most distinguished in Britain.

Spencer

The Spencer firm was founded in 1884 and quickly established itself. In forty years it produced 80,000 instruments of good musical quality and great durability. The Spencer pianos were supplied to the British Navy.

Chappell

In spite of the destruction of their premises in London by fire in 1964 this firm is still a leading establishment of pianoforte makers and music publishers. In 1810 Samuel Chappell, John Baptist Cramer and Francis Tatton became partners and a new firm was founded at the beginning of the following year at 124 New Bond

Street. The firm advertised its wares to "noble and genteel clients". In 1813 Cramer withdrew from the firm and, in 1825, Samuel Chappell dissolved the remaining partnership. Even in the early days Chappell was known as the "Prince of Publishers" and, in 1819, Beethoven wrote to Ferdinand Ries: "Potter[1] says that Chappell in Bond Street is now one of the best publishers."

Chappell died in 1834 and his son William continued as a director of the firm and was in association with the Philharmonic Society at 50 New Bond Street. Before 1850, Chappell had a factory in Soho and showrooms in George Street, Hanover Square, in a district which has been notable for its pianoforte showrooms for many years. The Chappell piano, well known in concert rooms and schools as well as in private houses, has been respected because of its fine craftsmanship, long life and good tone.

Wornum

R. Wornum (originally Wornham) was born in 1780. At the age of thirty he went into partnership in 1810 with George Wilkinson in a factory in Oxford Street, London. Two years later the factory was entirely destroyed by a fire, described by Thomas de Quincey in his famous essay on "Murder considered as one of the fine arts". S. T. Coleridge, the poet, had left his tea to see the fire and had felt himself unrewarded, not that "he was capable of wishing any ill to the poor man and his pianofortes (many of them, doubtless, with the additional keys)". After the fire Wornum continued alone in Store Street. Before the fire, he had produced his "unique" model, a diagonally strung pianoforte, and in 1813 he brought out his vertically strung Harmonie. Wornum was notable for his simplification and improvement of upright pianoforte actions.

George Rogers

This London firm has produced many beautiful instruments, distinguished both by tone and appearance. The firm was established in 1843 and throughout the years has used every development in construction and acoustics. Of great interest is the Rogers Frame which will withstand a tension of 30 tons.

A number of the most distinguished of the English nineteenth-century firms disappeared by absorption into others. The Longman

[1] Cipriani Potter: Principal of the Royal Academy of Music, London, during the years 1832–1859.

Plate nineteen

a. Broadwood Grand played by Chopin in London in 1848

b. Pianoforte by Streicher, Vienna, early 19th century. Probably played by F. Schubert

Plate twenty

a. The battered Broadwood at Beethoven's death, 26th March, 1827

b. W. A. Mozart at the age of seven (1763) with his father Leopold and sister Marianne

LEOPOLD MOZART, Pere de MARIANNE MOZART, Virtuose âgée de onze ans, et de J.G.WOLFGANG MOZART, Compositeur et Maître de Musique âgé de sept ans.

and Broderip and the Longman, Clementi firms became the Clementi and Collard firm until Clementi's death in 1832, when they were known as Collard and Collard. The firm of Kirkman, which made some of the finest harpsichords in the eighteenth century and pianofortes in the nineteenth century, was absorbed by Collard and Collard at the end of the nineteenth century. Collard and Collard had a considerable reputation in the present century.

SUPPLY HOUSES

Herrburger Brooks

In 1810, Henry Brooks first opened his action manufacturing business in London. In 1844 Jean Schwander founded his own firm in Paris which became famous throughout Europe. When he later took his son-in-law, Josef Herrburger, into the firm the great ability of the latter resulted in improvements to the actions and designs for machines and appliances for action manufacture. In the year 1920 the two firms became linked under the name of Herrburger Brooks, and in 1953 the London firm entirely absorbed the Paris Company. Herrburger Brooks can claim to be the oldest established action makers in the world, and their products are now in constant demand by the piano makers of many countries for their finest instruments. They are leading makers of the finest quality keyboards for pianos and organs. The firm is now associated with that of Kimball in America.

Louis Renner

This Stuttgart firm, now about eighty years old, produces every part of a piano. It is distinguished for the quality of its products, the variety of materials and parts which it handles and the size of its business. It also supplies tools and materials for piano technicians.

Fletcher and Newman

This London firm specialises in tuners' equipment, piano parts, repair materials and practice keyboards.

There are firms which specialise in piano felts, piano wire and other supplies.

Today there are fewer pianoforte firms than there were between the wars. In 1923 there were no fewer than 138 piano factories in North London alone. Nevertheless, the industry has been modernised, much research has been undertaken and the quality of the products

is generally very high. In England, in addition to those mentioned
already, there are the firms of Brasted; Eavestaff; Alfred Knight, a
world ambassador of the British pianoforte industry; Whelpdale,
Maxwell and Codd (Welmar); Monington and Weston; Stroud
Pianoforte Company (Bentley); Zender; Danemann; Renn; Kemble;
Barratt and Robinson. In Ireland, at Shannon and at Ede Holland,
are the factories of Rippen (Lindner); in Paris, G. Klein; in Switzerland (Berne), Schmidt-Flohr; in Czechoslovakia (Prague), Ligna,
which had made 100,000 instruments up to 1963; in Sweden the
Malmsjö Company; in Holland (Vries), Albert Hahn; in Japan,
Yamaha with modern production methods and large output; in fact,
the phenomenal rate of production in this country is second only to
that of America and may overtake it. In 1965 more than 150,000
pianos were produced—a 250 per cent growth in five years! In the
U.S.A. there are several manufacturing corporations which have
tended to associate former firms. The W. Knabe, Sohmer, Baldwin,
Kimball pianos, amongst others, including the firms already mentioned, produced a total of more than 200,000 a year. Some of the
fine U.S. firms have been united in the Aeolian American Corporation, others have connection with firms in Europe. The standard and
scope of American production, assisted by first class piano teaching
and performance, are things to be marvelled at.

In Germany there are still many firms at work in addition to those
historic houses which we have considered. C. Sauter of Spaichingen;
J. C. Neupert of Bamberg (many forms of keyboard instruments);
W. Schimmel of Brunswick; Euterpe of Langlau (Mittelfranken);
J. Feurich of Langlau; R. Lipp of Stuttgart; F. Manthey of Berlin;
B. May of Berlin; Steingraeber of Bayreuth; C. Bohn of Berlin;
Zimmermann of Berlin; Görs and Kallmann of Hamburg; Fuchs
and Möhr of Berlin; Geyer of Berlin; Weiss of Spaichingen;
Rönisch of Leipzig; Willis of Landshut; Seiler; Zeitter and Winkel-
mann of Kitzingen; VEB Sächsische Pianofortefabrik (Grunewald)
of Seifhennersdorf; Hoffmann of Langlau; Haegele of Aalen.

In Italy the Schulze-Pollmann firm is active at Bolzano; in
Finland, Musik-Fazer at Helsinki and at Kronach in Sweden the
Nordiska Piano factory.

CHAPTER VII

MUSICIANS AND THE PIANOFORTE

THE development of the pianoforte and the methods of playing and composing for it interacted with one another, particularly in the eighteenth and nineteenth centuries. Thus, it is interesting to think a little about the work of those musicians who were particularly associated with the instrument during this period. These will be considered only as far as their work throws some light on the development of the piano and the sounds which it makes.

C. P. E. Bach (1714–88)

I leave dexterity to the knights of the keyboard, preferring to sing upon my instrument; music ought principally to move the heart, and in this no performer on the pianoforte will succeed by merely thumping and drumming or by continuous arpeggio-playing. During the last few years my endeavouring has been to play the pianoforte, despite its deficiency in sustaining tone, as much as possible in a singing manner—this is by no means an easy task, if we desire not to leave the ear empty, or to disturb the noble simplicity of the cantabile by too much noise.

Thus wrote Carl Philipp Emanuel Bach in his important book: *An Essay on the True Method of Playing the Clavier*, the precursor of all systematic books on piano methods. "C. P. E. Bach was the pathfinder of the classic sonata form, blazing a trail that was broadened by Haydn to a thoroughfare and by Mozart and Beethoven to a highway." C. P. E. Bach said that he had no other teacher but his father. Nevertheless, he associated with the finest musicians at the Berlin Court, with the Graun brothers, Quantz, Agricola, Marpurg, Kirnberger and Sulzer. No doubt earlier works such as Mattheson's *General-Bass Schule*, Heinichen's *General-Bass*, Niedt's *Musicalische Handleitung*, and even F. Couperin's *L'Art de Toucher le Clavecin* were not without their influence on C. P. E. Bach's work, which in its turn was to be found as the background of the pianoforte "schools" of Türk (1789)[1] and Milchmeyer (1797).[2]

The following account, given by Forkel, describes the clavier playing of J. S. Bach, but he is referring to the clavichord and the harpsichord rather than to the piano. As we have noted already, Bach senior did not like Gottfried Silbermann's earlier pianos, and the improved models came too late in Bach's life for him to appreciate them. Moreover, even these later pianos, of which fifteen were bought for Frederick the Great, lacked the subtlety of the clavichord and the sonority of the harpsichord.

John Sebastian Bach's manner of keyboard playing was admired by all those who had the good fortune to hear him, and envied by all those who might themselves claim to be considered as good performers. That this method of playing on the clavier, so generally admired and envied, must have been very different from that in use among Bach's predecessors and contemporaries may be easily imagined; but hitherto nobody has explained in what this difference properly consisted.

If we hear the same piece played by ten equally skilful and practised performers, it will produce, under the hand of each, a different effect. Each will draw from the instrument a different kind of tone, and also give to these tones a greater or less degree of distinctness. Whence can this difference arise, if otherwise all the ten performers have sufficient readiness and practice? Merely from the mode of touching the instrument, which, in playing on the clavier, is the same thing as the pronunciation in speech. In order to make the delivery perfect in playing as well as in speaking or declaiming, the greatest distinctness is required in the production of the tomes as in the pronunciation of the words. But this distinctness is susceptible of very various degrees. Even in the lowest degrees we can understand what is played or said; but it excites no pleasure in the hearer because this degree of distinctness compels him to some exertion of his attention. But attention to single tones or words ought to be rendered unnecessary that the hearer may direct it to the ideas and their connection, and for this we require the highest degree of distinctness in the production of single tones as in the pronunciation of single words.

I have often wondered that C. Ph. Emanuel, in his *Essay on the True Manner of Playing the Clavier*, did not describe at length

[1] Clavierschule.
[2] Die wahre Art des Pianoforte zu spielen.

this highest degree of distinctness in the touch of that instrument, as he not only possessed it himself, but because in this consists one of the chief differences by which the Bach's mode of playing on the clavier is distinguished from all others. He says, indeed, in the chapter on the style of performance: "Some persons play too stickily, as if they had glue between their fingers; their touch is too long, because they keep the keys down beyond the time. Others have attempted to avoid this defect and play too short, as if the keys were burning hot. This is also a fault. The middle path is the best." But he should have taught and described to us the ways and means of attaining this middle path. I will endeavour to make the matter plain as far as such things can be made plain without oral instructions.[1]

According to Sebastian Bach's manner of placing the hand on the keys, the five fingers are bent so that their points come into a straight line, and so fit the keys, which lie in a plane surface under them, that no single finger has to be drawn nearer when it is wanted, but every one is ready over the key which it may have to press down. What follows from this manner of holding the hand is:

(1) That no finger must fall upon its key, or (as also often happens) be thrown on it, but only needs to be *placed* upon it with a certain consciousness of the internal power and command over the motion.

(2) The impulse thus given to the keys, or the quantity of pressure, must be maintained in equal strength, and that in such a manner that the finger be not raised perpendicularly from the key, but that it glide off the forepart of the key, by gradually drawing back the tip of the finger, towards the palm of the hand.

(3) In the transition from one key to another, this gliding off causes the quantity of force or pressure with which the first tone has been kept up to be transferred with the greatest rapidity to the next finger, so that the two tones are neither disjoined from each other nor blended together.

The touch is, therefore, as C. Ph. Emanuel Bach says, neither too long nor too short, but just what it ought to be.

The advantages of such a position of the hand and of such a

---

[1] The following passage incorporates information gathered from Quantz's *Versuch einer Anleitung die Flöte traversiere zu spielen* as well as from Philipp Emanuel Bach.

touch are very various, not only on the clavichord, but also on the pianoforte and the organ.[1] I will here mention only the most important.

(1) The holding of the fingers bent renders all their motions easy. There can therefore be none of the scrambling, thumping, and stumbling which is so common in persons who play with their fingers stretched out, or not sufficiently bent.

(2) The drawing back of the tips of the fingers and the rapid communication, thereby effected, of the force of one finger to that following it produces the highest degree of clearness in the expression of the single tones, so that every passage performed in this manner sounds brilliant, rolling, and round, as if each tone were a pearl. It does not cost the hearer the least exertion of attention to understand a passage so performed.

(3) By the gliding of the tip of the finger upon the key with an equable pressure, sufficient time is given to the string to vibrate; the tone, therefore, is not only improved, but also prolonged, and we are thus enabled to play in a singing style and with proper connection, even on an instrument so poor in tone as the clavichord is.

All this together has, besides, the very great advantage that we avoid all waste of strength by useless exertion and by constraint in the motions. In fact, Seb. Bach is said to have played with so easy and small a motion of the fingers that it was hardly perceptible. Only the first joints of the fingers were in motion; the hand retained even in the most difficult passages its rounded form; the fingers rose very little from the keys, hardly more than in a shake (trill), and when one was employed the other remained quietly in its position. Still less did the other parts of his body take any share in his play, as happens with many whose hand is not light enough.

A person may, however, possess all these advantages, and yet be a very indifferent performer on the clavier, in the same manner as a man may have a very clear and fine pronunciation, and yet be a bad declaimer or orator. To be an able performer, many other

---

[1] It should be noted that Forkel, while starting out to give a description of keyboard technique in general, has now chiefly the clavichord in mind. Of the following points, the third refers exclusively to this instrument. The action of the pianoforte in Forkel's day was, of course, lighter and shallower than it is today. His remarks cannot be taken as a guide to modern pianoforte technique.

qualities are necessary, which Bach likewise possessed in the highest perfection.

The natural difference between the fingers in size as well as strength frequently tempts performers, wherever it can be done, to use only the stronger fingers and neglect the weaker ones. Hence arises not only an inequality in the expression of several successive tones, but even the impossibility of executing certain passages where no choice of fingers can be made. John Sebastian Bach was soon sensible of this; and, to obviate so great a defect, wrote for himself particular pieces, in which all the fingers of both hands must necessarily be employed in the most various positions in order to perform them properly and distinctly. By this exercise he rendered all his fingers, of both hands, equally strong and serviceable, so that he was able to execute not only chords and all running passages, but also single and double shakes with equal ease and delicacy. He was perfectly master even of those passages in which, while some fingers perform a shake, the others, on the same hand, have to continue the melody.

To all this was added the new mode of fingering which he had contrived. Before his time and in his younger years, it was usual to play rather harmony than melody, and not in all the 24 major and minor keys. As the clavichord was still *gebunden*, which means that several keys struck a single string, it could not be perfectly tuned; people played therefore only in those keys which could be tuned with the most purity.[1] Through these circumstances it happened that even the greatest performers of that time did not use the thumb till it was absolutely necessary in stretches. Now when Bach began to unite melody and harmony so that even his middle parts did not merely accompany, but had a melody of their own, when he extended the use of the keys, partly by deviating from the ancient modes of church music, which were then very common even in secular music, partly by mixing the diatonic and chromatic scales, and learned to tune his instrument so that it could be played upon in all the 24 keys, he was at the same time obliged to contrive another mode of fingering, better adapted to his new methods, and particularly to use the thumb in a manner different from that hitherto employed. Some persons have pretended that Couperin taught this mode of fingering before him,

[1] The explanation is wrong, but it is true that unequal temperament on keyboard instruments gave way to one which approached equal temperament during Bach's lifetime.

in his work published in 1716 under the title of *L'Art de toucher le Claveçin*. But, in the first place, Bach was at that time above 30 years old and had long made use of his manner of fingering; and, secondly, Couperin's fingering is still very different from that of Bach, though it has in common with it the more frequent use of the thumb. I say only "the more frequent", for in Bach's method the thumb was made a principal finger, because it is absolutely impossible to do without it in what are called the difficult keys; this, however, is not the case with Couperin, because he neither had such a variety of passages, nor composed and played in such difficult keys as Bach, and consequently had not such urgent occasion for it. We need only compare Bach's fingering, as C. Ph. Emanuel has explained it, with Couperin's directions, and we shall soon find that, with the one, all passages, even the most difficult and the fullest, may be played distinctly and easily, while with the other we can, at the most, get through Couperin's own compositions, and even them with difficulty. Bach was, however, acquainted with Couperin's works and esteemed them, as well as the works of several other French composers for the harpsichord of that period, because a pretty and elegant mode of playing may be learned from them. But on the other hand he considered them as too affected in their frequent use of graces (or ornaments), which goes so far that scarcely a note is free from embellishment. The ideas which they contained were, besides, too flimsy for him.

From the easy, unconstrained motion of the fingers, from the beautiful touch, from the clearness and precision in connecting the successive tones, from the advantages of the new mode of fingering, from the equal development and practice of all the fingers of both hands, and, lastly, from the great variety of his figures of melody, which were employed in every piece in a new and uncommon manner, Sebastian Bach at length acquired such a high degree of facility and, we may almost say, unlimited power over his instrument in all the keys that difficulties almost ceased to exist for him.[1]

After the death of J. S. Bach in 1750 a reaction had set in against his scholarly and often complex basses to such an extent that the left hand was often confined to the playing of drum basses and

---

[1] Taken from the chapter, "Bach's Clavier Playing", in *On Johann Sebastian Bach's Life, Genius and Works* by Johann Nicolaus Forkel (1749–1818) (1802; translated by Stephenson, 1808).

"thumping". C. P. E. Bach warns against this pernicious style. He adds that it is at the clavichord that a keyboardist may be most exactly evaluated, for this reveals a sensitive, cultivated touch like no other instrument. Concerning methods of tuning, he says that if a barely noticeable amount of the purity of the fifths is removed all the twenty-four tonalities are then usable. Thus, in this he approaches the equal temperament system of tuning, but retains distinctive key-colour.

He devoted a large section of his work to the playing of ornaments. "They connect and enliven tones, and impart stress and accent; they make music pleasing and awaken our close attention. Expression is heightened by them; they give opportunities for fine performance. They improve mediocre compositions: the best melody is empty and ineffective without them." C. P. E. Bach wrote this before the dynamic and tone-colour possibilities of the piano had been realised fully.

His book had very great influence. Mozart spoke highly of it, Beethoven made it the groundwork of Czerny's studies with him, and Clementi, who had a notable line of pupils including Field, said that he owed all the new fingering and style to Bach. Haydn called it "the school of all schools" and the Czech teacher, composer and pianist J. L. Dussek, who was praised by Mendelssohn and had a wide influence, spent the year 1783 studying with C. P. E. Bach in Hamburg. Thus, much progress in keyboard playing from the style given by Diruta in *Il Transilvano*, in which the use of the extreme fingers was almost completely eschewed, to the foundation of a modern systematic method, with scale patterns, was achieved.

At the time of C. P. E. Bach it was considered that there was a great gulf fixed between his art and that of his father. Charles Burney said in his book on *The Present State of Music in Germany etc.*, of the playing of the son: "His performance today convinced me of what I had suggested before from his works, that he is not only one of the greatest composers that ever existed for keyed instruments, but the best player in point of expression; for others, perhaps, have had as rapid execution. However, he possesses every style, though he confines himself chiefly to the expressive." C. P. E. Bach was the chief exponent of the *Empfindsamkeit*[1] which stressed the expression of the feelings and emotions. The hearts of the listeners must be stirred by the subtlety of the playing, with its light and shadow. This was the German version of the style galant and

[1] Literally = sensitivity, sentimentality.

was opposed to the restrained grace of the rococo, and the "learned style" of his father. The "True art" is divided into three sections which concern correct fingering, good embellishments and a good performance which entails a knowledge of harmony, counterpoint, form and style, improvisation and accompaniment.

"More is lost by poor fingering than can be replaced by all conceivable artistry and good taste." In the new method of fingering, proper use must be made of the thumb, the fingers should be arched, the muscles should be elastic and relaxed and the motion of the hands barely noticeable in a good performer. The method of turning the thumb under the fingers was not new: it must have been employed by Domenico Scarlatti in the difficult passages of his sonatas. F. A. Maichelbeck[1] and Marpurg[2] employ the method but their work was not as well known in Europe as Bach's Essay of 1753. Nevertheless, this fuller use of the potentialities of the whole hand did not extend to turning the thumb under the little finger, crossing the second finger over the third, the third over the second, the fourth over the fifth and the fifth over the thumb. There was still no great use of the thumb and the little finger on the black keys.[3]

Wolfgang Amadeus Mozart (1756–91)

In Mozart, the sound should always have something noble and aristocratic about it. Mozart was indeed no stranger to sweet and voluptuous sounds, to the darker levels of sensibility; there is a measureless variety of moods in this music: but even in his most expressive moments the sound-picture remains translucent and beautiful. . . . Mozart's pianoforte writing contains trumpet flourishes, the gently melting tones of the flute, the veiled sound of the basset-horn, noisy orchestral tutti, just as it contains utterly magical sounds that could belong only to the pianoforte. But the most intimate and inward expression of all can be achieved by using the una corda tone of the pianoforte—as if the player were breathing the music into the listener's ear. To play Mozart without the magic of a richly varied tonal palette is not only inartistic, it is out of style.[4]

[1] Die auf dem Clavier Lehrende Caecilia (1738).
[2] Die Kunst das Clavier zu spielen (1750–51).
[3] W. J. Mitchell (1949) Edition of the "Essay on the true method of playing the clavier".
[4] Paul Badura-Skoda, *Interpreting Mozart at the Keyboard* (trans. London 1961).

Early in life Mozart played the pianofortes of the Regensburg
maker, Franz Jacob Späth, but when he tried the instruments of
Johann Andreas Stein, an organ-builder, in the line of Silbermann,
and piano maker, they became the pianos of his choice. As we have
seen in Chapter II, the durability of these instruments and the
reliable escapement of their action made clear and rapid playing
possible. These instruments reached perfection within their type.
They had a compass of five octaves from F, on the fourth leger line
below the bass clef, to f''' above the treble clef. The tone was
translucent, even when the pedal was down. The pitch was about
half a tone lower than the present standard pitch. For this type of
piano, Mozart wrote more than twenty sonatas, a similar number
of concerti, variations and other forms, most of which were of
sterling quality. Mozart played the instrument in concerts, improvised on it in masterly style and taught it, probably at times in-
differently. We can obtain an idea of his treatment of the piano as a
player from some of his letters in which he gives his opinions of the
playing of his contemporaries and pupils. He was rarely charitable.
He taught Stein's daughter Nanette, who was by no means incapable
as a pianist, and he wrote this about her:

But the best joke of all is that when she comes to a passage
which ought to flow like oil and which necessitates a change of
finger, she does not bother her head about it, but when the
moment arrives, she just leaves out the notes, raises her hand and
starts off again quite comfortably—a method by which she is
much more likely to strike a wrong note, which often produces a
curious effect. I am simply writing this in order to give Papa
some idea of clavier-playing and clavier-teaching, so that he may
derive some profit from it later on. Herr Stein is quite crazy
about his daughter, who is eight and a half and who now learns
everything by heart. She may succeed, for she has great talent for
music. But she will not make progress by this method—for she
will never acquire great rapidity, since she definitely does all she
can to make her hands heavy. Further, she will never acquire the
most essential, the most difficult and the chief requisite in music,
which is, time, because from her earliest years she has done her
utmost not to play in time. Herr Stein and I discussed this point
for two hours at least and I have almost converted him, for he
now asks my advice on everything. He used to be quite crazy
about Beecke; but now he sees and hears that I am the better

player, that I do not make grimaces, and yet play with such expression, that, as he himself confesses, no one up to the present has been able to get such good results out of his pianofortes. Everyone is amazed that I can always keep strict time. What these people cannot grasp is that in tempo rubato, in an Adagio, the left hand should go on playing in strict time.

And again:

The Andante (of the sonata K.309) will give us most trouble, for it is full of expression and must be played accurately and with the exact shades of forte and piano, precisely as they are marked. She is very smart and learns very easily. Her right hand is very good, but her left, unfortunately, is completely ruined. I can honestly say that I often feel quite sorry for her when I see her struggling, as she so often does, until she really gets quite out of breath, not from lack of skill but simply because she cannot help it, for she has got into the habit of doing what she does, as no one has ever shown her any other way. I have told her mother and I have told her, too, that if I were her regular teacher, I would lock up all her music, cover the keys with a handkerchief and make her practise, first with the right hand and then with the left, nothing but passages, trills, mordants and so forth, very slowly at first, until each hand should be thoroughly trained. I would then undertake to turn her into a first-rate keyboard player.

Mozart demanded insight and artistic integrity in the performer:

Besides, it is much easier to play a thing quickly than slowly: in difficult passages you can leave out a few notes without anyone noticing it. But is that beautiful music? In rapid playing the right and left hands can be changed without anyone seeing or hearing it; but is that beautiful? And wherein consists the art of playing prima vista? In this; in playing the piece in the time in which it ought to be played and in playing all the notes, appoggiaturas and so forth, exactly as they are written and with the appropriate expression and taste, so that you might suppose that the performer had composed it himself. Vogler's[1] fingering, too, is wretched; his left thumb is just like that of the late Adlgasser and he does all the treble runs downwards with the thumb and first finger of his right hand.

[1] Georg Joseph Vogler ("the Abbé") (1749–1814), composer, teacher, organist, "organ-expert" acoustician. An active man with more energy than supreme gifts. He inspired Browning's poem.

Mozart underestimated Muzio Clementi, who represented another school of playing:

> Clementi plays well, so far as execution with the right hand goes. His greatest strength lies in his passages in thirds. Apart from this, he has not a kreutzer's worth of taste or feeling—in short he is simply a mechanicus.

There can be little doubt that Mozart would not have approved of Beethoven's playing, though he complimented the youth of seventeen on his improvisation. Yet it was the Clementi–Beethoven–Czerny–Liszt tradition which dominated the nineteenth century, for good and ill.

Hummel was one of Mozart's pupils and he perpetuated and developed his methods, which were different from those of Beethoven. Mozart's pianos and piano-playing were well suited for his duet and chamber music playing. It is a revelation to hear his concerti played with small orchestra and a Viennese piano in a quiet village!

An amateur musician, Joseph Frank, a doctor, received twelve lessons from Mozart in 1790, and wrote:

> I found Mozart a little man with a large head and plump hand, and was somewhat coldly received by him. "Now," said he, "play me something." I played a Fantasia of his own composition. "Not bad," said he, to my great astonishment; "but now listen to me play it." It was a miracle! The piano became another instrument under his hands. It was strengthened by a second piano which served him as a pedal. Mozart then made some remarks as to the way in which I should perform the Fantasia. I was fortunate enough to understand him. "Do you play any other pieces of my composition?" "Yes," answered I; "your Variations on the theme 'Unser dummer Pöbel meint' (K.455), and a Sonata with accompaniments for violin and violon-cello." "Good, I will play you that piece; you will profit more by hearing me than playing them yourself."

This passage is interesting because it shows that Mozart used a pedal-board; in this case, working a second piano and not merely pulling down the low notes. This device, used also by Robert Schumann in his *Sketches* and *Canons*, is of considerable antiquity and was used by organists for practice in the form of two (or three) clavichords and two harpsichords, one of which was played by the feet.[1]

[1] Susi Jeans, *Proceedings of the Royal Musical Association*, 1952.

K

Franz Joseph Haydn (1732–1809)

Haydn was born almost a quarter of a century before Mozart and survived him by nearly two decades. In his lifetime Haydn saw the harpsichord and clavichord giving way to the Viennese pianoforte of the type which Mozart played. Haydn's immense gifts to the art of the pianoforte include the development of the sonata, the writing of so many examples (of which one edition offers forty-two) and other forms, including some beautiful sets of variations, and thirty-five piano trios.

Haydn, living in or near Vienna, was able to notice the development of the piano in that district. He had felt the need for a keyboard instrument with greater lyrical powers than the harpsichord and without the limitations of the clavichord. In 1771 he wrote the Sonata in C minor "for the pianoforte or harpsichord". This, his first sonata in a minor key, was also the first to show dynamic markings. Curiously, the sonata, in spite of its expressive character, was not published at the time and Haydn returned to producing works for the harpsichord. In 1798 he composed a sonata in E♭, which reveals his understanding of the pianoforte in its powers of shaping a melody dynamically, the playing of ornaments expressively and delicate contrasts produced by varieties of touch. The musical and historical values of Haydn's major keyboard works, produced at an interesting transitional period in keyboard techniques, have been long neglected until recent years.

Ludwig van Beethoven (1770–1827)

"*Thus he will live to the end of time, from now onward among the great of all ages, inviolate forever.*"—F. Grillparzer: Beethoven's funeral oration.

In the pianoforte works of Beethoven, a vast output sufficient in itself to ennoble the instrument, we can trace the development of pianoforte composition from the early sonatas which could be played on the harpsichord also, to the monumental later sonatas, such as the Hammerklavier, which seem to transcend the resources of the instrument and call for great powers of understanding and technique on the part of the performer. Beethoven's first sonatas for the piano as distinct from the harpsichord were Sonatas Opus 14, Nos. 1 and 2 (1799).

We can obtain an idea of Beethoven's approach to the piano from some of his letters and the impressions of his contemporaries, as well as from a study of his actual works. Chopin composed in terms of the human hand and the piano keyboard as he found it, but Beethoven did not think of or write for the instrument in such a felicitous manner. He was often frustrated by the limitations, even of the physical strength, of the pianos which he played.

If the modern pianoforte, with its great range of dynamics and tone, is a better medium for the performance of his works, in some respects, there are ways in which it differs from the later instruments used by the master. The introduction of cross-stringing brought some undeniable advantages to piano construction, but the parallel stringing of the older instruments and the avoidance of rather short, loaded bass strings were productive of a clear, well-defined bass of precise pitch and tone. A minor chord played at the very bottom of the compass could be distinguished from a major chord. It is an interesting experience to play some of the left-hand chords in the later sonatas on modern, short grands. The characteristic colours of minor, major, German sixth and other chords are not always readily apparent!

The tone of the pianoforte of Beethoven's time was generally more incisive than that of today. The soft pedal of the modern grand achieves its effect by the lateral displacement of the mechanism so that the hammer strikes two strings of the trichord. In Beethoven's time there was a genuine *una corda*, in which one string alone was struck and the others resounded with it. The upright piano, with its half-blow action, which should be unnecessary to a good pianist, makes no attempt to approach the beautiful *una corda* effect. Even the more powerful pianos possessed by Beethoven probably did not have the power of sustaining notes which is common today. It is said that Beethoven applied the pedal throughout whole movements. It is possible that this was deliberately his intention for he spoke of "singing in a cave". Often, his pedalling instructions were quite precise. Examples of these will be found in the Sonatas in B♭ Op. 106 (Hammerclavier) and in D minor Op. 31, No. 2.

We obtain a glimpse of Beethoven struggling with the Viennese piano, from Anton Reicha, a composer and teacher (*c*.1795):

He asked me to turn the pages for him. But I was mostly occupied in wrenching the strings of the pianoforte which snapped, while the hammers stuck among the broken strings. Beethoven insisted on finishing the concerto, and so back and forth I leaped, jerking out a string, disentangling a hammer, turning a page, and I worked harder than Beethoven.

In a letter to Johann Andreas Streicher, written in Vienna in 1796, Beethoven expresses his dissatisfaction with available pianos. (Streicher had married Nanette Stein, the daughter of J. A. Stein of Augsburg, a famous piano maker, and after 1794, with her husband and brother, established their firm in the Landstrasse, Vienna:)

Your little pupil, dear Streicher, apart from the fact that when playing my Adagio she drew a few tears from my eyes, has really astonished me. I congratulate you on being so fortunate as to be able to display through such a talent your own understanding of music; and, moreover, I am delighted that this dear little girl, who is so talented, has you for her teacher. I assure you in all sincerity, dear Streicher, that this was the first time it gave me pleasure to hear my trio[1] performed; and truly this experience will make me decide to compose more for the pianoforte than I have done hitherto. Even if only a few people understand me, I shall be satisfied. There is no doubt that so far as the manner of playing it is concerned, the pianoforte is still the least studied and developed of all instruments; often one thinks that one is merely listening to a harp.[2] And I am delighted, my dear fellow, that you are one of the few who realize and perceive that, provided one can feel the music, one can also make the pianoforte sing. I hope that the time will come when the harp and the pianoforte will be treated as two entirely different instruments. By the way, I feel sure that you can let your little pupil play anywhere and that, between ourselves, she will put to shame many of our commonplace but conceited organ-grinders.

Beethoven often played Streicher's pianos but did not own one. He had in his possession for some time a Viennese piano by Walter, and Czerny received lessons on it.

Another pianoforte owned by Beethoven and probably given to him by Prince Lichnowsky in 1803 was made by Érard of Paris. It failed to withstand Beethoven's treatment of it. Its compass is from F to c[4] and it has four pedals. It was formerly preserved in

---

[1] Possibly the pianoforte trio Opus 1, No. 1 in E♭, which has an Adagio Cantabile movement. The three trios, Opus 1, dedicated to Prince Karl Lichnowsky, were published by Artaria in the summer of 1795. The little girl was probably Fräulein von Kissow (1783–c.1864). The letter is No. 18 in Emily Anderson's collection.

[2] i.e., harpsichord.

Linz, but is now in the Musical Instrument Collection of the City of Vienna. Beethoven wrote to Streicher, whose work he admired, concerning this piano on several occasions:

> You promised to let me have a piano by the end of October; and now we are already half through November and as yet I haven't received one—my motto is either to play on a good instrument or not at all. As for my French piano, which is certainly quite useless now, I still have misgivings about selling it, for it is really a souvenir such as no one here has so far honoured me with.[1]

This Érard piano was modified by Streicher several times and finally given to Beethoven's brother.

Thus, Beethoven found the Viennese instruments to be lacking in sturdiness, sonority and compass. Only with the Waldstein Sonata did he command a six-octave instrument. In 1818, when John Broadwood sent Beethoven a grand piano, with a compass of six octaves and a more powerful tone, his hearing was practically nil. (The feat of transporting this instrument, now preserved in the Budapest Collection of musical instruments, from London to Vienna was no small one. It had to be delivered at the port of Trieste and taken by mule over poor roads and mountain passes to the capital of Austria.) The instrument was in a sad condition at the end of Beethoven's life. When Johann Andreas Stumpff, an instrument maker of note, visited Beethoven he wrote: "Quite a sight confronted me: the upper part of the compass was mute, and the broken strings in a tangle, like a thorn bush whipped by a storm."

Finally, Beethoven used a piano, now in Bonn, with a keyboard range C to f^4 by the Viennese maker Conrad Graf. The last mentioned piano was loaned to the composer in 1825, (i.e., two years before his death,) by the master piano maker. By this time, Beethoven had been deaf for years but nonetheless he agreed to accept the piano and set it up in his Viennese dwelling beside the Broadwood grand. It must be assumed that Beethoven played both the instruments in spite of his deafness, although it is known that they were not well looked after—especially the Broadwood piano—and even had torn strings. After 1827 the Graf piano was taken back to his workshop by the owner, overhauled and sold in 1849 to the Wimmer family in Vienna. From here the instrument, still in private hands,

---

[1] Written in Vienna, November 1810. The autograph is preserved in the H. C. Bodmer collection in the Beethoven House in Bonn.

moved to Berne in Switzerland and was bought in 1889 by the City of Bonn to be set up in Beethoven's birthplace.

Conrad Graf, born in Württemberg (1783–1851), was at that time the best known master piano maker in Vienna together with the celebrated firm of Nanette and Andreas Streicher. Graf made every effort to provide the composer with the best that was on the market in those days among German pianos, and it is also probable that he took Beethoven's wishes into account.

The instrument was heavy, very solidly built, and in view of Beethoven's defective hearing, equipped with four strings for every note.[1] The largest dimensions of those times were also given in respect of keyboard range, as it extends over 6½ octaves. The range which was at that time customary in Germany was from F to f⁴ and though 6 octaves were also preferred in England, the pitch was set a fourth lower from C to c⁴. Both ranges were included in Beethoven's instrument. The keyboard of the piano is set inside the walls of the casework (a mode of construction which comes from the harpsichord: the jutting-out keyboard did not become normal until a later period). The width of the keys of one octave is narrower than with modern pianos (the width of three octaves, or 21 keys, is only 47·9 cm., whereas it is about 50 cm. today).

The keys are covered with a thin layer of ivory, the heads of the keys measure 40 mm. and the natural keys 100 mm. in length. The piano has Viennese action with box damper extending as far as the final treble f⁴. The piano has 78 keys and 79 sets of strings.

The centre-most set of strings is not struck because a support between wrest-plank and bridge has been provided at this point to hold up the strings. The surface of the sound-board has a wooden dust protector. The left pedal works the shift, the second a "piano", and the third a damper lift. At that time other modifications could be found in Germany (bassoon registers etc.), but Beethoven thought nothing of them. Beethoven's playing contrasts with that of the fashionable composers of the day, Steibelt, Wölffl, Hummel. On the other hand it can be seen from transcribed conversations with the composer and from his directions for playing that he thought a great deal of the difference between playing with one-string, two-string, and three-string notes, and taught this. Above the keys can be read in a square bronze frame to the right and left of the double eagle:

---

[1] Only the first 14 notes have three strings.

Conrad Graf
Kaiserl. Kön. Hof-Fortepianomacher
Wien nächst der Carlskirche
im Mondschein
Nr. 102
(Fortepiano maker to the Imperial Court,
Vienna, beside the Charles Church, in Moonshine No. 102)

Three-sided "vase shaped" legs with castors were probably added in the period before 1889; the original ones must have been more slender (either straight or conical). There is a tradition that one of the pianos had for a while a horn-shaped sound-box designed to direct the sound waves towards the deaf composer. Whether this device was in fact on the Graf piano or on the piano by Broadwood can no longer be established today.

The instrument is 240 cm. (about 8 ft. long). In 1963 it was carefully restored by Bernhard Rochow of the firm of J. C. Neupert of Bamberg[1] (see PLATE 18). N.B. 1 inch is 25 mm. approximately.

To sum up the matter of Beethoven's piano, we may say that in his search for great contrasts of dynamic level, lower and more sonorous basses, higher and more brilliant trebles, Beethoven seems to have been irritated by the limitations of the piano of his earlier days; and even the instrument left at his death seems to have been a wreck unable to stand up to a struggle where the forces were so ill-matched. Twenty of his thirty Sonatas were composed for an instrument of five octaves compass, which was that of the larger eighteenth-century harpsichords. (FF to f^3 that is, from FF eight notes below the bottom line of the bass clef to f^3 an octave above the top line of the treble clef.) Apart from a solitary $f\sharp^3$ in the concerto in C, the early concerti in C and B♭ are contained within this compass. In the Waldstein Sonata the compass rises to a^3, the Appassionata to c^4 and in Les Adieux (Sonata in E♭ Opus 81ᵃ.) to f^4. The downward extension of the compass was slow in coming, and Beethoven welcomed it with honours, for in Opus 101, he built up a magnificent climax to it, and marked it boldly "Contra E" in the manuscript. In Opus 106 (the Hammerklavier Sonata), the compass is six octaves and a fourth CC to f^4, and only a further minor third below this was necessary to attain the present lowest note.

It is still the despair of the pianist to match Beethoven's intentions of loudness and softness, though he may easily satisfy the tenuous

[1] To whom the author is indebted for the photograph and this information.

brushwork of Debussy or the clamant idiom of Prokofiev. The protracted crescendo leading to the reprise in the first movement of the *Waldstein*, the towering heights of the *Appassionata*, the ineffably tender murmurs and ethereal lacery of the fourth variation in the Arietta of Opus 111 (the last Sonata): these were revelations that may indeed have struck contemporaries as extravagances of an inspired madman.[1]

Carl Czerny (1791–1857), the famous study writer and teacher of Liszt, was taken at the age of ten to play to Beethoven his Sonata Pathétique and the song Adelaïde, and was accepted as a pupil:

"First of all, however, get him a copy of Emanuel Bach's book on the true art of piano playing, for he must bring it with him the next time he comes," said Beethoven.

Then all those present congratulated my father on this favourable verdict, Krumpholz in particular being very happy, and my father at once hurried off to hunt up Bach's book.

During the first lessons Beethoven kept me exclusively on scales in all the keys, and showed me (something at the time still unknown to most players) the only correct position of the hands and fingers and, in particular, how to use the thumb, rules whose usefulness I did not learn fully to appreciate until a much later date. Then he went over the studies belonging to this method with me and, especially, called my attention to the legato, which he himself controlled to such an incomparable degree, and which at that time all other pianists regarded as impossible of execution on the fortepiano, for even after Mozart's day, the choppy, short, detached manner of playing was the fashion.[2] In latter years Beethoven himself told me that he had heard Mozart play on various occasions and that Mozart, since at the time the invention of the fortepiano was still in its infancy, had accustomed himself to a mode of playing on the claviers then more frequently used, which was in no wise adapted to the fortepiano. In course of time I also made the acquaintance of several persons who had taken lessons from Mozart, and found this remark justified by their playing.

Later in the passage, from which we have quoted, Czerny goes on to say:

[1] Ernest Hutcheson, *The Literature of the Piano*, London, 2nd Imp., 1958.
[2] However, Mozart's letters of June 27, 1781, and January 17, 1782, show him to have required the exact opposite.

Liszt at the Piano (Vienna Museum). An evening with Liszt. At his feet Marie d'Agoult, and behind him George Sand, dressed as a man, with Alexandre Dumas and, standing, Victor Hugo. Paganini and Rossini are in the background. The bust is of Beethoven

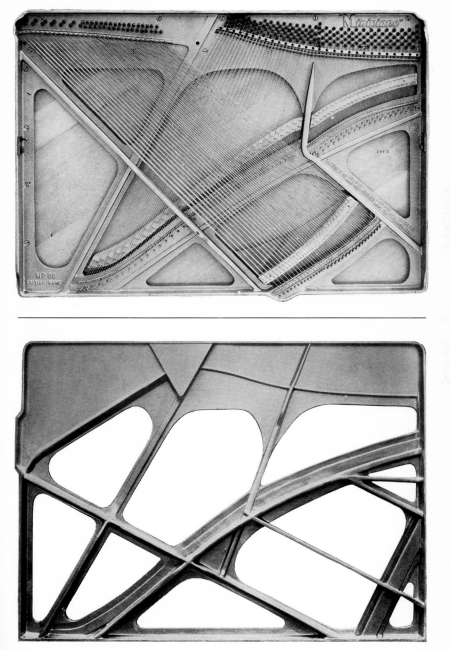

If Beethoven's playing was notable for its tremendous power, character, unheard-of bravura and facility, Hummel's performance, on the other hand, was a model of all that is clean and distinct, of the most charming elegance and delicacy, and its difficulties were invariably calculated to produce the greatest and most astonishing effect, since he combined Mozart's manner with the Clementi school so wisely adapted to the instrument. It was therefore quite natural that in the world at large he should have been reputed the better player, and that soon the devotees of the two masters formed two factions which assailed each other with great vigour. Hummel's followers reproached Beethoven with maltreating the fortepiano, said his playing was devoid of purity and distinctness, that his use of the pedal produced only a confused noise, and that his compositions were contrived, untuneful and irregular in form. Beethoven's partisans, on the other hand, asserted that Hummel lacked all real imagination, said his playing was as monotonous as that of a hurdy-gurdy, that he held his fingers like claws, spider-fashion, and that his compositions were mere inflations of Mozart and Haydn themes. Hummel's playing did not fail to influence me, since it spurred me on to play with greater purity and distinctness.

To his pupils Beethoven gave the advice: "Place the hands over the keyboard in such a position that the fingers need not be raised more than necessary. That is the only method by which the player can learn to generate tone." He told Tomaschek in 1814 that piano-music had to be something whole and integrated, "not like the players of today who run up and down the keyboard". Beethoven saw the superficiality of the music and playing of Steibelt and Vogler; Mozart he called old-fashioned and his style of playing "finger-dancing" or "manual air-sawing". He was pleased with the studies and playing of Cramer and Clementi.

Schindler[1] (1795–1864) says that in Beethoven's earlier days, before he became deaf, he had an adequate technique, which was dynamic and romantic and later lacked precision. "He threw tone out in detached notes, thus producing the effect of a fountain, gushing forth and dashing its spray on all sides, well contrasting with the melodious episodes he still preserved."

Ferdinand Ries (1784–1838) a piano student of Beethoven's, described his master's playing (1801–5):

---

[1] Anton Schindler, *Beethoven*, Vienna, 1840.

In general he played his own compositions in a very capricious manner, but he nevertheless kept strictly accurate time, occasionally, but very seldom, accelerating the tempo. On the other hand, in the performance of a crescendo passage, he would introduce a ritard, which produced a beautiful and highly striking effect. Sometimes in the performance of specific passages he would infuse into them an exquisite but altogether inimitable expression. He seldom introduced notes or ornaments not set down in the composition.

Friedrich Wieck (1785–1873) the father-in-law of Robert Schumann and a notable piano teacher, visited Beethoven in 1824 or 1826 and described the master's playing in the years shortly before his death:

> Then he improvised for me during an hour, after he had mounted his ear-trumpet and placed it on the resonance-plate which already stood on the pretty well battered, large grand piano, with its very powerful, rough tone, which had been presented to him by the city of London. He played in a flowing, genial manner, for the most part orchestrally, and was still quite adept in the passing over of the right and left hands (a few times he missed the mark), weaving in the clearest and most charming melodies, which seemed to stream to him unsought, most of the time keeping his eyes turned upward, and with close-gathered fingers.

The tragic picture of the deaf musician in his later years is vividly described by Sir John Russell.[1]

> The moment he is seated at the piano he is evidently unconscious that there is anything else in existence. . . . The muscles of his face swell and its veins stand out: the wild eye rolls doubly wild: the mouth quivers; and Beethoven looks like a wizard overpowered by the demons he has called up. . . . And, considering how very deaf he is, it seems impossible that he should hear all he plays. Accordingly, when playing softly, he does not bring out a single note. He hears it himself in his "mind's ear", while his eye, and the almost imperceptible motion of his fingers, shows that he is following out the struggle in his own soul through all its dying gradations. The instrument is actually as dumb as the musician is deaf. . . .

[1] Sir John Russell, *A Tour of Germany and Some of the Provinces of the Austrian Empire*, 1820–22, Edinburgh, 1828.

John Field (1782–1837)

Field, an Irishman, was a pupil and protégé of Clementi, for whom he acted as a piano salesman in Moscow, where he was also a much-esteemed music teacher. He adopted Clementi's style of playing and made his pupils practise with coins on the backs of their hands. He was intensely poetical. His compositions, called Nocturnes, as well as his playing in Paris in 1832, influenced Chopin. Here follow two impressions of his playing:

Field's playing was at once sweet and strong and characterised by admirable precision. His fingers fell on the keys as large drops of rain that spread themselves like iridescent pearls. Here let me say—and I am sure that my opinion is shared by many who have heard Field—that I do not share the view of Liszt, who told me on one occasion that he found Field's playing "sleepy". No! The playing of Field was not sleepy; on the contrary it was strong, capricious and improvised. In particular, he never descended to charlatanism to produce his effects.[1]

His pose, nearly immobile, his face without much expression held the attention . . . His playing flowed clear and limpid.

Those above all who have heard Field himself play, or rather dream these pieces, found him abandoning himself to his inspiration. He was not bound down to the notes which he had imagined but devised without ceasing new groups of ornaments which garlanded his melodies. Each time they were differently ornamented by him with these flowers showering like rain, but nevertheless never disappearing under the ornaments.[2]

Carl Maria von Weber (1786–1826)

Weber is remembered for his operas rather than for his pianoforte works. Nevertheless, he composed four sonatas for the instrument, concerti, a Concertstück in F minor and a Rondo Brilliant. He was a virtuoso performer and had a large hand, the span of which is reflected in his works. His influence in resisting the cult of the trivial piano fantasias of some of his contemporaries was valuable.

Franz Schubert (1797–1828)

I performed my variations (from Sonata Opus 42) not unsuccessfully, since several people assured me that my fingers had trans-

[1] Glinka, *Memoirs*.
[2] Liszt on Field's Nocturnes.

formed the keys into singing voices. If this is actually true, then I am highly delighted, since I cannot bear to listen to the damnable thumping which is peculiar to even the most distinguished pianists and which pleases neither the ear nor the mind.[1]

Schubert appears to have been satisfied with the Viennese piano, with its light touch, gentle singing tone and pedals which gave some variety of tone colour. To him it was an intimate instrument, far removed from the later grand pianofortes which were capable of duelling with full orchestras. Both in his own compositions and his playing there was no suggestion of virtuosity. The considerable bulk of his works for the piano as a solo, accompanimental and chamber instrument is extraordinary, especially when it is remembered that he died at the age of thirty-one. There are fifteen piano sonatas, excluding some early attempts but including the fine and lengthy works in A and B♭ written in the months before his death, several volumes of piano pieces, some of them short like the Moments Musicaux and Dances, and others of notable length, of which the Wanderer Fantasia is the best known. Amongst other forms, there are Duos for Violin and Piano, chamber works such as the "Trout" Quintet and the Trio in B♭, pianoforte duets of great merit, the most important contribution by any composer to this form, and the accompaniments to six hundred songs. Perhaps the word "accompaniment" does not convey enough, for many of the piano parts of his songs are in themselves little tone-poems which intensify the meaning and mood of the words of the songs. In his piano writing, Schubert was influenced by Haydn and Hummel and, to a lesser extent, by Mozart and Beethoven but, as Einstein has pointed out,[2] Schubert showed a general freedom from outside influences in his piano compositions.

Schubert set Schiller's "Laura at her piano" as a song, but it is evident that he thought of her piano as a late eighteenth-century Viennese instrument rather than as a more powerful "concerto" instrument of the nineteenth century. Schiller's raptures[3] are treated by Schubert with restraint, though he is more expansive in his song "An mein Clavier", the words of which were by Schubart.

[1] A letter written to his parents on July 25 (or 26), 1825.

[2] A. Einstein, *Schubert*, p. 89.

[3] "Rapturous harmonies swarm, in ecstatic profusion, from the strings, like new-born Seraphim, from the heavenly regions: as suns, loosed from the giant arm of Chaos, and aroused by the storm of creation, emerge, blazing, from the night, so streams forth the melody's magic power."

Schubert often used the piano orchestrally. He exploited the richness and clarity of chords in the lower part of the keyboard, he liked the flute and piccolo effects of high octaves, and the tone colours appropriate to melodies in the tenor region of the instrument.

Felix Mendelssohn-Bartholdy (1809–47)

Mendelssohn, a pupil of Moscheles, was a fine pianist, but in his short life had to devote most of his time to other activities. He composed a number of sonatas, some studies of little importance, variations, suites of shorter pieces, two piano concerti, of which one is still popular, chamber music and songs with piano parts. Mendelssohn delighted in an "elastic hand staccato", and this demands a supple, well-trained wrist.

Mendelssohn used, in a more artistic way, some of the devices of the virtuosi. Thalberg's method of playing a melody with the thumbs of both hands and decorating it on each side with arpeggii and other figurations is shown more artistically in Mendelssohn's Prelude in E minor. Instead of the cruder double octaves he used alternating octaves much more effectively, as in the Rondo Capriccioso. He did not advance the technique of the piano in the manner of a Chopin or a Liszt. With great facility he poured the new wine of romanticism into the old classical forms.

Mendelssohn's "Songs without Words" were immensely popular for a century after their date of composition, and even today they are not forgotten. An over-superior attitude to them might overlook their enormous propaganda value for the piano in the nineteenth-century. Most of them were well within the capacity of the amateur performer. They represent a number of styles which include the performance of singing melodies by both hands, the playing of octaves, rapid staccato passages, hymn-like movements, arpeggii and massive organ-like effects.

Robert Schumann (1810–56); Clara Schumann (1819–96)

Robert Schumann, who had literary as well as musical interests, was intended for the law. He became a rather wayward pupil of Friedrich Wieck, a conscientious, enlightened and effective teacher of the pianoforte, who was unwillingly to become Robert's father-in-law. Wieck, who claimed, probably not unjustly, that his daughter Clara at the age of eleven was the equal of any woman pianist, was not content with mere technical efficiency, but insisted on wide musical training in his pupils. We obtain a glimpse of his ideas on pianoforte teaching in a letter he wrote to Schumann's mother.

Robert very mistakenly thinks "that the whole of piano playing consists in pure technique"; what a one-sided conception! I almost infer from this, either that he has never heard a pianist of genius at Heidelberg or else that he himself has advanced no further in playing. My eleven-year-old Clara will show him something different. But it is true that for Robert the greatest difficulty lies in the quiet, cold, well-considered, restrained conquest of technique, as the foundation of piano playing. I confess frankly that when—in the lessons which I gave him—I succeeded after hard struggles and great contradictoriness on his part, after unheard-of pranks played by his unbridled fancy upon two creatures of pure reason like ourselves, in convincing him of the importance of a pure, exact, smooth, clear, well-marked and elegant touch, very often my advice bore little fruit for the next lesson. . . .

With instruction in the piano I always combine lessons in the practical study of simple chords by means of which I impart a beautiful and correct touch, etc., etc.—in a word, everything that is not and never will be found in any piano school.[1]

Schumann ruined any chances which he had of becoming a virtuoso pianist, by the use of a mechanical device which he hoped would give independence of the fourth finger of his left hand but which paralysed it, in spite of all the most advanced treatments of the time, including the use of electricity. Thereafter Schumann devoted his energies to composition and musical journalism. As a composer he seemed to be content with the best pianos of the time. He composed sonatas, fantasias, large-scale chamber works with piano part, a pianoforte concerto which is perhaps the most famous of this type of composition. He is seen at his best in his suites of miniatures such as Carnival, Papillons, Scenes of Childhood, Kreisleriana, Fantasy Pieces (Phantasiestücke). Like Brahms and Liszt he was attracted by the fiddle-playing of Paganini, and produced transcriptions of Paganini's pieces for which he wrote a preface on the methods of playing them on the pianoforte.

[1] Friedrich Wieck (1785–1873), writing to Robert Schumann's mother from Leipzig in August 1830.

Schumann did not exploit the resources of the pianoforte in the style of the virtuosi, but he enriched its literature with a great quantity of music mostly of first-rate quality and of all degrees of difficulty. Also, he composed a number of pieces for pedal-piano, some of which are esteemed by organists. Schumann liked to make the bass of the piano sing, and in order to enforce this he sometimes employed a bass in canon with a higher part of the work. He had a characteristic way of entrapping a melody in arpeggio figurations and, at the end of Papillons, made the final chord disappear gradually. Schumann's literary work in the *Neue Zeitschrift für Musik* made a contribution to the movement for the redemption of piano-music from the worthless piano fantasias beloved by many virtuosi. In the first issue of the journal in 1833 Schumann wrote: "At the piano nothing was heard but Herz and Hünten: and yet but a few years had passed since Beethoven, Weber and Schubert lived among us."

Clara Schumann was a first-rate pianist and musician, a worthy tribute to her father's teaching. She was an artist of integrity and interpreted her husband's compositions widely in Europe and England. Her outlook was classical and she eschewed the music of Liszt. She preferred the Grotrian–Steinweg piano to all others, delighting in its pure, singing trebles.

The *Neue Zeitschrift für Musik* in April 1848 made an analysis of the four leading pianists of the time, when already Chopin was too ill to be included. Clara, then twenty-eight years old, was considered with Liszt, Thalberg and Henselt.

The results of the analysis were:

Greatest purity of technique	Thalberg, Clara, Henselt, Liszt
Ability for improvising	Liszt, Clara
Warmth of musical feeling	Liszt, Henselt, Clara, Thalberg
Inborn artistry	Liszt, Clara
Highest soaring spirit	Liszt
Ease and sophistication	Thalberg
Affectation and mannerisms	Henselt
Uniqueness	Liszt
Complete absorption in music	Clara
Reading at sight	Liszt, Thalberg, Clara
Versatility	Clara, Liszt, Thalberg, Henselt
Scholarliness	Thalberg, Henselt, Clara, Liszt

Beauty of Touch	Thalberg, Henselt, Clara, Liszt
"Ego"	Liszt, Henselt
Dependence on finger practice	Liszt—none. Clara—free exercises. Thalberg and Henselt—slavish pedantry
Objective performance	None
Use of metronome	None
Most worthy of imitation by future artists	Thalberg, Clara
Correct note playing	Thalberg, Clara, Henselt
Proper concert preparation	Liszt, Thalberg, Clara
No hair-tossing or grimacing	Thalberg and Clara

Frédéric Chopin (1810–49)

> *"Homme exquis pour le coeur, et je n'ai pas besoin*
> *de dire pour l'esprit."*[1]

The music of Chopin mirrors the fine culture of his day. Chopin was no sentimentalist; the too-luscious interpretation frequently given of his music, by an older generation, does him injustice. At times indeed he touches great depths with a severely masculine strength, as, for example, in the G minor and the F minor ballades, in the famous sonata of the funeral march and in parts of the more stormy polonaises, where the sufferings of his country touched his patriotism to the heart.[2]

He had an instinct, amounting to genius, for inventing melodies that would be actually ineffective if sung or played on an instrument capable of sustaining tone but which, picked out in percussive points of sound each beginning to die as soon as born, are enchanting and give an illusion of singing that is often lovelier than singing itself.[3]

Failure to place him in his true line of descent—Couperin, Bach, Mozart—is to run the risk of repeating the error of George Sand, who reproached him with 'his innate respect for everything which was most narrowly conventional'. It is true that he resisted with all his might and mind the mirages of romanticism. . . . His

[1] Eugene Delacroix, *Diary*, 22/4/1849.
[2] Agnes Savill, *Music, Health and Character*, London, 1927.
[3] Gerald Abraham, *A Hundred Years of Music* (2nd Ed.), London, 1949.

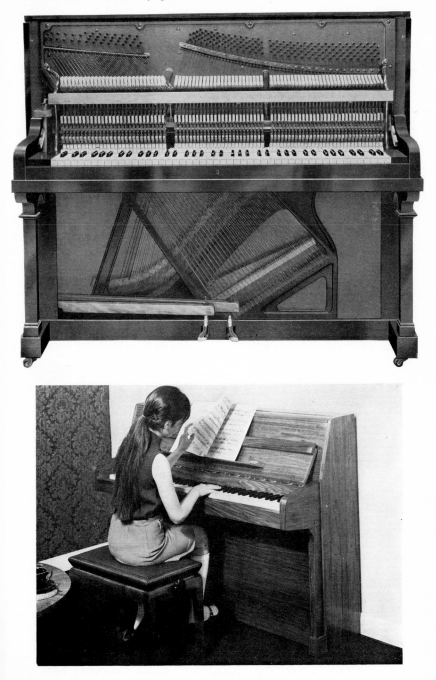

first piano teacher, the Czech Zwyny, instilled in him the cult of Bach, still so rare at that time. Thereafter Bach and Mozart were to remain for him the models of perfection.[1]

Until recent years the music of Chopin has suffered because of a misunderstanding of its nature, both by editors and performers. For decades, some solo pianists, who enjoyed a global reputation, did not hesitate to amend his music to suit their own ideas and technique, to use it as a vehicle for their idiosyncrasies and to play it on powerful pianos with over-romantic, "plummy" tone. Tempo rubato was exaggerated until the left hand of the performer did not know what the right was doing. One pianist, V. de Pachmann, went so far as to rewrite Chopin's basses and insisted that they were improved thereby. John Field called Chopin's music "the talent of the sick-room"; others saw in it pathological traits and, even where it should have been obvious that the nature of his compositions was intrinsically and solely musical, it was popular to supply romantic titles to his pieces. Hans von Bülow gave fanciful names to each of the twenty preludes, and the F minor Fantasia was programmed to represent episodes in the relations of Chopin and George Sand. Over the years the legends grew in a romantic atmosphere and were handed down from teacher to teacher. ("Leschetizky was told by Liszt who was told by Chopin!")

On the contrary, Chopin was dealing with purely musical and not romantic programme problems. His music is entirely wholesome, and his early death from consumption did not prevent him from achieving both maturity and distinction as a composer of the first rank. His ideas flowed naturally in terms of the pianoforte keyboard. His works for other media are of minor importance. His whole output of works is contained in a few slim volumes, yet they are amongst the priceless treasures of the Western Civilisation, and exercised a great influence in the development of the piano. Through him the Viennese tradition was finally broken and many modern trends in music were anticipated.

It has been said that Chopin's melodies were derived from and influenced by those of Bellini. This cannot be sustained, since some of Chopin's melodies preceded by a number of years those of Bellini, from which they were said to be taken. No doubt Chopin and Bellini drew their inspiration from the same source, that of the finest singers in the Italian style of the day. His appreciation of the

---

[1] Camille Bourniquel, *Chopin*, London, 1960.

great singers of the time, such as Sontag, Lablache, Rubini, Pasta and Malibran, was well known.

Here follow some impressions of Chopin's playing by contemporaries. Ignaz Moscheles wrote:

> Chopin has just been playing to me, and for the first time I understand his music. The rubato, which with his other interpreters, degenerates into disregard of time, is with him only a charming originality of manner; the harsh modulations which strike me disagreeably when I am playing his compositions no longer shock me, because he glides over them in a fairy-like way with his delicate fingers; his piano is so soft that he does not need any strong forte to produce his contrasts, and for this reason one does not miss the orchestral effects which the German School requires from a pianoforte player, but allows one's self to be carried away as by a singer, who, unconcerned about the accompaniment, entirely follows his emotions.[1]

Mendelssohn's impression of Chopin is of great interest, as written in a letter to his sister in 1835:

> His playing has enchanted me afresh, and I am persuaded that if you, and my father also, had heard some of his better pieces, as he played them to me, you would say the same. There is something thoroughly original in his playing, and at the same time, so masterly that he may be called a most perfect virtuoso; and as every style of perfection is welcome and acceptable, that day was most welcome to me. . . . It was so pleasant for me to be once more with a thorough musician, and not with those half-virtuosos and half-classics . . . but with one who has his perfect and well-defined phrase.

A. J. Hipkins in London:

> Here, in 1848, his compositions were almost unknown. Every time I heard him play, the pieces were strange to me, and I had to rush across Regent Street to Wessel, his English publisher, to discover what I had been hearing. Fancy the interest of this to me, a young man, who for the first time came in contact with genius!
>
> To return to pianos, he especially liked Broadwood's Boudoir cottage pianos of that date, two-stringed, but very sweet instruments, and he found pleasure in playing on them. He played Bach's "48" all his life long. "I don't practise my own com-

---

[1] Moscheles, *Diaries*, Leipzig, 1872.

positions," he said. "When I am about to give a concert, I close my doors for a time and play Bach."

Chopin never played his own compositions twice alike, but varied each according to the mood of the moment, a mood that charmed by its very waywardness; his playing resembling nothing so much as the tender delicate tints seen in mother-o'-pearl and rendered apparently without the least effort.[1] His touch was elusive, and his expression so new, that his art was little understood, and by the German School not at all, with the exceptions of Schumann and Henselt, the latter the finest interpreter Chopin ever had.

To show how different he was from the modern virtuoso; Mrs. Lyszczinska, his hostess in Edinburgh, told me when here in 1895 that when he stayed with her, he would of an evening retire into an adjoining room, where an old Broadwood square piano of her childhood stood, and play upon it with evident pleasure.[2]

Robert Schumann:

Let one imagine that an Aeolian harp had all the scales and that an artist's hand had mingled them together in all kinds of fantastic decorations, but in such a way that you could always hear a deeper fundamental tone and a softly singing melody—there you have something of a picture of his playing. It is wrong to suppose that he brought out distinctly every one of the little notes: it was rather a billowing of the chord of A♭, swelled here and there by the pedal; but through the harmonies could be heard in sustained tones a wonderful melody, and only in the middle section did a tenor part once stand out more prominently from the chords and the principal theme. When the study has ended you feel as you do after a blissful vision, seen in a dream, which, already half-awake, you would fain recall. . . .[3]

Schumann had heard Chopin play the A♭ Study, Opus 25, in Leipzig in 1836.

[1] Another enthusiastic admirer, Miss Sophy Horsley, compared his playing "to a gentle wind passing over the keys, so Aeolian was it in effect". And Heine, listening, asked: "If the trees at moonlight sang always so harmoniously?"

[2] A. J. Hipkins was a senior in the firm of Broadwood, an excellent acoustician and pianoforte expert. He tuned the pianos which Chopin played in England. His notes were collected and published as *How Chopin Played*. Hipkins was a young man at the time and his impressions were not always reliable, but there is no need to doubt the truth of the passage quoted here.

[3] R. Schumann, *Music and Musicians* (trans.), London, 1880.

Georges Mathias (a pupil):

Those who have heard Chopin may say that nothing approaching it has ever been heard. What virtuosity! What power! Yes, what power! But it only lasted a few bars and what exaltation and inspiration. The man's whole being vibrated. The pianoforte was animated by the most intense vitality: it sent a thrill through you.[1]

Carl Mikuli (a pupil):

The tone which Chopin drew from the instrument, especially in *cantabile* passages, was immense and a manly energy gave to appropriate passages an overpowering effect . . . energy without coarseness; but, on the other hand, he knew how to enchant the listener by delicacy, without affectation.[2]

A. M. Diehl wrote:

To save Chopin fatigue he was carried upstairs (he died the following year). Physical weakness was not, however, the cause of his tenderly-subdued style of playing. This was his own, and inseparable from his conception of pianoforte touch; it was incapable of modification from any influence whatever. His fortissimo was the full pure tone without noise, a harsh inelastic note being to him painful. His nuances were modifications of that tone, decreasing to the faintest yet always distinct pianissimo. His singing legatissimo touch was marvellous. The wide, extended arpeggios in the bass were transfused by touch and pedal into their corresponding sustained chords, and swelled or diminished like waves in an ocean of sound. He kept his elbows close to his sides, and played only with finger-touch, no weight from the arms. He used a simple, natural position of the hands as conditioned by scale and chord-playing, adopting the easiest fingering, although it might be against the rules, that came to him. He changed fingers upon a key as often as an organ-player.[3]

George Sand:

He spoke but little and rarely of his art, but when he did so, it was admirably clear and with so firm a judgment as to dispel the heresies he pretended to profess. But at the piano he was himself.

[1] C. Bourniquel, *Chopin.*
[2] Preface to Mikuli's edition of Chopin's works, Paris, 1890.
[3] A. M. Diehl, *Musical Memories*, 1897.

He said he intended to bring out a book, not only on his method, but of his theories. He was, above all else, a musician, his thoughts resolved themselves into music only: he had a receptive mind, but not for the fine arts; indeed, Michaelangelo scared him, and Rubens shocked him! He was a strange mixture.[1]

It was said that when Chopin was dying, he begged his friend Gutmann to destroy the notes for the intended book to which George Sand referred.

The following sheets have survived: they appear to be an introduction to a pianoforte tutor. If any notes were made by the composer on his theories of music they seem to have been destroyed.

"Its pitch being the business of the tuner the piano is free from the chief difficulties we meet with in the study of an instrument. Therefore, we have only to study a certain arrangement of the hand in relation to the keyboard in order to obtain the best quality of touch, to be able to play long and short notes, and to acquire the greatest dexterity.

"No admiration can be too great for the genius who was responsible for so cleverly adapting the construction of the keyboard to the shape of the hand. The black notes, intended for the long fingers, make admirable points of purchase. Could anything be more ingenious? Thoughtless people, knowing nothing of piano playing, have frequently suggested levelling the keyboard. This would do away with all the ease of movement and the support which the black keys give to the hands: it would, as a result, make the passage of the thumb extremely difficult in those keys involving sharps and flats. If the keyboard were levelled, it would be necessary to remove a joint from each of the long fingers in order to play a staccato passage. Legato thirds and sixths, indeed all legato passages, would be enormously difficult, and, since the tone is set by the tuner, the mechanical difficulty presented by a piano with a keyboard which assists the hand is less difficult than one would suppose. Of course, no question of musical feeling or style arises, it is purely a matter of technique—which I refer to as the mechanics of piano playing. I divide the technical aspects of piano playing into three parts:

1. The training of both hands to play chromatic and diatonic scales, that is to say to play notes a half tone and a tone's distance from one another.

[1] G. de Pourtalès, *Polonaise: the Life of Chopin*, New York, 1927.

2. Notes at a distance of more than half tone or tone from one another, that is to say from an interval of a minor third onwards. The octave divided into minor thirds so that each finger rests on one key.

3. Double notes, in two-part harmony—thirds, sixths and octaves. When we know thirds, sixths and octaves we can play in three-part harmony, and, knowing the distance between the notes, be able to play arpeggios.

"Having played the same chords with the left hand there is nothing further to study so far as the mechanics of the piano are concerned.

"To those who are studying the art of touch, I submit some very simple practical considerations which, in my experience, have proved to be of real value.

"Many abortive methods have been tried to teach to play the piano, methods which have no bearing on the study of the instrument. They are analogous to teaching someone to walk on their hands in order that they may go for a walk.

"As a result of this, people have forgotten how to walk properly and know very little about walking on their hands either. They are unable to play music in the real sense, and the difficulties they practise have nothing to do with the works of the great masters. These difficulties are theoretical. They are a new kind of acrobatics! I am not dealing with ingenious theories, however valuable these may be, but go straight to the root of the matter.

"Having some idea of notation, key signatures and the mechanism of the piano, the next step is to sit down in front of the keyboard, so as to be able to reach either end without leaning sideways. Placing our right foot on the pedal, without bringing the dampers into play, we find the position of the hand by placing our fingers on the notes E, F♯, G♯, A♯, B.

"The long fingers will be found to be on the black keys with the short fingers on the white. In order to obtain equality of leverage, the fingers on the black keys must be kept in line. The same applies to the fingers on the white keys. The resultant move will be found to follow the natural formation of the hand.

"The hand should remain supple and the wrist and forearm round themselves into a curve making for ease of movement that would be unobtainable if the fingers were outstretched.

"The pianist has nothing to do with the tuning of the instrument:

that is the province of the tuner. It is useless to begin to learn scales with that in C major. While it is the easiest to read, it is the most difficult for the hands, since it contains no purchase points. We shall begin with one that places the long fingers comfortably over the black keys—B major for example.

"Provided that it is played in time, no one will notice inequality of sound in a rapid scale. It has become customary to attempt to acquire equality of strength in the fingers, by flying in the face of nature. It is more desirable that the student acquires the ability to produce finely graded qualities of sound, or so it seems to me. The ability to be able to play everything at a level tone is not our object.

"Since each finger is formed differently it is far better to develop their special characteristics rather than attempt to destroy their individuality. The strength of each finger is relative to its shape. The extremities of the hand are formed by the thumb, which is its strongest member, and by the little finger. While the third finger has a greater freedom as a point of support, the fourth finger is bound to the third by the same tendon—like a Siamese twin—and is the weakest. One can try with all one's might to separate them, but this is impossible and, thank heaven, useless."

Chopin thought that three hours of practice each day was sufficient. The spontaneity of the music should not be destroyed by excessive attention to technique as more than a means to an end. For practice, Clementi's "Préludes et Exercices" and his "Gradus ad Parnassum", and J. S. Bach's Suites and Forty-Eight Preludes and Fugues were recommended.

Liszt said that Chopin preferred the Pleyel pianos because of their neutral tone, which did not stand in the way of his search for a "silvery and slightly veiled sonority". Chopin told Liszt, "When I am in a bad mood, I play on Érard's pianos and on them I can easily find a sound ready made. But when I am feeling in a good mood and strong enough to find my own sonorities, I use Pleyel's pianos." In more recent times Artur Schnabel expressed a similar sentiment concerning other types of piano, and liked the impersonal tone of the Bechstein piano. Chopin admired the Graf pianos, when he played in Vienna.

Chopin had remarkably elastic and extensible hands, which seemed to stretch, on occasion, "across a third of the keyboard". He ignored the older rules of fingering when it suited him, and respected the relative strengths of each finger in his phrasing. He would pass the third finger over the fourth and fifth fingers and would use the thumb and little finger for striking black notes. Marmontel says that he used both pedals simultaneously, thus producing "melodic rumblings". Chopin understood perfectly the subjective nature of a *forte* in relation to piano dynamics: Moscheles said: "His *piano* is so delicate that he does not need a strong *forte* to produce his contrasts." Chopin anticipated the impressionist style of Debussy and other later composers. He said to Lenz: "I only indicate, suggest and leave to my listeners the task of finishing the painting."

Chopin boldly shattered the Viennese tradition of harmonic progression, and it is not surprising that some of his chords were thought to be harsh by his friends and admirers. Editors and advisers mollified what they considered to be excessive harshness in his chords and progressions. We now see the logic and beauty of Chopin's intentions, and his dissonances seem relatively innocuous. Even in his time, the new and strange beauty of his work was usually apparent to all but the most conservative of listeners, when he played his own works. Chopin knew by instinct what the psychologists of musical experience have discovered only in the present century. Even when the resources of musical notation are strained to the limits it is difficult or impossible to convey more than the framework of a composer's intention, particularly when it is as subtle as that of Chopin. Chopin knew how to use selective and different dynamics for each note of a chord, when these were necessary; and by the use of the pedal, by slight differences of attack for each note, and by *tempo rubato* (which may be used to give the impression of slight dynamic changes, apart from its other uses), he was able to produce progressions of chords which were rare and fascinating.

The term *tempo rubato* has covered a multitude of sins, and until recent years has been the excuse for the most alarming deviations in playing Chopin's work. Singing of any sort which expresses emotional feeling cannot contain itself in strict time. The shapely nature of good phrasing demands a controlled amount of elasticity in its time values. Although Berlioz felt that Chopin had "pushed rhythmic independence too far", Chopin insisted that "your left hand be the conductor and maintain the beat" and that there should be freedom of expression in the singing tone, which was usually played by the right hand.

Liszt, amongst many performers who have given versions of the nature of *tempo rubato*, said: "Imagine a tree bent by the wind.

Between its branches the sun's rays pass; the trembling light which results is *rubato*."

The study of Chopin's ornaments in their relation to tone production on the piano is important. They are not the "baroque excrescences" of the older composers. Chopin's ornaments give great tone-colour as well as expression to his melodies. The rich interplay of the harmonics of the ornaments with the notes of the melody produce new tonal hues: sometimes the melody itself is suggested by rich ornamentation and delicate filigree figures. Beautiful examples of these devices occur, for example, in the Impromptu in A♭ and the Berceuse. Such methods of ornamentation are peculiar to the pianoforte, and, like Chopin's melodies, do not bear transcription for any other instrument.

Franz Liszt (*1811–86*)

Liszt was born two years after the death of Haydn; he died a year before the birth of Alban Berg, and in a way he may be said to bridge the gap between those two musical worlds. When one thinks of the long road that he had to travel between his early Czernian pieces and late works like *Nuages Gris* and *Unstern* his achievement becomes even more astonishing.[1]

The influence of Liszt on the destiny of the piano has been immense. In his supernatural playing there was evidence of a great variety of gifts. When he played "Saint Francis de Paul walking on the waters" he had the appearance of an apostle. It is certain that his prodigious technique was only one of the factors of his talent.[2]

In his endeavour to acquire on the keyboard the standard of virtuosity which Paganini manifested on the violin, Liszt worked for several hours each day in preparation for his pianoforte concerts, at technical exercises which included "thirds, sixths, cadences and tremolos". He continued his practice with Bach's "Forty-eight preludes and fugues" and Clementi's "Studies". His own studies for the pianoforte advanced even further, in their technical requirements, than those of Chopin.

The stature of Liszt does not diminish with the passage of years. He was a musician of the widest sympathies, and a full and just

[1] Humphrey Searle, *Franz Liszt*.
[2] C. Saint-Saëns, *Portraits et Souvenirs*.

estimate of his services to the art has not yet been made. For instance, his four major compositions for the organ ought to have restored the aesthetic and technique of that instrument, after nearly a century of aridity from the death of Bach.

In his desire to publicise the works of other composers, as is done today by broadcasting and the gramophone record, he arranged orchestral pieces, symphonies, songs, movements from operas, Bach's organ works for the piano and other works. With great generosity and nobility of spirit he did not take fees for his piano concerts or his classes in the second half of his life. His humility was such that he rarely played his own compositions in public during this time. Much of his published keyboard music was thought to be difficult and did not sell well in his lifetime. A survey of his remarkable output of music creates amazement that, like Bach, he could have written down all of it, quite apart from the time and labour of composition.

Liszt was well endowed physically. He had long, flexible fingers and exceptionally long thumbs. His musculature was supple and he brought into use the wrist, the whole arm and the shoulder, calling into play, when necessary, an integration of the energy supplied by each. He used a higher position of the arms than had hitherto been thought compatible with good tone production. "This," said Camille Saint-Saëns, "separates the old school of playing, which relied only on the phalanges of the fingers, and the new which used the forces and movements of the upper part of the body and the arms in a co-ordinated way." In his search for great dynamic contrasts, Liszt's keyboard tuttis might well have damaged the feeble mechanism and broken the thin strings of the older pianos. "I contemplate the battlefield. I count the wounded and the dead," said Camille Mooke-Pleyel, herself an excellent pianist, when observing the condition of the pianos at the end of a Liszt concert. Nevertheless, to imagine that Liszt's playing lacked subtlety is to do him an injustice. His beautiful singing tone was renowned. "I listen night after night to the greatest singers," he said. Liszt was not a piano smiter: the heavier and more destructive style was a later manifestation. Much of his pianoforte music looks more difficult to play than it is. Even his transcriptions are remarkably pianistic and lie felicitously under the fingers. He experimented ceaselessly to evolve new sounds from the instrument. He imitated the wind, the sea, fountains and the sounds of Nature, and was fond of bells. "In my time I have made some discoveries," he said to Miss Amy

Fay[1] and, on the piano, demonstrated various ways of playing the Angelus to the Revd. H. Haweis.[2]

If much of Liszt's published music was too difficult for most contemporary pianists, his concerts did much to popularise the instrument. Piano manufacturers and salesmen were always pleased when he visited their neighbourhood.

Sir Charles Hallé, a pianist of great attainment, said of Liszt:

He was a giant, and Rubinstein spoke the truth when, at the time his own triumphs were greatest, he said that, in comparison with Liszt, all other pianists were children—Liszt was all sunshine and dazzling splendour, subjugating his hearers with a power that none could withstand. For him there were no difficulties of execution, the most incredible seeming child's play under his fingers. One of the transcendent merits of his playing was the crystal-like clearness which never failed him for a moment, even in the most complicated and, for anybody else, impossible passages; it was as if he had photographed them in the minutest detail upon the ear of his listener. The power he drew from his instrument was such as I have never heard since, but never harsh, never suggesting "thumping". His daring was as extraordinary as his talent. At an orchestral concert given by him and conducted by Berlioz, the "March to the Scaffold", from the latter's Symphonie Fantastique, that most gorgeously orchestrated piece, was performed, at the conclusion of which Liszt sat down and played his own arrangement, for the piano alone, of the same movement, with an effect even surpassing that of the full orchestra, and creating an indescribable furore.[3]

Professor Dent, in his biography of Busoni, describes the great pianist playing Liszt:

The greater works of Liszt, which minor pianists turn into mere displays of virtuosity because their technique is inadequate for anything beyond that, often sounded strangely easy and simple when they were played by Busoni. The glittering scales and arpeggios became what Liszt intended them to be—a dimly suggested background, while the themes in massive chords or singing melodies stood out clear. Liszt evidently realised the danger of the extreme technical difficulty of some of his works,

[1] Amy Fay, *Music Study in Germany*, London and New York, 1888.
[2] H. Haweis, *My Musical Life*, London, 1880.
[3] S. Sitwell, *Liszt*, London, 1955.

and therefore revised them in later life, but even so a great deal
of his music is in the unfortunate position of being playable in the
way Liszt meant it to be played by only a handful of pianists in
each generation, while remaining at the mercy of every pianist
who has enough technique and nothing more; and thereby the
misleading impression, to which we are so well accustomed, is
perpetuated. Liszt did not invent his transcendental technique
merely in order to dazzle his hearers and show that he was a
better pianist than his rivals; he did it because he was able to
draw new and almost orchestral effects from the piano which
incomparably widened its range of expression—and all subsequent
composers for the piano are grateful to him.

Mendelssohn[1] compared the playing of Thalberg and that of
Liszt:

A fantasia by Thalberg (especially that on Rossini's Lady of the
Lake) is an accumulation of the finest and most exquisite effects, a
crescendo of difficulties and embellishments that is astonishing.
Everything is so calculated and so polished, and shows such
assurance, skill and superlative effects. At the same time the man
has incredibly powerful hands and such practised, light fingers
that he is unique.

Liszt, on the other hand, possesses a certain suppleness and
differentiation in his fingering, as well as a thoroughly musical
feeling that cannot be equalled. In a word, I have known of no
performer whose musical perceptions so extend to the very tips
of his fingers and emanate directly from them as Liszt's do. With
his directness, his stupendous technique and experience, he could
far have surpassed the rest, were not a man's own thoughts in
connection with all this the main thing. And these, so far, at
least, seem to have been denied him by nature, so that in this
respect most of the great virtuosi equal, or even excel him. But
that he, together with Thalberg, alone represents the highest class of
pianists of the present day, seems to me indisputable.

Liszt taught the piano in Paris, Weimar (where there is a Liszt
museum with some of his pianos), and at Budapest. He was one of
the first teachers to recommend a free and relaxed condition of the
arm, particularly of the forearm, so that it could be used in a free,

---

[1] Letter from Leipzig, 30/3/1840, but Liszt had still forty-six years of life
ahead of him, and in this period acquired depth of character, intellectual powers
and artistic insight.

FIG. 15. Liszt's finger exercises.

rolling or rotational movement. In the difficult semi-quaver passage in C♯ minor in the Chopin Ballade in A♭ Opus 47, Liszt said to Siloti: "Shake it out of your sleeve, and you'll find it quite easy." He found some of the volumes of the velocity studies of his own teacher, Czerny, to be of good pedagogical value. According to Mlle Boissier,[1] Liszt gave the fingerings on page 173 to exercises which were used by his pupils Siloti, Scharwenka, D'Albert, who in turn gave them to their own pupils.

Siloti related how that, in Weimar, Liszt gave only a few private lessons and preferred to give lessons in class three times a week. As the group contained such artists as Rosenthal, Reisenauer, Friedheim, Sauer and others it was a proving experience—"if you could play in that critical circle you could play anywhere".

Johannes Brahms (1833–97)

Brahms made a major contribution to the music of the piano. His noble output contains sonatas, variations (including, like those of Schumann, Liszt and Rachmaninoff, a set on Paganini's themes), ballades, waltzes, études, a few arrangements of pieces by other composers and many shorter pieces. In addition there are two pianoforte concerti of considerable length, sonatas for clarinet, cello, violin and piano respectively, chamber works and song accompaniments, duets and music for two pianos.

His music does not lie under the pianist's fingers like that of Chopin, and some of it appears to be ungrateful and unpianistic. Brahms was the son of a double-bass player, and in his own work sought for sonorous basses. The compass of his piano terminated at C, a minor third above the present lowest note, and it did not have the turgid thickness of sound which is evident in some modern instruments. He was opposed to the music and influence of Liszt. In his search for organ-like sonority Brahms often doubled the melody in two or three octaves, and loved the reedy growl of the tempered thirds and sixths of the keyboard. The tempered keyboard is often an awkward partner for the silky consonance of the best string-playing. Brahms's early experience as an accompanist to the violin playing of Remenyi and Joachim was valuable to him, and he achieved in his compositions for strings and piano a perfection of blend which had hardly been attained previously.

In spite of his self-discipline as a composer, Brahms could write

[1] Mlle Valerie Boissier, *Liszt—Pedagogue*.

long, romantic melodies, suitable for "singing" on the keyboard and, like those of Chopin, spoilt by transcription. An excellent example is the Andante from the Sonata in F minor.

Brahms wrote a number of studies adapted from works by Chopin, Weber, and Bach, and in addition to two tremendous sets of Paganini variations, which he called Studies, he composed fifty-one Exercises (*Übungen*) which make no pretence at any musical qualities but are intended to develop the technical skill necessary for the playing of his works. These contain many devices of fingering, the use of two varieties of touch simultaneously with the same hand, and the playing of as many as four different metrical patterns with the two hands. Undoubtedly, the publication of these exercises, which he originally intended for his own practice, pointed to methods of playing which looked to the future.

Claude Achille Debussy (1862–1918)
"Le piano sans marteaux"

In the years after the first world war the writer sometimes visited the shop of Debussy's publishers, Durand, in the Place de la Madeleine, Paris. Here was a grand piano which Debussy used to play in the earlier years of the century. The head of the firm often heard him: "You forgot that the piano had hammers when Debussy played." Although doubtless this was true, Debussy used every resource of the piano and could play with a martellato touch when it was required. Nevertheless, he extended Chopin's use of the pedal and used the subtle washes of colour which are produced by the sympathetic vibrations of unstruck strings. In his later piano works, in particular the Études, he explored, in a systematic manner, all his harmonic devices through the tone-colour of the instrument. In his music there are the soft, blurred edges of the French impressionist painters, such as Monet, and writers, such as Mallarmé. There is also the analysis into tiny details and the synthesis of the *pointillistes*, of whom Seurat is the best-known. Debussy did not limit himself to such impressionism, but he could write very definite tone pictures in his "Spanish" music. His Études are studies, not only of technical performance but of new sounds, and they were one of the great sources of inspiration for twentieth-century composers in various parts of the world. Debussy analysed afresh the whole of the tonal resources of the piano: the sympathetic vibrations of strings which picked up the harmonics of those lower in the scale, the use of the pedal, including half-pedalling, the veiled tone-qualities yielded by the soft pedal, a further study of chords and a new conception of harmony. The illusion of a static, statuesque effect, as of a marble figure in a moonlit garden, could be produced by the repetition of similarly compounded chords on different notes. Debussy explored the sensuous beauty of a piano chord, as a thing in itself. Overstrung instruments in particular yield a particularly rich, if somewhat indefinite, sensuous tone-colour when gentle discords, well spread over the keyboard, are played, and the sustaining pedal is then used to permit the strings of the instrument to resound to any of the harmonics which are contained in the notes which have been played. Here there is an interplay of the great chord of the harmonics of the strings and the actual chord of the music. Debussy's pianoforte art required much sensitive analysis of the nature of piano tone and intelligent experiment on his part; and, for the fullest realisation of his music, similar efforts must be expected from the performer. There is an abstract quality in much of his music which gives scope to the sensitive mind, if it will, to fill in the details. Such analysis and abstraction were also suggestive to successors who find therein a direction and an inspiration towards new methods and progress.

An impression of Debussy's playing is given by Maurice Emmanuel:

> His playing had incomparable grace. He was a charmer at the piano. He conjured from the keys all the diverse sounds of the orchestra, and his touch was perfectly delicate and apparently limitless in its wealth of shading. He was a master of pedalling and understood how to combine the most disparate chords in the most natural way by means of his legato.[1]

Some of the leading composers of the twentieth century tended to think of the piano solely as a percussion instrument. In particular Igor Stravinsky said, "It has hammers, why try to alter its nature?" Prokofiev and Bartok both explored this aspect of its nature, but there are singing passages in Prokofiev's sonata, and Bartok, who had been nurtured in an older school of pianoforte playing, did not put lyricism out of court altogether and never resorted to key-hitting. Nevertheless, beauty and subtlety of tone quality seemed to be less important to the anti-romantics than the production of sounds of definite pitches and dynamic levels.

A great variety of piano effects is required in the music of Bartok.

[1] Inghelbrecht, *Claude Debussy*, Paris, 1953.

These can be studied at an elementary level in his Mikrokosmos, which is much more worthy than the insipid material which is so often used for teaching purposes. Here are 153 short pieces which give an introduction to modern harmony and rhythms. If the ear is at first repelled by some of the sounds, it is well worth the listener's while to persist in an endeavour to reach an understanding of their nature.

In the works of Henry D. Cowell, an American composer, the fist, elbow and forearm are all used to produce tone-clusters. In Charles E. Ives's piano sonata "Concord Mass 1845" passages of great charm are contrasted with intentional cacophony and brutality. Wood blocks of a prescribed size are used to force down clusters of notes. Tone-clusters, for which the piano is very suitable, can be used both because of their direct effect of a dazzling spectrum of fundamental and harmonic notes, and as generators of overtones which can be picked up by resonance and used in strings of higher pitches. There are some passages in Scarlatti's sonatas which anticipate the use of tone-clusters in the lower part of the keyboard. The piano has proved to be a favourite instrument for the works of the atonalists and the "tone-row" composers.

Stravinsky has pointed out that systems of tuning have not been exploited fully by modern composers. There is unlimited scope here, and new temperaments are constantly being devised. Because so few performers and composers tune their own pianofortes, or would care to subject them to constant experimental tunings, the electronic production of notes of various and adjustable pitches may prove more convenient and acceptable, for such work.

STUDY WRITERS AND MINOR COMPOSERS
FOR THE PIANO

The "study writers" of the early nineteenth century, who were usually piano virtuosi, did not have the musical statures of Beethoven, Chopin, Schubert or Schumann, but generally they have an honourable place in the story of the piano because they did much to popularise the instrument and to produce music which had a wide vogue for teaching purposes.

Ignaz Moscheles

Moscheles, as a musician, scholar and composer, was superior to most of the study writers. He was born in Prague in 1794 and died

M

in Leipzig in 1870. He left much piano music, including seven
concerti and some volumes of studies. He was the teacher and
colleague of Mendelssohn, who was an excellent pianist.

Johann Nepomuk Hummel

Hummel, who was born in Pressburg in 1778 and died in Weimar in
1837, had great influence on the next generation of pianists. His
compositions were greatly esteemed and his influence on the development of keyboard techniques was outstanding. He produced two
books of twelve studies in various styles which, for many years,
were very attractive to students. He produced a logical system of
fingering, more rational methods of playing ornaments and a routine
of daily piano practice.

Muzio Clementi (1752–1832)

He was feeling his way into styles which were afterwards to be
perfected by composers of a later age. Among the fascinations
of the *Gradus* are its forward vision and its lively anticipation of
musical things to come—of Chopin's sensuous harmonies and
Schumann's tonal scene-painting; of Brahms's rugged massive-
ness and suave tenuity, Debussy's evanescent colour-schemes and
even Scriabin's veiled mysteries. Pieces which might easily bear
the signatures of these composers are to be found scattered
throughout the *Gradus*, bringing musical refreshment to the student
who has diligently mastered the more numerous technical studies,
the pieces in sonata form, the canons and the fugues.[1]

Clementi, a Roman, showed great talent at an early age, and was
brought to England by the wealthy Mr. Beckford. He became a
composer and touring recitalist before he was twenty, and as a
young man had a piano-playing competition in Vienna with Mozart,
in which he was not worsted. Clementi probably influenced Beethoven in his use of the piano as a cantabile instrument. Amongst
his many pupils were Cramer and Field. Clementi settled in England and developed a successful pianoforte manufacturing and
music publishing business. He was a partner of the firms of Longman and Broderip and Collard. In spite of the loss of a factory by
fire in 1807, which reduced his capital by £40,000, he died a wealthy

[1] Kathleen Dale, "The Three C's (Clementi, Czerny, Cramer) Pioneers of
pianoforte playing", in *Music Review*, vol. VI, No. 3, 1945.

man. He died at Evesham and was buried in the cloisters of Westminster Abbey in 1832.

In addition to the *Gradus ad Parnassum* (by Degrees to Parnassus) of 1817, he published in 1800 an *Introduction to the Art of Playing on the Pianoforte*, which was the successor to C. P. E. Bach's *Essay* and contained examples from the works of Bach, Corelli, Couperin, Domenico Scarlatti, Rameau, Haydn and other "old masters". He was a prolific composer and wrote in several forms: he composed over a hundred piano sonatas. He represented the classical C. P. E. Bach–Beethoven school of pianoforte playing. Carl Tausig (1841–1871), a great pianist, said that Clementi's *Gradus* and Chopin's *Studies* were the only piano works which were entirely indispensable to the pianist.

Carl Czerny (1791–1857)

"I spend a part of every day with the Master," said Liszt, with reference to Czerny's School of Velocity.

Czerny was a pupil of Beethoven and the teacher of Liszt and Leschetizky, who in their turn taught the majority of the leading pianists of the next generation. Czerny was a man of outstanding energy and industry and produced more than a thousand opus numbers, many of which were substantial volumes.[1] Some of his sets of piano studies have endured to the present day. He understood the resources of the pianoforte, and his influence on the teaching and popularisation of the instrument is incalculable, in spite of the common association, in recent decades, of his works with piano drudgery.

John Baptist Cramer (1771–1858)

Our master [Beethoven] declared that these studies were the chief basis of all genuine playing. If he had carried out his intention of writing a pianoforte school these studies would have formed in it the most important part of the practical examples, for on account of the polyphony predominant in many of them, he looked upon them as the most fitting preparation for his own works.[2]

---

[1] His *Opus 500*, dedicated to Queen Victoria, ran to 542 pages.
[2] *Selection of Studies*, by J. B. Cramer, with comments by L. van Beethoven, and preface, translation, explanatory notes, and fingering by J. S. Shedlock, London, 1893. The quotation is from Anton Schindler.

Cramer, born in Mannheim, was brought to England at the age of twelve months and made his home here for the whole of his life. His father was a violinist of note and influenced the boy's musical development. Cramer commenced his career as a music publisher by becoming a partner in the firm of Chappell, in 1812. In 1824 he joined R. Anderson and T. F. Beale as music publishers in Regent Street, and the firm was known as Cramer and Company. J. B. Cramer was a man of considerable musical abilities, but he is remembered for his pianoforte studies, forty-two exercises for the pianoforte, Opus 30, 1804. In addition, he composed a hundred and five sonatas, at least eight concerti and a large number of "display pieces". Moscheles spoke of his artistic piano playing: he had a touch of velvet and produced a lovely singing tone "like the air from the sweet South". He was said to be unrivalled as an interpreter of Mozart, but Hummel insisted that he was the first to reveal the spirit of Beethoven's sonatas. "Never until now have I heard Beethoven," he said. "Though not of the fathers of the church of pianoforte playing, he was worthy of consultation at all times."[1]

Beethoven added comments, for his nephew, to twenty-one of Cramer's studies. Beethoven stressed the necessity for concentrating on rhythm and accent, for then technical ability would follow.

Sigismond Thalberg (1812–71)

Thalberg, who was born in Geneva and died in Naples, was the natural son of a nobleman and his surname was synthetic (Thal—a valley, Berg—a mountain). His noble origin manifested itself in the elegance, charm, evenness and perfection of his playing. He received lessons from the chief bassoon player of the Vienna Opera, but his piano-style derived from that of Hummel. He was famous because his piano technique gave the impression of a third hand, by playing a melody which was well marked and surrounding it both above and below with arpeggii. This he exploited in his own compositions, but it was put to more artistic uses by Mendelssohn, Liszt and César Franck in his Prelude, Choral and Fugue. From about 1836 there was a strong rivalry between Thalberg and Liszt as performers, which was manifested in Thalberg with nobility but was the occasion for jealousy in Liszt. The piano in the hands of Thalberg was an instrument which could produce a beautifully phrased singing line and accompany it at the same time.

[1] E. Dannreuther in *Grove's Dictionary of Music* (1st ed.).

Jan Ladislav Dussek

Dussek was born in 1760, spent much of his life in Prague, and died near Paris in 1812. He composed much pianoforte music which at the time seemed forward looking and is now not quite forgotten. He was famous for his beautiful cantabile style of playing: "His fingers were like ten singers," and in his search for a perfect legato he often changed fingers on one key. He was the first to play one of Broadwood's six octave pianos in 1794.

Friedrich Wilhelm Kalkbrenner

Kalkbrenner was born in Berlin in 1788 and died near Paris in 1849. He was a piano and harmony student at the Paris Conservatoire and, like Beethoven and Hummel, received lessons in counterpoint from Albrechtsberger. Also, he was taught the piano by Clementi. He prospered greatly as a partner in the piano firm of Pleyel and as a teacher and performer. Kalkbrenner is remembered chiefly because he wished Chopin to become his pupil. Chopin praised Kalkbrenner's charming, even touch, and his quiet, self-possessed manner; but Chopin was wise, as Mendelssohn pointed out, in going his own way.

Adolf Henselt (1814–89)

Henselt was born and died in Germany. He studied for a time with Hummel but later taught himself. He possessed wonderful technique and musicianship but did not like playing in public. He had "a soft velvety touch" admired by Liszt. Henselt worked hard at his studies and devised exercises for extending the stretch of his hand and for independent finger movement. In spite of the fact that his fingers were short, he could play with ease tenths, with a deep touch. He used Cramer's studies as a basis for his method: he required perfect legato and a full tone.

Stephen Heller (1813–88)

Heller was born in Pesth in Hungary. For a short time he was a pupil of Czerny and later of Kalkbrenner, when he lived in Paris. His compositions, which were almost exclusively for piano, reached an opus number of 158, and while they were not of the quality of those of Mozart or Beethoven, they showed a sincerity and musicianship which was not to be found in the shallow fantasias of contemporary piano virtuosi such as Herz and Kalkbrenner. Heller wrote some pleasant sets of variations and some Études intended to prepare for the study of Chopin's works. Isodor Philipp, a great French pianist, said of him: "His talent may have been small, but it was pure and bore a stamp of its own, essentially the music of good breeding. His music occupies a distinctive and important place in the literature of the piano. It is music replete with imagination, charm and sincerity."

At the beginning of the nineteenth century there were many piano showmen who specialised in fantasias of little musical value but much pianistic effect and superficially attractive. Daniel Steibelt (1765–1823) specialised in tremolo effects imitating string playing, and battle scenes. C. V. Alkan[1] (1813–88) produced very difficult works of a somewhat better standard, which he was able to play.

[1] A pseudonym for Morhange. See H. Bellamann. *The pianoforte works of C. V. Alkan.* Musical Quarterly, (1924) pp. 251–62.

CHAPTER VIII

THE TECHNIQUE OF PLAYING

"'Tis more by Art, than force of numerous strokes."—Homer.

THE history of keyboard playing methods, since the time of C. P. E. Bach's famous essay, shows that teachers with very diverse or opposite views produced pupils of the first quality as pianists, and often were themselves brilliant and artistic performers. The single-minded mutual devotion of master and pupil, and of both to the art of music, would point to a success which could not be found in a mere manipulation of mechanism, however scientifically this might be achieved.

When the harpsichord was yielding its place to the pianoforte, it was not realised for a time that there was a difference between pushing a plectrum past the string and throwing a hammer at it. It was said that "depressing a pianoforte key was a thrust and playing a harpsichord key was a grasp". The early sonatas of Beethoven were playable on the harpsichord, but the difference in the styles of the two instruments was seen in the ornamentation of some of Haydn's keyboard pieces, for example, the variations in F minor, where a graduation of tone, impossible on the harpsichord, is required in the ornaments. With the heavier "English" piano actions the finger had to be vertical when meeting the key and leaving it. The schools of Cramer and Clementi demanded a calm hand position, and much practice was necessary to strengthen weak fingers and to produce evenness of tone. The keyboard music of the eighteenth century, which left a legacy in the early nineteenth, made much use of scale passages, and any defects in the playing of these would be apparent. Nevertheless, the strengthening of weak fingers could lead to stiffness. Mechanical devices and dumb keyboards, with heavy "spring" touch, were used by pianists, sometimes with disastrous results. The fate of Schumann as a pianist is well-known.

The position of the performer at the keyboard was a matter of disagreement. Clementi made his pupils sit in the middle, Dussek to the left and Kalkbrenner to the right, because he thought that the performer would then be able to give more energy to the feeble trebles.

Clementi and his pupils practised with coins on the backs of their hands. Field, one of the pupils, handed on this method to his own students. In more recent times, Artur Schnabel stated that he learnt nothing more useful in piano playing than by this method. The pupil, successful in keeping the coin on his hand during his playing of a work, was sometimes rewarded with the coin! Dussek maintained that the hands should lean towards the thumb in order to give the shorter third and fourth fingers a better chance to play: conversely Hummel said that the hands should lean outwards in order that the thumb should reach the keys more easily. Kalkbrenner taught that the wrist should be loose in the playing of sixths and octaves, but Moscheles kept the forearm and wrist as motionless as possible. Fétis believed that the wrist should not be overworked, lest it become tired and this would inhibit all finger action. Hummel taught that the ends of the thumb and little finger should make a line parallel to the front of the keyboard. The elbows should be in advance of the body, and a line from the elbow to the second joint of the fingers should be horizontal. C. P. E. Bach insisted on the importance of carefully worked out fingering, and Dussek, with other teachers, carefully preserved "symmetrical" fingering, that is, similar fingering in both ascending and descending passages. This was to give way to less rigid methods.

Czerny, the pupil of Beethoven and the teacher of Liszt and Leschetizky, aimed at velocity, smoothness and brilliance, which, if it was not well considered, might lead to superficiality. Already we have noted the popularity of "singing on the piano" notable in the teaching and performance of many of the early nineteenth-century pianists. Thalberg wrote a method entitled, "The art of singing applied to the piano". Érard repetition action and its modifications, other actions of similar type, "tremolo" actions, which allowed the pianist, who had sufficient digital skill, to exploit various effects until then the exclusive property of violin players, were a mixed blessing. Superficial fantasias, ephemeral but able to dazzle, became very popular. Robert Schumann had warned his readers against this, and for many years his wife Clara nobly demonstrated a more worthy approach to the piano, with her restrained brilliance, her beautiful control of tone and dynamics and her scholarly insight into the nature of the finest piano music. Chopin, in contrast to Field, did not wish to force the player's hand to conform unnaturally to the keyboard. The weakness of certain fingers was used to advantage. His music is always pianistic, and suitable fingerings are usually apparent. Liszt, unique at the time as a projector of piano tone in all its varieties, and a concert pianist *par excellence*, adopted a higher seat in order to give himself a larger dynamic range. Nevertheless, with him beautiful tone was never sacrificed to power, although some of his pupils may have been at fault. It is generally believed that a high position of the wrist is inimical to good tone, because it restricts the free and sensitive movements of the fingers.

In a desire to secure beautiful legato tone, much finger changing on the same key was resorted to. Chopin was said "to change his fingers as often as an organ player". Brahms's exercises, to which reference has been made already, probably did much to produce a freer approach to the problem of fingering. As Brahms grew older his piano playing became more subtle and well graduated. The sturdy grand pianos of the late nineteenth century, with great sound output and "built like battleships", tempted some performers to sacrifice tone-quality to noise, and musical perception to prestidigitation. This was frequent, but there were voices, such as those of Saint-Saëns, Tchaikovsky and Sgambati, which were raised against the "piano beaters". Apart from Liszt, the most famous teachers of the pianoforte in the late nineteenth century and until the First World War were Deppe, Leschetizky and, in France, Philipp.

Miss Amy Fay, a spirited American young lady, left an account of the foremost piano teachers in Germany of the time of Liszt, and shamelessly went from one teacher to another.[1] She seems to have preferred Deppe to all others because of the manner in which he considered the individual needs of each of his students. Ludwig Deppe (1828–95) made a study of the muscular action of the fingers and arms, in minute detail. The player's position was rather lower than usual, and every movement of the fingers was carefully prepared. The low position forced the co-operation of the muscles of the upper arm, shoulder and back. The normal playing position of the hand was such that an india-rubber ball might be held in the palm. The third finger regulated the balance of the hand, and everything had to be unforced and calm. For staccato and octave playing the "arm should carry the hand", and he did not like the extreme lifting of the fingers. "Let the finger just fall. Do not strike the key. The notes will be inaudible at first but gain in power will come with practice. The fingers should be curved so that they play on the tips."

[1] Amy Fay, *Music Study in Germany*, New York and London, 1888. (New Edition, 1965.)

The hands are turned outwards with the knuckles of the third and fourth fingers higher than those of the first and second. The elbow should not be moved outwards but the turn should be made from the wrist. The thumb should be independent; the moment it contracts the whole hand is enfeebled. He began with the scale of E major. The finger end should be pivoted on the key and turned until the next finger is brought over its own key. The direction of the hand in running passages is always oblique. "In playing the scale you must gather your hand into a nut shell as it were, and play on the finger tips. In taking a chord, on the contrary, you must spread the hands as if you were going to ask for a blessing!" Deppe was one of the first teachers to give a systematic treatment to the pedal.

Deppe insisted that the eye and the ear were the true arbiters of good piano playing. The eye should be charmed by the gracefulness, economy and efficiency of the movements: the ear should constantly listen, analyse, criticise, and direct.

Until 1914, the best-known teacher of the piano in Europe was Theodor Leschetizky (1830–1915), a Pole who lived in Vienna. He was instructed by Czerny and inherited to some extent the Clementi and Beethoven tradition, but as a young man he heard Schulhoff playing in Vienna, and was at once attracted by his beautiful singing tone, his firm finger-tips and light wrist. Leschetizky, a superb pianist himself, taught some of the greatest exponents of the art. The end of the romantic period of piano playing was dominated by the pupils of Liszt and Leschetizky. Paderewski was the most famous product of the Leschetizky school and was its most effective advertisement, but there were better pianists from the same, such as Moiseiwitsch, Schnabel, Friedman, Gabrilowitsch, Fanny Bloomfield, Zeisler, to select a few from a large galaxy.[1]

Several books have been written concerning Leschetizky's "method", and it is amusing to find that they largely disagree with one another. He said: "I am personally against any fixed principle in instruction. Every pupil must, in my opinion, be treated differently according to circumstances. . . . My motto is that with a good, yes, a very good teacher, no printed method will be effective, and only he is a good teacher who can practically demonstrate every possibility to his pupils."[2]

Paderewski said: "The method of Leschetizky is very simple. His

[1] Harold C. Schonberg, *The Great Pianists*, New York, 1964.
[2] A letter dated June 6, 1915 (the year of his death), to Carl Stasny of the New England Conservatory of Music.

pupils learn to evoke a fine tone from the instrument and to make music not noise. There are principles that are uniformly inculcated in every pupil—that is, breadth, softness of touch and precision in rhythm. For the rest, every individual is treated according to the nature of his talent. In one word it is the method of methods."

And Schnabel said of his teaching: "It was a current which activated or released all the latent vitality in a student's nature. It was addressed to the imagination, to taste and to personal response. It was not a blueprint or a short-cut to success. It did not give the student a prescription but a task. What he arrived at was truthfulness of expression and he would not support any violation or deviation from what he felt to be true. He thought your ears were untrained or not talented if your tone was not adequate. To project music the technique employed has to be a technique which from the outset is used exclusively in the service of this projection."

Like Liszt, Leschetizky would say to his pupils who hurried their playing, "You do not know this well enough to play it slowly."

Leschetizky made a careful study of his pupils' hands and seems to have remembered these when he had forgotten their faces. He worked out by his insight and experience the best approach to the keyboard for each hand. He seems to have believed that for producing a beautiful tone the heavy and fat hand had a natural advantage, but for lightness and brilliance thin, supple hands like those of Liszt were best. He kept the hand rather low, a pliable wrist, curved fingers with firm tips and a light thumb. "There is no method for the wrist except to get the easiest way to the next note— every hand is different and everyone must decide his own fingering."[1]

Amy Fay gives an impression of the training in various German Conservatories about the year 1870. Of Tausig's Conservatory she says:

> First we had to go through Cramer, then through the 'Gradus ad Parnassum', then Moscheles, then Chopin, Henselt, Liszt and Rubinstein. . . . When I went to Kullak I studied Czerny's *Schule des Virtuosen*, which teaches you to play out your passages: you do not hurry or blur over the last notes but play clearly and in strict time to the end of the passage.

At the Stuttgart Conservatory the "Well-Tempered Clavichord" was made the foundation of everything. Bach strengthens the fingers and equalises them and gives an easy and eloquent execution. The Gradus trains the arm and wrist and gives a much more power-

[1] Ethel Newcombe, *Leschetizky as I Knew Him*, New York, 1919 and 1966.

ful execution. The Stuttgart system stressed execution, but Kullak tried to secure musical perception and insight.

Attempts, which would have been thought unnecessary by Chopin, to modify the keyboard in order to make it conform to the human anatomy were many and ingenious, but they failed to displace the arrangement which had persisted for centuries. Thus, it is not surprising that several important teachers of the instrument undertook detailed analyses of the anatomical and physiological processes which were involved in playing the pianoforte, and that there were many differences of opinion in these matters.

Tobias Matthay (1858–1946), a successful and revered teacher in England, produced a number of books on piano technique. In his book *The Act of Touch* he analysed touch into its elements and then reintegrated it. Obviously the artistic pianist could not have his performance constantly inhibited by conscious attention to these elements which by practice were absorbed into his technique. Matthay and R. M. Breithaupt[1] were known for their relaxation methods, which were adopted and used by some other leading pianists. Relaxation was sometimes misunderstood. Briefly, it meant the use of intelligent economy in the effort of sound production: it told of the evils of "key-bedding", for when the hammer has left the mechanism, no further pressure on the key can affect the tone; and if the note is to be held down it should be done with the minimum of effort to keep it down. Matthay insisted that his pupils should "play upon the strings" and "think through" to the actual source of the sound. Matthay considered the use of the leverage of fingers, hand, forearm and upper-arm, and thought of six methods of using the arm—poised, forearm rotation, forearm weight, whole arm weight, forearm down exertion and full weight and upper arm forward drive. He warned against the possibilities of bad tone in using forearm down exertion. "Understanding and mastery of rotation is usually the solution of most finger work troubles." Stiffness of the fingers and other parts of the body, used in playing the piano, was due to a "tug of war" of opposing muscles and could be resolved. Matthay preferred hard hammers in his pianos, for these would encourage the touch to become more sensitive. He would never permit his pupils to hit down a key or to attack the keyboard from a height. He realised that fortes are not absolute, but only relative to the accepted level in the particular circumstances of quiet playing. The decibel gain, from soft to loud,

[1] *Natural Pianoforte Technique*, Berlin and New York, 1912.

is that which is accepted by the ear, not the energy output of the fortissimo. Matthay realised that piano tone tends to lose its beauty if its dynamic level is too high.

Matthay's pupils number some of the most artistic players of the present. Matthay always made technique subservient to musicianship. His method was an obvious reaction against the German muscular and heavyweight techniques. The relaxation methods did not go unchallenged. Otto Ortmann, who had made a neuromuscular analysis of methods of manipulating the keys, wrote: "Undue stress on relaxation has seriously restricted velocity and technical brilliance."

In a recent work, Professor József Gát of Budapest, Hungary, has again considered the anatomical processes of touch in relation to piano mechanism, and synthesised the elements of touch in the performance of passages from the works of chief composers for the pianoforte. He has used high-speed cinema photography to show the action of the hands and fingers in "slow motion". He has suggested a number of physical exercises, away from the keyboard and not confined to the hands and arms, for assisting the performer.

Chopin affirmed that the correct use of the pedal was a life-long study and, later, Anton Rubinstein has said: "There are places where the pedal means everything—the longer I play, the more convinced I am that the pedal is the soul of the piano."

In Chapter IV we have noted the three possibilities of tone colouring by means of the sustaining pedal. Firstly, the rhythmic pedal, for a long time considered the normal way, in which the dampers are raised at the moment of striking a chord. Secondly, raising the dampers immediately after the chord has been played. This is known as syncopated pedalling, and was used after 1870 by Liszt, Kullak and Deppe. This is now considered to be the normal method. The pianoforte methods of Hans Schmidt and Köhler of 1875 mention syncopated pedalling; and in 1890, von Bülow, in his Beethoven edition, writes: "If the sound is to be clear, do not depress the pedal until after the chord has been struck."

Thirdly, the use of the pedal before the playing of the chord (the anticipated, acoustic or timbre pedal) gives a luminous glow to the sound. It can be used to compensate for dryness and deadness in upper notes. The tone becomes resonant, fuller but less defined. Even the resultant tones generated in the lower part of the compass from two or more upper notes are heard. Debussy makes use of the phenomenon in "La Cathédrale Engloutée". The anticipated pedal is sometimes used to make an easier attack, for then the fingers do not have to raise the dampers, for this has been done already by the foot. A well-known optical phenomenon is that a colour is modified by the nature of its background. Similarly, the tone colour of a melody may be modified by a "tonal wash" in the background accompaniment or even the accompanying voice. Tone-colour is not absolute and objective. The anticipated pedal may be used to supply "background washes of colour".

The pedal is susceptible to very refined treatment. A quickly reiterated, shallow movement of the pedal does not allow time for the melodic lines to become indefinite but will enliven and aerate the music. The use of the pedal must be modified to suit the type of pianoforte which is being used. Pedalling instructions given by composers and editors in the nineteenth century must be modified in relation to the modern piano with its longer sustaining power. The pedal must be considered in accordance with a composer's style and intentions, but here there is not always agreement between leading authorities. Gieseking would apply the pedal sparingly or not at all in playing Mozart. In Casello's edition of Mozart the pedal is hardly used at all:

> The pedal must consequently be treated with tremendous control and caution (especially in quick movements) with a view to improving the resonance of a chord or to exercising a legato which on many occasions cannot be managed by the hand. Above all, it is necessary to take special care with arpeggio passages. Mozart's arpeggios are always melodic in character, not harmonic. The ordinary "Alberti basses" in the left hand, too, must always be played without pedal, as they ought to sound as if they were being played by a clarinet or bassoon.

On the other hand Margit Varo wrote—"Even many ethereal melodies by Mozart will come into their own more graciously if we play the individual notes portata and with syncopated pedal. By means of this floating pedal, the melody notes, one after the other, will coalesce."

Several modern treatises have analysed many pianoforte compositions in terms of the pedal. They all agree that the pedal must never be used to try to cover poor finger technique, and that the ear must always be listening critically. Artistic pedalling demands more than attention to the bass and changes of harmony. Tone colour, dynamics, rhythm and both the vertical and linear aspects of the progression of the music must all be studied before an effective and artistic system of pedalling can be worked out. In addition to this, the sustaining power of the piano in different parts of the compass, the acoustical environment, and the type of projection of tone which is required in the circumstances of performance are all important. In broadcasting, a more sparing use of the pedal than in ordinary circumstances is usually satisfactory. Authors of works on piano playing mention the vagueness of some editors of pianoforte music, whose directions and symbols for the use of the pedal are misleading (c.f. Ernst Bacon, *Notes on the Piano*, p. 54).

The number of both introductory and advanced methods of playing the piano is legion, and the fact that they are extant is symptomatic of the enormous amount of piano-teaching which must be going on in the world. No doubt there are still a number of "best methods". In the final analysis there can be no general method. Each student must be considered as an individual. His hands, musculature and other physical attributes, his sensory and motor nervous systems and his reactions must be considered in relationship to his psychological traits—his intelligence, temperament, speed, quality and persistence of thinking, his general musicianship and insight, his aural acuity and his cultural background.

CHAPTER IX

SOME BYWAYS

Keyboards

The use of the semitone keys above the level of the naturals is credited to Guido d'Arezzo (990–1050), and it appears, in the present shape, in Praetorius's drawings of the Halberstadt keyboards of 1361. The present arrangement brings the scale within the stretch of the human hand. Chopin said that the size and arrangement of the black and white notes of the piano were so convenient that they might have been conceived in terms of the anatomy of the human hand. The hands of pianists vary from those of Harriet Cohen, who could hardly stretch an octave, to those of Rachmaninoff, who could encompass an eleventh with apparent ease.

The keyboard brings within reach of the fingers the resources of a large and complex sound producer. The piano keyboard has the possibility of a lateral movement of the hands of a total of four feet, a breadth away from or toward the player of a few inches and a vertical rise of sharp from natural of a part of an inch. Thus, it is not surprising that inventors have devised from time to time arrangements of keys which appeared to them to be more convenient or to offer greater facilities for technical achievements.

In 1882 Paul von Janko constructed a keyboard of six tiers, one above the other, and this was improved by Paul Perzina of Schwerin, Germany, so that there was a single leverage to each key. On this keyboard tenths and twelfths can be produced with extreme ease, the finger reaching up or down the range above or below the notes. Arpeggii through the whole compass of the keyboard can be given by a sweep of the wrist.

Quarter-tone pianofortes have been made by August Förster of Löbau, Germany. Actually, two pianofortes, differing in pitch by a quarter of a tone, were placed one over the other. Grotrian Steinweg of Brunswick also made a quarter-tone pianoforte. The firm described it in the following words: "In effect this instrument is really two ordinary pianofortes joined together, one of them being tuned a quarter of a tone higher than the other." Both pianofortes are played

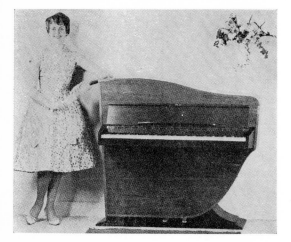

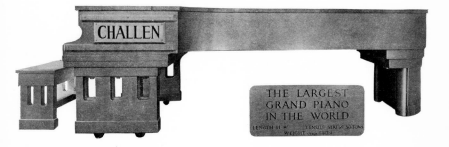

by means of one keyboard with three sets of keys, black, white and brown, the brown keys comprising the quarter-tone scale. This special keyboard contains twenty keys to the octave instead of the usual twelve. By an elaborate system of levers, it is possible to play in the ordinary way on the normal part of the pianoforte or on the quarter-tone part, or on both sections together, thus producing combinations of inexhaustible variety.

In the years after the First World War, the Bechstein firm collaborated with the physicist Nernst to produce the "neo-Bechstein". In this instrument the strings, which had little sound-board loading, would vibrate for a comparatively long period after striking. Their feeble tones were picked up by a number of microphones and the degree of amplification, obtained by electronic means, which was controlled by a pedal, could produce the effect of a crescendo on a note or chord. This device permitted a considerable prolonging of the sound, but the effect was foreign to that of the piano, where each note diminishes after striking. This may be a limitation to the scope of the piano but it is certainly not a defect.

Many other attempts have been made to modify the tone and keyboard of the piano. In spite of Chopin's complete satisfaction with the piano keyboard as he found it, attempts to modify it have been made from time to time. In 1780 Neuhaus, in Vienna, produced a concave keyboard so that, as he believed, the extreme bass and trebles could be played more conveniently. The added difficulties in making the keyboard and the problems of key leverage which it introduced, quite apart from the conservatism of manufacturers and players which has always been alleged, prevented its wide acceptance.

The Emanuel Moor duplex coupler piano had two identical keyboards, similar to those of a double manual harpsichord, immediately in contact with each other. Each white key of the lower keyboard had a raised portion at its back which rose to the level of the black keys and formed a convenient step in the upper keyboard. There was only one action and set of strings and, while the instrument could be played in the normal manner, octave and sub-octave coupling were readily accomplished.

The instrument was championed in Britain by Professor Donald Tovey of the University of Edinburgh, who felt that its wide acceptance had been inhibited because it had never been demonstrated widely or effectively. Nevertheless, the mechanical uniform addition of an octave to its note is far removed from the vitality and variety of tone which a good player can produce by varying the relative

N

dynamics, colour and even the timing of the two notes when he is playing both of them. Moreover, the device cannot produce the effective tremulando sounds which result from the rapid alternation of a note with its octave or sub-octave.

It seems that these new and ingenious devices did not become general because most pianists did not find them necessary. The great corpus of music which had developed over centuries, in terms of a keyboard which had changed little over the period, seemed to be more conveniently played with the traditional arrangement. The music had grown up in ecological relationship to the keyboard; and the traditions of composition, performance and keyboard were so intertwined that the inertia of the whole triune system resisted attempts to change it.

The Player Piano

Mechanically produced music has been known since the eighth century at least, when automatic organs blown and actuated by water power were known to the Arabian civilisation in Byzantium. Instruments of various kinds, including carillons, played by barrels, were popular in the seventeenth and eighteenth centuries. A slowly rotating barrel was pinned or pegged so that the projections, in turn, actuated the playing mechanism of the instrument. W. A. Mozart composed three excellent extended pieces for a small Viennese mechanical organ: Handel, Haydn and Beethoven and others of lesser stature composed pieces for mechanical instruments.

Sometimes the "dumb player" was so arranged that projections from the machine would fit the keys of the stringed instrument or small organ and thus play it directly. The player piano, actuated by a different mechanism, flourished at the end of the nineteenth century and in the twentieth, until it was ousted by the long-playing gramophone record and wireless receiver. Vertical holes or slits were cut in a roll of paper, and this unwound itself slowly over a tracker-bar behind the music-rest of the player piano. In the tracker-bar was a horizontal line of holes equal in number to the notes of the piano (or those which it was desired to play), and each of these holes was connected separately to a pneumatic exhaust mechanism, which worked the action of the corresponding note by means of a pneumatic motor. Pressure or exhaust wind was supplied by foot-bellows like those of an harmonium or American organ, and this wind also rotated the roll and unwound it at a fixed speed. If pressure wind was forced through the corresponding holes in the tracker-bar, the roll had to be enclosed in a glass-fronted chamber which would hold pressure wind. A suction (exhaust) mechanism was more popular because the roll did not need to be enclosed.[1]

Some little expression was possible by modifying the wind pressure at the treble or the bass, but at times this could be of more hindrance than help. The rolls could be cut by reference to the score without the aid of a keyboard or a pianist. Although this method had extraordinary vogue for several decades it was obviously incapable of subtle performances. For more than twenty-years, until after the First World War, the number of patents which related to player-piano mechanism was extraordinary. Improvements were made by using electricity both for "tracking" and, through the media of solenoids or magnets, actuating the mechanism. Remarkable progress was made when pneumatic, electro-pneumatic or electrical mechanism was devised so that a pianist could actually cut a roll (or make a paper-recording so that a roll could be cut by using this as a template) while in the act of playing. The Ampico, Welte-Mignon and, to a lesser extent, the Duo Art would actually reproduce on the player piano the performances of the virtuosi, with most of the nuances of their playing and all the wrong notes. With regard to the last, a certain amount of correction was feasible before the record was released. A few enthusiastic amateurs still use player pianos and collect sets of rolls. Historically, the player piano is useful because it enables us to assess the playing of some of the later virtuosi of the "golden age of piano-playing" in a manner which the early gramophone records do not permit. It is necessary to be certain that the rolls are played at the proper speed, for, unlike the gramophone, the pitch of the composition is not dependent on the speed of running the roll. Some pianists may seem to acquire speeds of performance which in fact they did not achieve![2]

Transposition Devices

Transposition devices in the pianoforte date from the beginning of the nineteenth century. There would have been no need for transposition before instruments were tuned to equal temperament, or, failing that, a temperament in which playing in all keys would be

[1] Ernst Simon, *Mechanische Musikinstrumente früherer Zeiten und ihre Musik*, Wiesbaden, 1960.
[2] Sidney Grew, *The Book of the Player Piano*, London, 1927.

tolerable. The transposing pianoforte was popular amongst less skilful pianists for accompanying voices, and wind instruments which have large pitch changes with changes of temperature. Transposing pianofortes are not often made today. The original transposing pianofortes by Edward Ryley had a movable keyboard which, on being shifted laterally, would engage with projections on the action. Érard invented a transposing pianoforte in which a wooden cylindrical sound-board was moved by four rollers so that strings of higher or lower pitch than those in the normal playing position would be struck by the respective hammers when the cylinder was moved. Instead of moving the keyboard, Woolley of Nottingham made a transposing piano in which the strings on their frame were moved laterally by means of a foot pedal, so that the hammers would then strike one, two or three semitones above or below the normal pitch as required.

Other modifications to the standard keyboard were suggested from time to time in the nineteenth century. Keyboards with narrow keys, which could be made to engage with the ordinary keyboard by means of splayed stickers, were devised, and were imagined to be suitable for children. There were even inventions which prevented the playing of wrong notes, in any particular key, but it is obvious that such devices would mean that the notes to be played would be confined to the scales of those keys without accidentals! It is hardly surprising that the idea was not widely accepted.

CHAPTER X

THE PIANOFORTE TODAY

In view of the enormous scope of the piano, which has been noted in the earlier part of this book, it must be confessed that not enough is done with it and for it in Britain. It ought to be the gateway to so much creative musical experience. For a time, more limited portable instruments such as the recorder and guitar may have tended to displace it, but really they should be regarded as being complementary to it and not in place of it. There is much private pianoforte teaching at a junior level going on in Britain, but apart from professional musicians, the harvest which this yields in adolescence and adulthood is still disappointing. Martin Cooper has spoken of an aristocracy, an élite of those who have been ennobled by contact with good music. Such a state of personal and social culture is more and more necessary in the climate of increasing technological progress, which at the best produces a means to, but not an end in, a way of rich living, and at the worst a spiritual vacuum and a death of mind and spirit. Passive enjoyment of the arts is not enough. Real, creative contact with great art, even at a level of modest technical achievement, which can be secured, for example, in playing the piano, is necessary. No more satisfying indoor hobby can be imagined. The co-ordination of muscles, ears and eyes, thereby cultivated, tends to physical stability and the joy which results from the effective use of the human body. The absorption of the mind in music fortifies, stabilises and enriches the human personality.

If the fruit which is yielded by so much music teaching in and out of school is much less than it should be, it is useful to enquire into the reasons for this, which will be considered as far as the pianoforte is concerned only. In doing this we recognise the importance of other forms of musical activity, outside the scope of this book.

Because of the nature of the organisation of official education in Britain, there is still a tendency to regard music as a subject of much less importance than mathematics, languages and the sciences, and one to be dropped when the stresses of school examination preparation become demanding. Until educators of all types, parents, and our society in general, believe in and understand the importance of music, as a part of the fabric of living, it will be pushed into a secondary position in our education. We need many more good teachers who are also good musicians, and musicians who are good teachers. The popularity and incalculable value of the teaching of the piano in class and Sidney Harrison's television lessons (in all of which the acquisition of keyboard technique goes hand in hand with an improvement of general musicianship) indicate what might be done if there were a greater availability of such resources. Facilities are still too few, and there are not enough teachers who can present the matter enthusiastically and adventurously to the young.

There are some aspects of school music teaching which may be a matter of opinion, but it could be asked whether too much of the already limited time which is spent on it is devoted to what is known as "musical appreciation", which, aided and abetted by out-of-date examination bodies, often involves the soulless dissection of masterpieces, bar by bar. This has even less validity in the flesh and blood of great music and its human implications, than the revelations made by the scalpel on the anatomist's table, for the living human organism with its inexhaustible variety and richness. Not only have the superb achievements of the great composers, writers and visual artists suffered by this analytical method, often applied unintelligently, but many young mathematicians and scientists have had their minds closed, their spontaneous thought stifled and their initial interest destroyed in a similar manner. When analysis is necessary, it must be complementary to synthesis, to creative and divergent activities and a vision, even an imperfect one, of the whole. The true road to musical appreciation, if there is such a subject, is through creation or re-creation as composer, singer and performer on an instrument.

This leads to a matter of paramount importance. Teachers of the piano are constantly pointing out the extent of the harm which is done by a bad instrument. It is obvious that many professional pianists nobly try to do their best with inferior pianos, but they cannot achieve what is impossible with instruments which have a bad tone and inferior or worn action. It should be apparent that poor pianos, both in school and in the home, will kill enthusiasm in all but the most ardent pupil, and even here will ruin the sensitivity of touch and hearing habits which are essential to good performance.

Not only should the piano be in tune, but it should be regulated in evenness both of touch and tone. The young pianist should be conscious that the instrument can produce a beautiful sound and that this is produced economically; in other words, that the mechanism is sensitive to gradations of touch and gives a good return in sound for the energy which is imparted to the key. It is bad pedagogy to think that an indifferent piano is good enough for a learner. The cost of good pianos and their adequate maintenance is not great in comparison with that of other teaching media, laboratories, gymnasia and craft workshops. Pianos are not of less importance!

All the factors of piano tone and mechanism which have been noted in this book should be kept in mind when the pupil's instrument is considered. Pianos do not mature like violins, and defective pianos should be replaced by good instruments. Noisy, loose keys which need rebushing, hammers and jacks with loose centres, hammers which need re-covering, loose covered strings, springs which are broken and fatigued, damp, dirt and rust, cracked soundboards and wrest-planks and loose pins which render tuning impossible are some of the defects which should not be tolerated in any instrument used for teaching or the performance of legitimate piano music. The supply of pianoforte tuners is not adequate in England; that of pianoforte technicians capable of maintaining and adjusting the mechanism is even less. The piano should be accorded the respect and care which is shown not only to a pleasing article of furniture but to a subtle mechanism and an elegant instrument.

Although damp is the enemy of the structure and mechanism of the piano, a very dry, warm atmosphere, such as is provided by modern space-heating, will do more damage and do this more quickly. Wood which has been stored and worked at a relative humidity of sixty to seventy per cent will shrink, twist and split if it is subjected to a much drier atmosphere. A cool temperature, in an atmosphere which is neither dehydrated nor saturated, is necessary. The state of tuning of a piano is not much affected by moderate changes of temperature but changes of humidity upset its pitch. Many first-class instruments have been irretrievably ruined by modern "central heating". It is a matter of pride and hygiene that the case and keyboard are kept clean, unmarked and polished. Where there is any tendency for infestation with moths, woodbeetles and even mice, care and regular inspection of the interior of the instrument are necessary. The dust and grit common in many places will create trouble both inside and on the outside of the piano.

Pianofortes are made in many sizes, and the smaller examples are readily moved. Research work is constantly going on, and remarkable improvements have been made both to the tone and mechanism of small pianofortes. Thus, even in small rooms a pianoforte may find a place. Makers have advertised their small pianos as having a large tone. This is not always required. It should not be beyond the skill of the maker to produce an instrument with a bright, satisfying tone at a smaller dynamic level. It is not necessary to produce a powerful fundamental tone in order to give the aural impression of vitality, majesty and power. A good harmonic development in the tones will produce this in a more artistic and less exhausting manner than an obese ground tone. The excessive toning of the felt of the hammers of a piano, by softening it with needles in an attempt to reduce the sound of the instrument, spoils the hammer-coverings permanently and produces a dull, indefinite tone quality which is not only unpleasant but gives a feeling of wastage of energy in the performer. Very small horizontal pianos, "grand" only in name, may have bass strings which are shorter than those of an ingeniously over-strung small upright. With such miniature grands there is a lack of satisfying, musical tone in the bass.

Although individual study of the instrument as a matter of personal reaction between pupil and teacher must take place, acquaintance with the keyboard and a study of musical scales and other rudiments can be undertaken in class. The class teaching of the pianoforte may take several forms. The members of the class each have a dummy keyboard, or a "solid keyboard" made of plastic material with raised sharps, and a chart above the keyboard which relates each keyboard note with one on the treble or bass clef. The pupils take turns at the real piano. A refinement of this method, which is more expensive, is to have each keyboard connected via a switchboard, which is controlled by the teacher, to an "electric piano" or electronic organ. The teacher can "switch in" to the sound-producer, the playing of a particular pupil at any time, by means of a switchboard. Moreover, he has a keyboard of his own for purposes of demonstration. It is true that the subtleties of pianoforte touch cannot be taught by this method, but it will produce a useful first acquaintance with a keyboard, and the relation of its notes to those printed for performance on the piano. A useful co-ordination of eye, ear and hands should result, also.

It seems probable, since healthy human beings demand constant activity, that, in the long run, television may contribute to the wider

Plate thirty-one

a. The influence of the piano keyboard (Hohner)

b. Keyboard lessons in class in Germany

playing of the piano. Good camera-work enables the listener to see the work of the skilled performer at close quarters, and this would be difficult or impossible in the concert room. Mr. Sidney Harrison, in England, and other inspiring teachers in Europe, America and Japan have given very successful series of television lessons on the groundwork of pianoforte playing. The subsequent work undertaken by pupils of all ages, has been of great value to the cause of the pianoforte and pianoforte playing. Such courses should be available at frequent intervals on any "college of the air".

Children should be encouraged to respect and love instruments of music as amongst the noblest products of the craftsman. The skilled technicians, often single-minded artists in their own way, who maintain musical instruments, should be accorded the respect and remuneration due to those who practise a skilled profession. Because of the ever-presence of the noises of civilisation, the loudspeaker and degraded popular music, the failure of some teachers to develop in their pupils a critical ear or because of a reaction against romanticism, the beauty of tone of a musical instrument is often overlooked. If children are introduced to the piano with good touch and tone in school, many will wish to continue making music at the keyboard of a good instrument at home.

Today throughout the world there are more competent as well as brilliant keyboard players than at any time in history. The popularity of the pianoforte in central Europe is well known, as is the phenomenal increase in the interest of the Japanese in the instrument, the number of instruments made each year by modern production methods, and the enormous amount of piano-teaching, particularly in class, which takes place in that country. A few other examples taken at random from musical journals at the time of writing this book may be indicative. The Czechoslovak firm of Petrof announced the completion of its 100,000th piano in 1963. In America there are 14 million amateur keyboard players. Half of the ten million children who are learning to play a musical instrument in the U.S.A. play the piano. In Britain 180,000 musical examinations at all grades take place each year, and of these 150,000 concern the piano.[1] The manufacture of new pianos in England was nearly 16,000 in 1969, of which half were exported. American manufacture amounts to about 210,000 each year. It is true that in absolute numbers there is a considerable shrinking in the western

[1] These figures are taken from 1969 issues of *Das Musikinstrument*, Frankfurt, W. Germany.

world since the days before the First World War. In North London alone, at this time, there were a hundred and fifty separate establishments of manufacturers. If numbers of instruments are less, they find more serious users. Scientific research and materials and methods of manufacture have improved the products of the best establishments.

New "centres", which are resistant to atmospheric changes, and frictionless and durable, are now used in the action; plastic bonding materials have replaced glue; woods have been subjected to research to find optimum acoustic properties; non-tarnishing and rustproof metals are available to manufacturers. Constant progress in manufacture is made. Jacks and flanges can now be made from nylon, which is resistant to damp and can be machined with precision. Polytetrafluorine, a synthetic, anti-friction material, can be applied to the action bushings of the piano, where it ensures ease of movement and prevents wear. Wood can be sealed against humidity changes.

It is entirely wrong to suppose that the influence and use of the piano are waning. It is true that it is no longer a status symbol in the drawing-room and that small and cheap stringed and wind instruments, which are readily portable, have become enormously popular. Further, it must be admitted that high-quality performances, multiplied millions of times by television, sound-broadcasting and gramophone records may, for a period of time, tend to produce a passive attitude. Nevertheless, intelligent and active human beings will not be satisfied by such a condition, and sooner or later will be stimulated to try to make music for themselves. There is still much scope for composers and arrangers. New pianoforte sounds still await to be discovered. The beautiful effects of the evanescent piano tone against sustaining instruments, as in concerti and sonatas for piano and other instruments, are well known.

Although duet-playing is important and delightful, "three-hand" playing, as an alternative, has a clarity and simplicity of approach for the pupil which is refreshing. The tonic effect on both mind and body of being able to play the piano, even at a humble level in the home, cannot be over-estimated. Many of the physical and mental ills of the present are due to a passive, non-creative attitude to life which is completely contrary to the nature of a human being. The piano offers an ivory portal to an inexhaustible treasure-house whose riches will never fail to satisfy.

APPENDIX

THE CHIEF CLAVICHORD AND HARPSICHORD COMPOSERS

England and the Netherlands

Thomas Tallis 1505–85
William Byrd 1543–1623
Thomas Morley 1557–1603
Peter Philips 1560–1633
Jan Pieterszoon Sweelinck 1562–1621
John Bull 1563–1628
Giles Farnaby 1565–98
Orlando Gibbons 1583–1625
Matthew Locke 1632–77
John Blow 1648–1708
Henry Purcell 1658–95
Thomas Arne 1710–78

France

André de Chambonnières 1602–72
Jean Henri d'Anglebert 1628–91
Antoine le Bègue 1630–1702
François Couperin 1668–1733
Louis Marchand 1669–1732
Jean Philippe Rameau 1683–1764
Jean François Dandrieu 1684–1740
Claude Daquin 1694–1772

Germany

Konrad Paumann 1410–73
Elias Nikolas Ammerbach 1530–97
Hans Leo Hassler 1564–1612
Heinrich Schütz 1585–1672
Samuel Scheidt 1587–1654
Johann Jakob Froberger 1616–67
Johann Adam Reinken 1623–1722
Johann Kaspar Kerl 1627–93

Johann Dietrich Buxtehude 1637–1707
Georg Muffat 1645–1704
Johann Kaspar Fischer 1605–1746
Johann Krieger 1651–1735
Johann Pachelbel 1653–1706
Johann Kuhnau 1660–1722
Georg Böhm 1661–1733
Franz Xaver Murschhauser 1663–1738
Johann Mattheson 1681–1764
Georg Philipp Telemann 1681–1767
Georg Friedrich Handel 1685–1759
Johann Sebastian Bach 1685–1750
Gottlieb Muffat 1690–1770
Philipp Emanuel Bach 1714–88
Friedrich Wilhelm Marpurg 1718–95

Italy

Adrian Willaert 1490–1562
Jacques Buus d 1565
Andrea Gabrieli 1510–86
Claudio Merulo 1533–1604
Luzzasco Luzzaschi 1545–1607
Giovanni Gabrieli 1557–1612
Adriano Banchieri 1567–1634
Girolamo Frescobaldi 1583–1643
Bernardo Pasquini 1637–1710
Francesco Durante 1684–1756
Domenico Scarlatti 1685–1757
Nicolo Antonio Porpora 1686–1766
Giovanni Battista Martini 1706–84
Baldassare Galuppi 1706–85
Pietro Domenico Paradisi 1710–92

THE CHIEF COMPOSERS OF PIANOFORTE MUSIC

A century of development
Carl Philipp Emanuel Bach
(1714–1788)
Franz Joseph Haydn (1732–1809)
Muzio Clementi (1752–1832)
Wolfgang Amadeus Mozart
(1756–1791)
Jan Ladislav Dussek (1761–1812)
Ludwig van Beethoven (1770–1827)
Johann Baptist Cramer (1771–1858)
Johann Nepomuk Hummel
(1778–1837)
John Field (1782–1837)
Carl Maria von Weber (1786–1820)
Carl Czerny (1791–1857)
Ignaz Moscheles (1794–1870)
Franz Schubert (1797–1828)
Felix Mendelssohn (Bartholdy)
(1809–1847)
Frédéric François Chopin
(1810–1849)
Robert Schumann (1810–1856)
Franz Liszt (1811–1886)
Charles V. Alkan (Morhange)
(1813–1888)
Johannes Brahms (1833–1897)

French Composers
César Auguste Franck (1822–1890)
Camille Saint-Saëns (1835–1921)
Emmanuel Chabrier (1841–1894)
Gabriel Fauré (1845–1924)
Claude Achille Debussy (1862–1918)
Maurice Ravel (1875–1937)
Francis Poulenc (1899–1966)
Oliver Messiaen (1908–)

Russian Composers
Anton Rubinstein (1830–1894)
César Cui (1835–1918)
Mili Balakirev (1837–1910)
Modest Mussorgsky (1839–1881)
Peter Ilich Tchaikovsky (1840–1893)
Anton Arensky (1861–1906)

Alexander Scriabin (1872–1915)
Sergei Rachmaninoff (1873–1943)
Serge Prokofiev (1891–1960)
Dmitri Shostakovich (1906–)
Nicholas Medtner (1879–1951)
Igor Stravinsky (1882–)
Alexander Tcherepnin (1899–)
Aram Khatchaturian (1903–)

Polish Composers
Xaver Scharwenka (1850–1924)
Moritz Moszkowski (1854–1925)
Karol Szymanowski (1883–1937)
Ignace Jan Paderewski (1860–1941)

Hungarian Composers
Stephen Heller (1813–1888)
Béla Bartók (1881–1945)
Ernst von Dohnányi (1877–1967)
Zoltan Kodaly (1882–1966)

Bohemian Composers
Bedrich Smetana (1824–1884)
Antonin Dvořák (1841–1904)

Scandinavian Composers
Edvard Grieg (1843–1907)
Niels Gade (1817–1890)
Selim Palmgren (1878–1951)
Christian Sinding (1856–1918)

U.S.A. Composers
Edward MacDowell (1861–1908)
Daniel Gregory Mason (1873–1953)
Charles E. Ives (1874–1954)
Charles T. Griffes (1884–1920)
George Gershwin (1898–1937)
Aaron Copland (1900–)
Abram Chasins (1903–)

German School
Adolf Jensen (1837–1879)
Joachim Raff (1822–1882)
Adolf Henselt (1814–1889)

Max Reger   (1873–1916)
Eugen d'Albert   (1864–1932)
Arnold Schönberg   (1874–1951)
Paul Hindemith   (1895–1963)

Spanish Composers
Isaac Albeniz   (1860–1909)
Enriques Granados   (1867–1916)
Manuel de Falla   (1876–1946)
Joaquin Turina   (1882–1949)

British Composers
William Sterndale Bennett
   (1816–1875)
Balfour Gardiner   (1887–1950)
Cyril Scott   (1879–   )

Arnold Bax   (1883–1953)
John Ireland   (1879–1967)
Arthur Bliss   (1891–   )
Herbert Howells   (1892–   )
Howard Ferguson   (1908–   )
Alan Rawsthorne   (1905–   )
Michael Tippett   (1905–   )

Italian Composers
Giovanni Sgambati   (1841–1914)
Ferrucio Busoni   (1866–1924)
Ottorino Respighi   (1879–1936)
Alfredo Casella   (1883–1947)
This list excludes many hundreds of
minor composers who wrote much,
and some major composers who wrote
little pianoforte music.

BIBLIOGRAPHY

Pianoforte Construction and Maintenance

BLÜTHNER, J. and GRETSCHEL, H., *Der Pianofortebau* (Leipzig, 1872, 1909).

British Standards 3499.4A, *Pianofortes* (London, 1967).

DIETZ, R., *The Regulation of the Steinway Grand Action* (Frankfurt, 1964)

FEASTER, C. R., *The Dynamic Scale and How to Tune It* (Frankfurt, 1960).

FENNER, K., *Determination of Piano String Tensions* (Frankfurt, 1959).

FISCHER, J. C., *Pianoforte Tuning, Regulating and Repairing* (Philadelphia, 1907).

FUNKE, O., *The Piano and How to Care for it* (Frankfurt, 1962).

GOEBEL, J., *Grundzüge des modernen Klavierbaus* (Frankfurt, 1960).

HAUTRIVE, G. M., *La Facture du Piano* (Brussels, 1939).

HOWE, A. H., *Scientific Piano Tuning and Servicing*, 3rd ed., (New York, 1955).

Institute of Musical Instrument Technology, *Occasional Papers* (London, 1934–1965).

JANKO, P. Von, *Eine neue Klaviatur* (Vienna, 1886).

JUNGHANNS, Herbert, *Der Piano und Flügelbau*.

MICHEL, N. E., *Michel's Piano Atlas* (U.S.A., 1953).

Musical Opinion (Publication), "Repairing the Pianoforte" (London, n.d., c. 1925).

NALDER, L. M., *The Modern Piano* (London, 1927).

NALDER, L. M., *Essays in Pianoforte Technology* (London, 1927).

NORTON, E. Q., *Construction, Tuning and Care of the Piano* (5th ed., New York, 1892).

PFEIFFER, W., *Vom Hammer* (Frankfurt, 1963).

PFEIFFER, W., *Über Dampfer, Federn und Spielart* (Frankfurt, 1963).

STEINWAY, *The Steinway Grand Action* (New York, 1950).

STEINWAY, *The Steinway Upright Action* (New York, 1950).

WHITE, William Braid, *Piano Tuning and Allied Arts* (Boston, U.S.A., 1953).

WOLFENDEN, J., *The Art of Pianoforte Construction* (London, 1924).

The History of Keyboard Instruments

ADLUNG, J., *Musica Mechanica Organoedi* (Berlin, 1768; facsimile ed. C. Mahrenholz, Kassel, 1931).

BIE, O., *Klavier, Orgel und Harmonium* (Leipzig, 1910).

BIE, O., *A History of the Pianoforte and Pianoforte Players* (Leipzig, 1899, New York, 1966).

BEIJNUM, B. van, *Bouw en Geschiedenis van het Klavier* (Rotterdam, 1932).

BOALCH, D. H., *Makers of the Harpsichord and Clavichord to 1840* (London, 1956).

BRINSMEAD, E., *The History of the Pianoforte* (London, 1889).

CASELLA, A., *Il pianoforte* (Rome and Milan, 1937).

CLOSSON, E., *Histoire du piano* (Brussels, 1944).

DALE, W., *Schudi, the Harpsichord Maker* (London, 1913).

DOLGE, A., *Pianos and their Makers* (Covina, Cal., U.S.A., 1911).

DUFOURCQ, N., *Le claveçin* (Paris, 1949).

FISCHHOF, J., *Versuch einer Geschichte des Clavierbaues* (Vienna, 1851).

GOUGH, H., "The Classical Grand Pianoforte 1770–1830", *Proc. Royal Mus. Ass.* (1952).

HARDING, R. E. M., *The Pianoforte* (Cambridge, 1933).

HARICH-SCHNEIDER, E., *The Harpsichord* (London 1960).

HIPKINS, A. J., *A Description and History of the Pianoforte and the Older Keyboard Stringed Instruments* (London, 1896).

HIRT, F. J., *Meisterwerke des Klavierbaus* (Olten, 1955).

JAMES, P., *Early keyboard instruments* (London, 1930).

JUNGHANNS, H., *Der Piano und Flügelbau* (Leipzig, 1932).

KENYON, M., *Harpsichord Music: A Survey of the Virginals, Spinet and Harpsichord* (London, 1949).

KINSKY, G., *Katalog des musikhistorischen Museums vom Wilhelm Heyer* (Cologne, 1910).

KREBS, K., "*Die besaiteten Klavierinstrumente bis zum Anfang des 17. Jahrhunderts*", *Vierteljahrschrift für Musikwissenschaft*, vol. VIII (1892).

KROPP, E. A., *Das Zupfklavier* (Berlin diss., 1925).

KULLAK, A., and NIEMANN, W., *Aesthetik des Klavierspiels* (Berlin, 1905).

LÖSSER, A., *Men, Women and Pianos* (New York, 1954).

MARMONTEL, A., *Histoire du Piano* (Paris, 1885).

NEUPERT, H., *Vom Musikstab zum modernen Klavier* (Bamberg, 1926).

NEUPERT, H., *Harpsichord Manual* (Kassel, New York, London, 1960).

NEUPERT, H., *Das Klavichord, Geschichte und technische Betrachtung des "eigentlichen Claviers"* (Kassel, 1948).

NORLIND, T., *Systematik der Saiten instrumente* (2 vols., Hannover, 1936–1939).

PAUL, O., *Geschichte des Claviers* (Leipzig, 1868).

PONSICCHI, C., *Il pianoforte, sua origine e sviluppo* (Florence, 1876).

PONSICCHI, C., *Il primo pianoforte verticale* (Florence, 1898).

PRAETORIUS, M., *Syntagma musicum*, vol. II (Wolfenbüttel, 1618–1620; facsimile ed. W. Gurlitt, Kassel, 1929).

RAPIN, E., *Histoire du Piano et des Pianistes* (Lausanne, 1904).

RIMBAULT, E. F., *The Pianoforte: its Origin, Progress and Construction* (London, 1860).

RUSSELL, R., *The Harpsichord and Clavichord* (London, 1959).

RUSSELL, R., *Victoria and Albert Museum. Catalogue of Musical Instruments* (London, 1969).

SCHAFHAUTL, K. F. E., *Die Pianofortebaukunst der Deutschen* (Munich, 1855).

SACHS, C. R., *Reallexikon der Musikinstrumente* (Berlin, 1913).

SACHS, C., *Handbuch der Musikinstrumentenkunde* (Leipzig, 1920).

SACHS, C., *Das Klavier* (Berlin, 1923).

SCHMITZ, E., *Klavier, Klaviermusik und Klavierspiel* (Leipzig, 1919).

SEIFFERT, M., *Geschichte des Klavierspiels* (Leipzig, 1879).

SEIFFERT, M., *Geschichte der Klaviermusik* (Leipzig, 1899).

SPILLANE, D., *History of the American Pianoforte* (New York, 1890).

STEINWAY, Th., *People and Pianos* (New York, 1953).

VIRDUNG, S., *Musica getutscht und ausgezogen* (Basel, 1511; facsimile Bärenreiter Verlag).

WÖRSCHING, J., *Die historischen Saitenklaviere* (Mainz, 1946).

The Technique of Piano-playing

BARDAS, W., *Zur Psychologie der Klaviertechnik* (Berlin, 1927).

BOWEN, YORK *Pedalling the Modern Pianoforte* (London, 1936).

BREE, M., *Bas de la Méthode Leschetizky* (Paris, 1902); trans., *The Groundwork of the Leschetizky Method* (New York, 1902).

BREITHAUPT, R. M., *Die natürliche Klaviertechnik* (Leipzig, 1912).

CHING, J., *Piano Technique: Foundation Principles* (London, 1948).

CHING, J., *Piano Playing: A Practical Method* (London, 1950).

CORTOT, A., (trans. Jacques), *The Rational Principles of Pianoforte Technique* (New York, 1940).

DICHLER, J., *Der Weg zum Künsterischen Klavierspiel* (Vienna, 1948).

FIELDEN, T., *The Science of Pianoforte Technique* (London, 1949).

FOLDES, A., *Keys to the Keyboard* (New York, 1948).

GÁT, J., *Technique of Piano Playing* (Budapest, 1961).

JAELL, M., *Le Mécanisme du toucher. L'étude du piano par l'analyse expérimental de la sensibilité tactile* (Paris, 1936).

KOCHEVITSKY, G., *The Art of Pianoforte Playing* (New York, 1968).

KREUTZER, L., *Das Wesen der Klaviertechnik* (Berlin, 1923).

KREUTZER, L., *Das normale Klavierpedal* (Leipzig, 1928).

LEIMER, K., *Rhythmic, Dynamik Pedal nach Leimer–Gieseking* (Mainz, 1938).

LEIMER and GIESEKING, *The Shortest Way to Pianistic Perfection* (London, 1930).

LEVINSKAYA, M., *The Levinskaya System of Pianoforte Technique* (London, 1930).

MARTIENSSEN, C. A., *Die individuelle Klaviertechnik auf der Grundlage des schöpferischen Klangwillens* (Leipzig, 1930).

MATTHAY, Tobias, *The Act of Touch* (London, 1924).

MATTHAY, Tobias, *The Visible and Invisible in Piano Technique* (new ed., Oxford, 1962).

ORTMANN, O., *Physiological Mechanics of Piano Technique* (London and New York, 1937).

PHILLIP, I., *Le Piano et la virtuosité* (Paris, 1926).

PHILLIP, I., *Réflexions sur l'art du piano* (Paris, 1927).

PHILLIP, I., *Quelques considérations sur l'enseignement du piano* (Paris, 1927).

RIEFLING, R. (trans. K. Dale), *Pianoforte Pedalling* (London, 1962).

ROES, P., *Essai sur la technique du piano* (Paris, 1935).

ROES, P., *La Technique fulgurante de Busoni* (Paris, 1935).

ROES, P., *L'Elément fondamental de la technique du jeu chez Liszt et Chopin* (Paris, 1939).

SCHMITZ, E. R., *The Capture of Inspiration* (New York, 1948).

STEINHAUSEN, W., *Les Erreurs physiologiques et la transformation moderne du piano* (Paris, 1914).

WOODHOUSE, G., *The Artist at the Piano* (London, 1925).

WOODHOUSE, G., *Creative Technique* (London, 1930).

WHITEMORE, C., *Commonsense in Pianoforte Technique* (London, 1948).

Teaching and Learning the Piano

BOLTON, H., *On Teaching the Piano* (London, 1954).
BOLTON, H., *How to Practise* (London, 1952).
D'ABREU, *Playing the Piano with Confidence* (London, 1962).
EVERHART, P., *The Pianists' Art* (Atlanta, 1958).
FERGUSON, D., *Piano Interpretation* (London, 1955).
FOWLES, E., *Centre Points in Pianoforte Study* (London, 1935).
HARRISON, S., *Beginning to Play the Piano* (London, 1950).
HARRISON, S., *Piano Method* (2 vols.) (London, 1960).
HARRISON, S., *Piano Technique* (London, 1953).
KIRKBY-MASON, B., *Modern Piano Course* (London, 1960).
LAST, J., *The Young Pianist* (London, 1960).
LAST, J., *Interpretation for the Piano Student* (London, 1960).
LOWE, G. Egerton, *Pianoforte Practising* (London, 1951).
MERRICK, F., *Practising the Piano* (London, 1960).
MOORE, G., *The Unashamed Accompanist* (London, 1958).
REEVES, B., *Approach to Piano Teaching* (London, 1950).
RUBINSTEIN, A., *Outline of Piano Pedagogy* (New York, 1929).
TOBIN, R., *How to Improvise Piano Accompaniments* (London, 1956).
WATERMAN, F., and HAREWOOD, M., *First Year Piano Lessons* (London, 1967).

The Music Teacher (Evans Bros.), monthly, deals with the problems of the music teacher, particularly the piano teacher.

Miscellaneous Works

BACON, E., *Notes on the Piano* (Syracuse, N.Y., 1963).
BLOM, E., *The Romance of the Piano* (London, 1928).
BRIGGS, G. A., *Pianos, Pianists and Sonics* (Bradford, 1951).
CLUTTON, C., Section in *Musical Instruments through the Ages* (*Pianoforte*) (London, 1962).
DART, T., Section in *Musical Instruments through the Ages* (*Clavichord*) (London, 1962).
FAY, A., *Music Study in Germany* (London, 1886. New edition 1965).
GOTTSCHALK, L. M., *Notes of a Pianist* (New York, 1964).
HAMBOURG, M., *The Eighth Octave* (London, 1951).
HAACKE, W., *Am Klavier* (Konigstein, 1969).
JEANS, J., *Science and Music* (Cambridge, 1937).
LOCARD, P., *Le Piano* (Paris, 1948).
RENNER, L., *75 Jahre Louis Renner* (Stuttgart, 1965).
SCHNABEL, A., *My Life and Music* (New York, 1960).

SCOTT, C., *My Years of Indiscretion* (London, 1924).

Pianists and Composers of Pianoforte Music

APEL, W., *Masters of the Keyboard* (Cambridge, Mass., 1947).
BROOK, D., *Masters of the Keyboard* (London, 1946).
CHASE, G., *The Music of Spain* (New York, 1959).
CHASINS, A., *Speaking of Pianists* (New York, 1953).
COOPER, M., *French Music from the Death of Berlioz to the Death of Fauré* (London, 1951, 1961).
CORTOT, A., *La Musique française de Piano* (Paris, 1930).
DALE, K., *Nineteenth-century Piano Music* (Oxford U.P., 1954).
DEMUTH, N., *French Piano Music* (London, 1961).
EHRLICH, A., *Celebrated Pianists of the Past and Present* (New York, 1895).
FILLMORE, J. C., *History of Pianoforte Music* (London, 1885).
FRISKIN and FREUNDLICH, *Music for the Piano* (New York, 1954).
HUTCHESON, E., *The Literature of the Piano* (reprint, London, 1958).
KIRBY, F. E., *A History of Keyboard Music* (London, 1965).
KREHBIEL, H. E., *Pianoforte and its Music* (London, 1911).
MODENHAUER, H., *Duo-Pianism (Two-piano Music)* (Chicago, 1950).
RUTHARDT, A., *Wegweiser durch die Klavierliteratur* (10th Ed. Zürich, 1925).
SCHÖNBERG, Harold C., *The Great Pianists* (London, 1964).
TEICHMULLER, R., and HERMANN, K., *Internationale Moderne Klaviermusik* (Leipzig, 1927).
WEITZMANN, C. F., *History of Pianoforte Playing and Pianoforte Literature* (London, 1897).
WESTERBY, H., *History of Pianoforte Music* (London, 1924).

Bach, J. S. and C. P. E.

BACH, C. P. E. (ed. Mitchell), *Essay on the True Art of Playing Keyboard Instruments* (London, 1949).
BODKY, E., *The Interpretation of Bach's Keyboard Works* (Cambridge, Mass., 1960).
DAVID and MENDEL, *The Bach Reader* (London, 1945).
DAVID, J. N., *Die dreistimmigen Inventionen von J. S. Bach* (Göttingen, 1959).
DAVID, J. N., *Das Wohltemperierte Klavier* (Göttingen, 1962).

EMERY, W., *Bach's Ornaments* (London, 1953).

ERNST, F., *Bach und das Pianoforte* (Frankfurt, 1962).

ERNST, F., *Der Flügel Johann Sebastian Bachs* (Frankfurt, 1964).

KELLER, H., *Die Klavierwerke Bachs* (Leipzig, 1950).

SCHWEITZER, A. (trans. Newman), *J. S. Bach* (2 vols., London, 1947).

SPITTA, P., *Johann Sebastian Bach* (3 vols., London, 1952).

TERRY, C. S., *The Music of Bach. An Introduction* (London 1933).

Mozart

BADURA SKODA, Paul, *Interpreting Mozart at the Keyboard* (trans., London, 1961).

BRUNNER, Hans, *Das Klavierklangideal Mozarts and die Klaviere seiner Zeit* (Augsburg, 1933).
Some of Brunner's conclusions were disputed in an article by Rudolf Steglich: "Studien an Mozarts Hammerflugel" in *Neues Mozart Jahrbuch* (1941).

EINSTEIN, A., *Mozart* (London, 1944).

FRANZ, Gottfried, von "Mozarts Klavierbauer Anton Walter" in *Neues Mozart Jahrbuch* (1941).

GIRDLESTONE, C. M., *Mozart and his Piano Concertos* (Paris, 1939; trans., London, 1950).

HAAS, R. M., *Bach und Mozart in Wien* (Vienna, 1951).

HERTZ, Eva, *Johann Andreas Stein* (Wolfenbüttel, 1937).

HYATT KING, A., *Mozart in Retrospect* (Oxford, 1956).

RUSSELL, John F., "Mozart and the Pianoforte" in *Music Review*, Vol. 1, No. 3 (August, 1940).

Beethoven

ANDERSON, E., *The Letters of Beethoven* (London, 1961).

BEKKER, P. (trans. M. M. Bozman), *Beethoven* (New York, 1932).

COOPER, M., *Beethoven: the Last Decade* (Oxford, 1970).

FISCHER E. (trans. P. Hamburger), *Beethoven's Pianoforte Sonatas* (London, 1959).

MATTHEWS, D., *Beethoven Piano Sonatas* (London, 1967).

ROSENBERG, R., *Die Klaviersonaten Ludwig van Beethoven* (Olten, 1957).

SONNECK, O. C. (ed.), *Impressions of Contemporaries* (Oxford, 1927).

THAYER, A. W. (revised E. Forbes), *Life of Beethoven* (2 vols., Princeton, 1964).

TOVEY, D. F., *Beethoven* (London, 1944).

TOVEY, D. F., *A Companion to Beethoven's Sonatas* (Oxford, 1927).

Schubert

ABRAHAM, G. (ed.), *Schubert, a Symposium* (London, 1950).

DEUTSCH, O. E., *Schubert* (trans., London, 1928).

EINSTEIN, A., *Schubert* (trans., London, 1951).

FLOWER, N., *Franz Schubert, the Man and his Circle* (New York, 1928, 1935).

HUTCHINGS, A., *Schubert* (London, 1964).

RADCLIFFE, P., *Schubert Piano Sonatas* (London, 1967).

SCHNEIDER, M., *Schubert* (New York and London, 1959).

WESTRUP, J., *Schubert Chamber Music* (London, 1967).

Chopin

ABRAHAM, Gerald, *Chopin's Musical Style* (London, 1939).

BIDOU, Henri, *Chopin* (trans. C. A. Phillips, New York, 1927).

BOURNIQUEL, Camille, *Chopin* (trans. S. Road, London, 1960).

BROWN, M. J. E., *Chopin—An Index to his Works in Chronological Order* (London, 1960).

CORTOT, Alfred, *In Search of Chopin* (trans. C. and R. Clarke, New York, 1949).

HEDLEY, Arthur, *Chopin* (2nd ed., London, 1964).

HIPKINS, A. J., *How Chopin Played* (London, 1937).

HUNEKER, James, *Chopin, the Man and his Music* (New York, 1924).

LISZT, Franz, *Life of Chopin* (London, 1913 and 1963).

MAINE, Basil, *Chopin* (London, 1933).

NIECKS, Frederick, *Frederic Chopin, as a Man and Musician* (2 vols., London, 1888).

POURTALÈS, Guy de, *Polonaise, the Life of Chopin* (trans. Ch. Bayly, New York, 1927).

WEINSTOCK, Herbert, *Chopin, the Man and his Music* (New York, 1949).

WHEELER, Opal, *Frederic Chopin, Son of Poland* (London, 1949).

Schumann, Robert and Clara

ABRAHAM, Gerald, *Schumann, a Symposium* (London, 1952).

BEAUFILS, M., *La Musique de Piano de Robert Schumann* (Paris, 1951)

CHISSELL, Joan, *Schumann* (London, 1948).

FULLER-MAITLAND, J. A., *Schumann's Concerted Chamber Music* (London, 1929).

FULLER-MAITLAND, J. A., *Schumann's Pianoforte Works* (London, 1927).

HARDING, Bertita, *Concerto: The Story of Clara Schumann* (London, 1962).

REIMANN, H., *Robert Schumanns Leben und Werke* (Leipzig, 1887).

REHBERG, W. and P., *Robert Schumann: Sein Leben und Sein Werk* (Zurich, 1954).

YOUNG, P. M., *Tragic Muse* (London, 1961).

Liszt

FRIEDHEIM, PHILLIP, *The Pianoforte Transcriptions of Liszt* (Studies in Romanticism) (New York, 1962).

HUNEKER, J. G., *Franz Liszt* (New York, 1911).

KAPP, J., *Liszt, Eine Biographie* (Berlin, 1916).

RAABE, P., *Franz Liszt* (2 vols., Stuttgart, 1931).

SEARLE, H., *Liszt* (London, 1957).

SITWELL, S., *Liszt* (2nd ed., London, 1955).

Bartok

MOREUX, S., *Bartok* (New York, 1964).

STEVENS, H., *The Life and Music of Bela Bartok* (New York, 1964).

Berg

REICH, R., *The Life and Work of Alban Berg* (New York, 1965).

Brahms

GEIRINGER, K., *Brahms, his Life and Work* (London, 1936).

MAY, FLORENCE, *The Life of Brahms* (London, 1948).

MURDOCH, W., *Brahms, with an Analytical Study of the Complete Piano Works* (London, 1938).

NIEMANN, W., *Brahms* (New York, 1929).

SPECHT, R., *Johannes Brahms, Leben und Werke eines deutschen Meisters* (Leipzig, 1928).

Busoni

DENT, E. J., *Ferruccio Busoni* (London, 1936).

Clementi

PARIBENI, G. C., *Muzio Clementi Nella Vita e Nell' Arte* (Milan, 1921).

Debussy

INGHELBRECHT, G. and D. E., *Claude Debussy* (Paris, 1953).

LOCKSPEISER, E., *Debussy. His Life and Mind* (London, 1962 and 1965).

SCHMITZ, E. R., *The Piano Works of Claude Debussy* (New York, 1950).

THOMPSON, O., *Debussy, Man and Artist* (New York, 1937).

Dvořák

CLAPHAM, JOHN, *Antonin Dvořák: Musician and Craftsman* (London, 1966).

COHEN, HARRIET, *The Pianoforte Compositions of Antonin Dvořák* ed. V. Fisdel (London, 1942).

ROBERTSON, A., *Dvořák* (London, 1964).

Falla

TREND, J. B., *Manuel de Falla and Spanish Music* (New York, 1929).

Fauré

KOECHLIN, C., *Gabriel Fauré 1845–1924* (trans. London, 1945).

SUCKLING, N., *Gabriel Fauré* (London, 1948).

Field

DESSAUER, H., *John Field, sein Leben und seine Werke* (Langensalza, 1912).

Franck

D'INDY, Vincent, *César Franck* (Paris, 1907).

VALLAS, L., *César Franck* (trans. London, 1951).

Grieg

FINCK, H. T., *Grieg and His Music* (New York, 1904).

MONRAD-JOHANSEN, D., *Edvard Grieg* (Oslo, 1934; Eng. trans., 1938).

SCHJELDERUP, G. and NIEMANN, W., *Edvard Grieg* (Leipzig, 1936).

Handel

CHRYSANDER, F., *G. F. Handel* (Leipzig, 1858–67).

DEUTSCH, E. O., *A Documentary Life of Handel* (London, 1948).

TOBIN, J., *Handel at Work* (London, 1964).

WEINSTOCK, H., *Handel* (New York, 1946).

Haydn

BRENET, M., *Haydn* (trans. London, 1926).

GEIRINGER, K., *Haydn: A Creative Life in Music* (New York, 1946).

PARRISH, C., *Haydn and the Piano*. Journal of the Am. Mus. Soc. I. No. 3, (1948).

Macdowell

GILMAN, L., *Edward Macdowell* (New York, 1909).

Mendelssohn

ERSKINE, J., *Song Without Words: the Story of Felix Mendelssohn* (New York, 1941).
JACOB, H. E., *Felix Mendelssohn and his Times* (London, 1963).
WERNER, E., *Mendelssohn: a New Image of the Composer and the Age* (London, 1963).

Mussorgsky

CALVOCORESSI, M. D., *Mussorgsky, the Russian Musical Nationalist* (trans. London, 1931).
RIESSEMANN, O. von, *Mussorgsky* (New York, 1935).

Paderewski

LANDAU, R., *Paderewski* (New York, 1934).
PADEREWSKI, I. J., and LAWTON, Mary, *The Paderewski Memoirs* (London, 1939).

Prokofiev

NESTYEV, I. V., *Sergei Prokofiev, His Musical Life* (trans. New York, 1946).

Rachmaninoff

CULSHAW, J., *Sergei Rachmaninoff* (London, 1949).
BERTENSSON, S. and LEYDA, J., *Sergei Rachmaninoff* (London, 1965).

Ravel

GOFF, M., *Bolero: the Life of Ravel* (New York, 1940).
JANKELEVITCH, V., *Ravel* (London and New York, 1959).
JOURDAN-MORHANGE, M., and PERLEMUTER, V., *Ravel d'après Ravel* (Lausanne, 1953).
ROLAND-MANUEL, *Maurice Ravel* (trans. London, 1947).

Saint-Saëns

LYLE, W., *Saint-Saëns: His Life and Art* (London, 1923).

Schönberg

WELLESZ, E., *Arnold Schönberg* (London, 1950).

Shostakovich

SEROFF, V. I., *Dmitri Shostakovich* (New York, 1943).

Sibelius

GRAY, C., *Sibelius* (London, 1934).

JOHNSON, H. E., *Sibelius* (London, 1959).

Smetana

RYCHNOVSKY, ERNST, *Smetana* (Stuttgart, 1924).

Stravinsky

STRAVINSKY, I. (with Robert Croft), *Stravinsky* (London, 1958).
STRAVINSKY, I., *Chronicle of my Life* (London, 1936).

Tchaikovsky

ABRAHAM, G. (ed.), *Tchaikovsky: a Symposium* (London, 1946).
NEWMARCH, R., *Tchaikovsky: his Life and Works* (London, 1908).

Weber

BENEDICT, J., *Weber* (New York, 1913).
GEORGII, WALTHER, *Karl Maria von Weber als Klavier Komponist* (Leipzig, 1914).
SAUNDERS, W., *Weber* (London, 1940).

See also *Master Musicians*; a series of books published by Dent, London.

Miscellaneous

BEDBROOK, G. S., *Keyboard Music from the Middle Ages to beginnings of Baroque* (London, 1949).
CZERNY, C., *Letters to a Young Lady in the Art of Playing the Pianoforte* (1846. London reprint, 1967).
DEAN, HOWELL, W., *Professional Piano Tuning* (New York, 1967).
DESCAVES, L., *Un Nouvel Art du Piano* (Paris, 1966).
KAISER, J., *Grosse Pianisten in unserer Zeit* (Frankfurt, 1965).
KOH, MURATA, *Sectional Tuning of the Piano* (Frankfurt, 1967).
MICHEL, N. E., *Historical Pianos, Harpsichords and Clavichords* (U.S.A., *c.* 1960).
MOISEIWITSCH, M., *Biography of a Concert Pianist* (London, 1964).
ROBILLIARD, E. D., *The Persistent Pianist* (Oxford, 1967).
SAERCHINGER, C., *Artur Schnabel* (London, 1957).
SCHIMMEL, K., *Piano Nomenclature* (Frankfurt, 1967).
Schweizerischen vereinigung für Hausmusik, *Das Klavier: Ein Wegweiser zu Instrument und Spiel* (Zurich, 1967).
THOMMA, L. and FENNER, K., *Slide-rule for Calculating String Tensions* (Frankfurt, 1965).

INDEX